From ILO Standards to EU Law

From ILO Standards to EU Law

The Case of Equality between Men and Women at Work

By

Eve C. Landau
Yves Beigbeder

MARTINUS
NIJHOFF
PUBLISHERS

LEIDEN • BOSTON
2008

This book is printed on acid-free paper.

Library of Congress Cataloging-in-Publication Data

Landau, Eve C.
From ILO standards to EU law : the case of equality between men and women at work / by Eve C. Landau, Yves Beigbeder.
p. cm.
Includes bibliographical references and index.
ISBN 978-90-04-15718-7 (hardback : alk. paper)
1. Women—mployment—Law and legislation—European Union countries. 2. Sex discrimination in employment—Law and legislation—European Union countries. I. Beigbeder, Yves. II. Title.

KJE2945.W66L36 2008
344.2401'4133—dc22

2008038795

ISBN 978 90 04 15718 7

PRINTED IN THE NETHERLANDS

CONTENTS

Part II – The Role of European Organizations

Part III – Selected Issues

Part IV – New Challenges and the Decent Work Agenda

FOREWORD

The book which I have the pleasure to preface is the work of two experienced colleagues specialized in the fields of international organizations, of international labour relations and of the law of the European Union (EU). It deals with the issue of the equality of workers, men and women, and the delicate equilibrium between the work place and the family, viewed from the angle of international law, including human rights law. The focus of the study is on the historical process which led to where the matter stands today and, in particular, the ways in which legislation and recommendations of the International Labour Organization (ILO) have influenced that process.

The work begins by recalling the history and functioning of the main agencies involved: the United Nations and the ILO, on the one hand, and the Council of Europe and the EU, on the other. It also examines the relationship between the two main actors the ILO and the EU (Parts I and II).

The study next proceeds (Part III) to analyze a series of specific problems within the framework of its general theme, including: equal pay for equal work; equal treatment of women and men, and protective measures for women; pregnancy, maternity and parental care; the treatment of workers – women *or* men, as well as the burden of proof for allegations of discrimination; the protection of workers from harassment, and the issue of positive or affirmative action. In principle each of these chapters sets out, for the topic addressed, ILO legislation and, the law of the EU, the latter being peppered by liberal sprinklings of case-law of the European Court of Justice. Finally, in Part IV, the book provides a glance into the future and shows – predictably – that while much has been achieved, much remains to be done.

The interest of the work presented here lies in its subject and the way it is being presented. It deals with issues in which gender equality really counts, and it does so matter-of-factly, which makes the message conveyed ever so much stronger.

The book is of considerable academic interest. It is also, and perhaps more so, a reliable and up-to-date guide for all those who, in their professional activities, have to deal with issues of discrimination at work and the relationship between professional and family life. It is built upon a very clear and logical outline; and the writing is simple and lucid. One of its main qualities lies in the balance achieved by the authors and in the absence of ideological bias.

The study does not exclusively focus on women but deals with "workers" generally. It shows, for instance, that equality does not always improve the status of women but may work to their detriment; that the lifting of certain prohibitions (such as that of night work) may increase professional opportunities for women, that – as in the case of part-time employment – increased protection may be necessary for both female and male workers; and that harassment at the work place, though undoubtedly more serious for women than for men, is a general problem of international and domestic labour law.

In short, the book prefaced here achieves high academic and practical standards. It deserves to be read, studied and used.

Lucius Caflisch
Emeritus Professor, Graduate Institute of International Studies in Geneva
Former Judge, European Court of Human Rights
Member of the International Law Commission of the United Nations
Geneva, March 2008

PREFACE

Equality and equal opportunity are the core issues of social justice, which has been the main aim of the International Labour Organisation (ILO) since its creation in 1919 by the Treaty of Versailles. That same year it started protecting women at work in Convention No. 3 concerning Maternity Protection. The 1944 ILO Declaration of Philadelphia, now part of its Constitution, states: "All human beings, irrespective of race, creed or sex, have the right to pursue both their material well-being and their spiritual development in conditions of freedom and dignity, of economic security and equal opportunity." The ILO then elaborated standards of equality in two major Conventions as early as 1951 and 1958.

In the European Community (EU), equality and equal opportunity came in through the window and not through the door. In the words of Sir Francis Jacobs, Advocate General: "The [EU] law on sex equality developed from a principle set out in a relatively obscure provision of the original EEC Treaty, Article 119, which called for equal pay for men and women for equal work. The inclusion of that principle in the Treaty was not then seen as a matter of fundamental rights, but rather had an economic rationale"[1] The approach of the 1957 Treaty of Rome was not based on protecting fundamental rights or pursuing justice, but on economic considerations.

In this study the authors wish to examine the profound change that has transformed the values and focus of EU law on gender equality and to reveal the impact of ILO standards on EU legislation and case law. The study aims to trace five decades of piecemeal promotion of equality between men and women at work, culminating when the EU recognized that equality is a fundamental right and a fundamental principle of Community law, now enshrined in the EU Charter of Fundamental Rights.

That the study has been undertaken in the year 2007 is no coincidence, for it is the European Year of Equal Opportunities. The book, however, focuses only on gender equality in the EU and does not cover the extension of equality on the

---

1 General Editor's Foreword to E. Ellis, *EU Anti-Discrimination Law*, 2005, Oxford University Press.

new grounds, promoted by Article 13 of the 1997 Treaty of Amsterdam, that empowered the Community to establish a wider regime of non-discrimination on the basis of racial or ethnic origin, religion or belief, disability, age and sexual orientation.

The hidden guiding spirit of the ILO will be shown as it fosters the fundamental principles of equal pay for work of equal value, equal treatment in all conditions of work, reconciliation of the dual role of women at home and at work, protection of pregnancy and maternity, and the abolition of protective measures that have lost their purpose, such as the ban on night work for women and the prohibition of women workers in underground mines.

More recent developments prohibiting direct and indirect discrimination will also be examined, such as part-time work and its impact on employment of women, an issue that was concurrently dealt with in the last decade of the Twentieth Century by both the ILO and the EU. Finally, the topics of affirmative-positive action and sexual harassment will be examined in the light of ILO theory and practice and in the light of recent EU legal provisions and case law.

The aims and values of the ILO and the EU are now converging as the EU Charter on Fundamental Rights, 2000 becomes legally binding and enters into force. Equality will become a fundamental right enshrined in Chapter III, Article 23 of the Charter: "Equality between men and women must be ensured in all areas, including employment, work and pay."

In addition, the consolidating 2006 Directive on Equal Treatment and Equal Opportunities recalls in its Preamble Recital (2) that "Equality between men and women is a fundamental principle of law under Article 2 and Article 3(2) of the Treaty and the case law of the Court of Justice. Those Treaty provisions proclaim equality between men and women as a "task" and an "aim" of the Community and impose a positive obligation to promote it in all its activities." There is no question that the EU has undergone a profound reform in its attitude towards equality as a core principle of human rights.

The study will compare ILO standards (Conventions Nos. 100, 111, 156 and 175) and the social *acquis communautaire* of the EU, as expressed in Directives, and the Community Court's case law. The similarities of the definitions, scope and criteria for derogations between the Conventions and the Directives will be pointed out.

Along with the substantive rules that are common to the ILO and the EU, the study will examine the impact of the ILO tripartite system on the procedures adopted by recent EU legislation. The growing role of the social partners in the preparation of Framework Agreements backed by Community Directives will be traced, especially in relation to the Parental Leave Directive, the Part-time Work Directive, and others adopted in the last decade of the twentieth century.

The EU is privileged to have machinery for effective enforcement that accelerates the implementation of its standards and principles through judicial control by the Court of Justice of the European Community (ECJ). The ILO has no such binding enforcement infrastructure. It merely has a supervisory role over nationally ratified and implemented Conventions. The study wishes to unveil the ECJ's vital contribution to uniform application and interpretation of the law throughout the Member States, which systematically guarantees justice and equality to five hundred million people. The unique procedure of preliminary rulings, detailed in this study, has created a consistent *corpus juris* on equality at work which cannot deny its roots in the ILO standards.

The topic of social security is not treated in this study for several reasons. First, it is already the subject of a number of books. Secondly, the issue is complex and the ECJ itself has on occasion excluded it from the scope of Article 119 of the Treaty of Rome, now Article 141 of the EC Treaty.

Overall, our study aims to familiarise lawyers, students, and practitioners, as well as the social partners, with the rich and consolidated progress of EU legislation and case law in the quest for equality. At the same time we will show that without the heritage bestowed by the ILO, the EU's implementation of equality would have been slowed down. Furthermore, without the inspiration of ILO norms, EU law would have been much poorer. New trends unite the ILO and the EU in the recent ILO Global Decent Work Agenda.

So far, not enough credit has been given to the ILO, the pioneer in the field of social justice and equality. The authors wish to remedy this *lacuna* in their modest way and pay tribute where tribute is due.

The authors are grateful to Webster University Geneva for its interest and support.

Geneva, January 2008.

List of Abbreviations

CEEP	Centre Europeen des Entreprises Publiques
CFI	Court of First Instance
EC	European Community/Communities
ECHR	European Convention on Human Rights
ECJ	European Court of Justice
ECR	European Court Reports
EEC	European Economic Community
ESC	European Social Charter
ECSC	European Coal and Steel Community
EP	European Parliament
ETUC	European Trade Union Confederation
EU	European Union
ILO	International Labour Organization
OJ	Official Journal of the European Communities
SEA	Single European Act
TEC	Treaty establishing the European Community
TEU	Treaty of the European Union
UN	United Nations
UNICE	Union of Industrial and Employers Confederation of Europe

PART I
THE ROLE OF GLOBAL ORGANIZATIONS

Chapter 1

THE UNITED NATIONS

Overview

The equality of men and women at work is mainly implemented at the national level through legislation. General principles have however been designed and promoted at the international level, both by global and regional intergovernmental organizations. At the global level, the International Labour Organization's Conventions have played an essential role in defining standards and monitoring their implementation by states. At the regional level, the creation and growth of the European Union and its rule-setting and judicial systems have obliged EU Member States to apply common employment rules and establish judicial sanctions through the European Court of Justice for states and enterprises that breach their obligations.

Our first two Chapters review the role of the United Nations (UN) system of organizations in setting standards and affirming general principles of non-discrimination by sex in employment. The use of reporting and/or monitoring systems is explained.

The first Chapter focuses on relevant UN Declarations, Conventions and World Conferences, and the second one on the International Labour Organization (ILO), the UN agency specially entrusted with employment issues.

The Origins of Equal Rights for Women

The transformation in the status of women came with the Industrial Revolution, with the access of girls and women to education at all levels, which led to the advancement of women's human rights. At the end of the nineteenth century, women workers began to organize movements demanding better working conditions. The right to vote was granted to women in a few countries and the first international convention related to the protection of women was adopted in 1910: the International Convention for the Suppression of the White Slave Trade.

Women acquired more visibility in Western countries as a result of events during World War I, and more so during and after World War II.[1] The equality of women then overcame the more limited focus on the protection of women.

First, women replaced the fighting men in the work force during the war, establishing a new social pattern. After the war, this pattern became irreversible for economic reasons. Many women became joint breadwinners with their husbands or heads of family, or became heads of one-parent families. This gave women a degree of economic independence and enhanced their social and home status.

Second, as decolonization proceeded after the war, many women assumed important political roles in building and shaping independence in newly emerging countries. For instance, Golda Meir, Indira Gandhi and Chandrika Bandaranaike became heads of government respectively in Israel, India and Sri Lanka. They became role models for women in many countries.

Third, the development of family planning meant that women could control reproduction, facilitating new activities outside the home.

Fourth, the revolutionary advances in information and communications technology and modern service economies enabled women to work in jobs previously reserved for men, for which they could claim equal financial compensation.

The League of Nations

The Covenant of the League of Nations of 10 January 1920, an integral part of the Treaty of Versailles, has a short reference to labour conditions but it does not prescribe equality between men and women:

> "Article 23 ... the Members of the League:
>
> (a) ... will endeavour to secure and maintain fair and humane conditions of labour for men, women and children, both in their own countries and in all countries to which their commercial and industrial relations extend, and for that purpose will establish and maintain the necessary organisations."

The League adopted two Conventions dealing with the protection of women, albeit not related to employment conditions.[2]

---

1 See Eve Chava Landau, "Opening Address: Equality and Human Rights" in *The Status of Women at the Dawn of the Twenty-first Century – Proceedings of the Conference Held under the Auspices of the International Association of Legal Science and the Minerva Center for Human Rights* (UNESCO, 2001), p. 10.

2 The International Convention for the Suppression of the Traffic in Women and Children 1921, the International Convention for the Suppression of the Traffic in Women of Full Age 1933.

The International Labour Organization was set up in 1919 by the Paris Peace Conference as an autonomous organization, initially as part of the League of Nations. Its contributions are described in Chapter 2.

The Human Rights Regime of the United Nations

Following World War II and its widespread horrors and suffering the United Nations created and developed an international human rights regime through Declarations, Conventions and World Conferences. The regime affirmed two important principles concerning the employment of women: the equality of men and women at work, and the need for protection of women.

The UN Charter, which came into force on 26 June 1945, was the first international instrument to refer specifically to sex equality. Its Preamble reaffirms "... faith in fundamental human rights, in the dignity and worth of the human person, in the equal rights of men and women ...". Article 13 (b) refers to "the realization of human rights and fundamental freedoms for all without distinction as to ... sex ...". Articles 55 (c) and 76 (c) refer to the promotion of universal respect for human rights and fundamental freedoms for all without distinction as to sex, as well as to race, language or religion.

In 1946 the Economic and Social Council (ECOSOC) set up the Commission on the Status of Women to report and make recommendations on the promotion of the human rights of women and to recommend measures to achieve equal rights for men and women. In the same year, the UN created the Division for the Advancement of Women in its Secretariat.

Declarations and Conventions

Over the years the UN has promulgated a series of instruments promoting women's equality with increasing vigour.

The Preamble to the Universal Declaration of Human Rights adopted in 1948 states that it is essential that human rights should be protected by the rule of law. It clearly affirms that the peoples of the United Nations believe in the equal rights of men and women and are determined to promote social progress. The 'no-distinction' on the basis of sex is reaffirmed in Article 2. Everyone's right to work, and everyone's right to equal pay for equal work are affirmed in Article 23, but without specific reference to men and women. Motherhood is entitled to special care and assistance but not in reference to employment (Article 25.2).

The International Covenant on Economic, Social and Cultural Rights, adopted by the General Assembly on 16 December 1966, affirms the non-discrimination clause on the basis of sex for the exercise of the rights included in the instrument and the equal rights of men and women to the enjoyment of these rights (Articles 2.2 and 3). More relevant to the subject of this book, Article. 7 (a) (i) imposes upon States Parties to provide equal pay for equal work, 'in particular women being guaranteed conditions of work not inferior to those enjoyed by men'. Special protection should be accorded to working mothers during a reasonable period before and after childbirth through paid leave, or leave with adequate social security benefits (Article 10 (2)).

The Covenant requires that States Parties submit reports on measures adopted, progress made and difficulties encountered. Reports are submitted to ECOSOC and the specialized agencies through the UN Secretary-General. ECOSOC may transmit these reports to the Commission on Human Rights for study and recommendations.

The International Covenant on Civil and Political Rights, also adopted on 16 December 1966 by the UN General Assembly, affirms the equal rights of men and women to the enjoyment of all civil and political rights set out in the Covenant. It specifies that all persons are equal before the law and are entitled without any discrimination to the equal protection of the law (Articles 3 and 26).

The 1967 Declaration on the Elimination of Discrimination against Women was followed by the binding Convention on the Elimination of All Forms of Discrimination against Women, adopted by the Assembly in 1979.[3] The most important Convention on the issue, it entered into force on 3 September 1981.

Article 1 of this Convention defines 'discrimination against women' as:

> "Any distinction, exclusion or restriction made on the basis of sex which has the effect or purpose of impairing or nullifying the recognition, enjoyment or exercise by women, irrespective of their marital status, on a basis of equality of men and women, of human rights and fundamental freedoms in the political, economic, social, cultural, civil or any other field."

States Parties should embody the principle of equality of men and women in their national constitutions or other appropriate legislation, including sanctions prohibiting all discrimination against women where appropriate. They should establish legal protection of the rights of women on an equal basis with men and ensure through competent national tribunals the effective protection of women against any act of discrimination. They should take all appropriate measures to eliminate discrimination against women by any person, organization or enterprise, and they should repeal all national penal provisions which constitute discrimination against women (Article 2).

Temporary affirmative action to accelerate *de facto* equality between men and women is allowed by the Convention (Article 4). In the field of employment, the Convention affirms:

- the right to work as an inalienable right of all human beings,

---

3 Res. 34/180.

- the right to the same employment opportunities, including the same criteria for selection,
- the right to free choice of profession and employment, the right to job security and other conditions of service,
- the right to equal remuneration, to social security, to protection of health and to safety in working conditions, including the safeguarding of the function of reproduction.

Dismissal on the grounds of pregnancy or of maternity leave is prohibited, subject to the imposition of sanctions. States Parties should introduce maternity leave with pay or with comparable social benefits without loss of former employment, seniority or social allowances (Article 11).

The Convention established a Committee on the Elimination of Discrimination against Women, composed of twenty-three experts elected by States Parties for a four year term. States Parties undertake to submit a report every four years to the UN Secretary-General for consideration by the Committee on the legislative, judicial, administrative or other measures they have adopted to give effect to the provisions of the Convention. The reports may indicate factors and difficulties affecting the degree of fulfilment of obligations under the Convention. The Committee reports on its activities annually to the General Assembly through ECOSOC and may include suggestions and general recommendations. The UN Secretary-General transmits these reports to the Commission on the Status of Women for information. The Committee may invite specialized agencies to submit reports on the implementation of the Convention in their areas of activities.

On 6 October 1999, the General Assembly adopted the Optional Protocol to the Convention on the Elimination of Discrimination against Women,[4] which entered into force on 22 December 2000. State Parties recognize the competence of the Convention's Committee to consider communications submitted by individuals or groups of individuals who are under the jurisdiction of a State Party and claim to be victims of a violation of any of the rights set forth in the Convention by that State Party. Communications are in writing and not anonymous. All available domestic remedies must first have been exhausted unless the application of these remedies has been unusually prolonged or is unlikely to bring effective relief. Further action by the Committee involves confidential transmission of the communication to the State Party concerned, written explanation or statement clarifying the matter and possible remedy. The cooperation of the State Party concerned is sought at all stages of the review.[5]

---

4 Res. A/54/4.

5 Articles 1, 2, 8.

In 1993 the General Assembly adopted the Declaration on the Elimination of Violence against Women.[6] Its Preamble affirms in part that:

> "... violence against women constitutes a violation of the rights and fundamental freedoms of women and impairs or nullifies their enjoyment of those rights and freedoms ..."

It recognizes:

> "... that violence against women is a manifestation of historically unequal power relationships between men and women, which have led to domination over and discrimination against women by men and to the prevention of the full advancement of women, and that violence against women is one of the crucial social mechanisms by which women are forced into a subordinate position compared with men."

Article 2 of the Declaration includes sexual harassment and intimidation at work as an element of the physical, sexual and psychological violence occurring within the general community. Article 3 includes the right to just and favourable conditions of work as one of the rights to which women are entitled.

World Conferences and Plans of Action

The World Conference of the International Women's Year, held in Mexico in 1975, adopted the Declaration of Mexico on the Equality of Women and their Contribution to Development and Peace and the World Plan of Action for the Implementation of the Objectives of the International Women's Year.[7]

The Conference recommended, in part, that governments ensure the equality of women and men before the law and the equality of opportunities in employment. As proposed in Mexico, the General Assembly proclaimed 1976-1985 the United Nations Decade for Women, Equality, Development, Peace.

Other World Conferences followed: the World Conference of the United Nations Decade for Women: Equality, Development, Peace, held in Copenhagen in 1980, and the World Conference charged to examine and evaluate the results of the United Nations Decade for Women: Equality, Development, Peace, held in Nairobi in 1985.

Also in 1985, the Voluntary Fund for the United Nations Decade for Women became the United Nations Fund for Women (UNIFEM) whose main tasks are to improve the economic capacities of women as entrepreneurs and producers, increase the participation of women in decisions concerning them, and to promote women's rights.

---

6 Res. 48/104.

7 See *Human Rights of Women: A Collection of International and Regional Normative Instruments*, prepared by Janusz Symonides and Vladimir Volodin (UNESCO, 1999), pp. xiv-xvii.

The 1993 Vienna World Conference on Human Rights called, in part, for the eradication of all forms of discrimination against women and for the elimination of violence against women. The Fourth World Conference on Women, held in Beijing in September 1995, adopted a Platform for Action which endorsed gender mainstreaming as a major strategy for the promotion of gender equality. It included, in part, the elimination of job discrimination.

Two years later, ECOSOC defined gender mainstreaming as the process of assessing the implications for women and men of any planned action, including legislation, policies and programmes, in all areas and at all levels, as a strategy for making women's as well as men's concerns and experiences an integral dimension of the design, implementation, monitoring and evaluation of policies and programmes in all political, economic and social spheres.[8]

In 2000, the 23rd special session of the General Assembly titled Women 2000: Gender Equality, Development and Peace for the Twenty-First Century was held in New York. It adopted a Political Declaration and an outcome document entitled Further Actions and Initiatives to Implement the Beijing Declaration and Platform for Action. General equality was re-affirmed as an underlying principle. One target was the creation and maintenance of a non-discriminatory, gender sensitive legal environment through reviewing legislation with a view to striving to remove discriminatory provisions as soon as possible, preferably by 2005. However, also in 2000, ECOSOC noted with concern the persistent problems in addressing the challenges of poverty eradication, employment, gender inequalities, empowerment and the advancement of women, as reflected in the five-year reviews of the Fourth World Conference and the World Summit for Social Development.[9]

The 2005 World Summit reiterated the resolve of world leaders to eliminate discrimination against women and renewed a commitment to the gender mainstreaming strategy.

Conclusion

The United Nations have played an important role in promoting women's rights at the global level through Declarations, Conventions, Resolutions of the General Assembly and World Conferences, and through the initiation and development of a human rights regime.

While Declarations, Resolutions and World Conferences may have helped in promoting equal rights for men and women and in fighting against sex

8 ECOSOC agreed conclusions 1997/2 on "Mainstreaming the gender perspective into all policies and programmes in the United Nations system".

9 ECOSOC res. E/2000/26.

discrimination, only binding Conventions, ratified by countries and translated into national laws providing judicial remedies have a legal effect on Member States' citizens. International implementation of the International Covenant on Economic, Social and Cultural Rights is limited to requiring countries to submit reports on measures adopted.[10]

Countries' reports are submitted to the Committee on the Elimination of Discrimination against Women, set up by the Convention on the Elimination of All Forms of Discrimination against Women: the mechanisms for complaints brought by individuals or groups of individuals under the Protocol are also limited to reviews and the submission of reports and possible remedies by State Parties under strictly defined conditions.

10 As of 2004, 178 States had ratified the Convention, but many appended reservations.

Chapter 2

THE ILO

This Chapter surveys the major ILO Conventions relevant to the protection of women and to the equality of women and men at work, and their review or control mechanisms.

The Origins

In 1919 the States Parties to the Treaty of Versailles created the International Labour Organization on the basis of several considerations inscribed in the Preamble of its Constitution.[1] The motivations were political, humanitarian and economic.

The first was that social justice was linked to peace: "... universal and lasting peace can be established only if it is based upon social justice". In comparison, the documents creating the UN specialized agencies after World War II deem peace and world order dependent on social progress achieved through international organizations in such fields as health, education and (for the ILO) labour.

A second consideration in the ILO Constitution, partly humanitarian and partly political, was that:

> "... whereas conditions of labour exist involving such injustice, hardship and privation to large numbers of people as to produce unrest so great that the peace and harmony of the world are imperilled; and an improvement of those conditions is urgently required ..."

Thus the ILO was also created as a preventive buffer against communism, two years after the 1917 Russian Revolution: there was an urgent need to improve the workers' conditions in Western countries in order to prevent or resolve social conflicts, or even to pre-empt communist revolutions.

---

1 The original text of the ILO Constitution of 1919 has been modified by Amendments of 1922, 1945, 1953, 1962, 1972.

A final motivation was economic. Because of its effect on the cost of production, any industry or country adopting social reform would find itself at a disadvantage with its competitors. The Preamble states that "the failure of any nation to adopt humane conditions of labour is an obstacle in the way of other nations which desire to improve the conditions in their own countries": a very relevant concern in the present globalization conditions.

Technically, the Paris Peace Conference incorporated the Constitution of the ILO into the Treaty of Versailles in response to pressures from several international workers' conferences held during World War I. The new organization became part of the League of Nations (Part XIII of the Treaty).[2]

On 10 May 1944 the General Conference of the ILO, meeting in its 26th Session in Philadelphia, adopted a Declaration concerning the aims and purposes of the Organization and the principles which should inspire the policy of its Members.[3] It reaffirms the fundamental principles on which the Organization is based and, in particular, that:

1. labour is not a commodity;
2. freedom of expression and of speech are essential to sustained progress;
3. poverty anywhere constitutes a danger to prosperity everywhere;
4. all human beings, irrespective of race, creed or sex, have the right to pursue both their material well-being and their spiritual development in conditions of freedom and dignity, of economic security and equal opportunity.

It recognizes, as one of several solemn obligations of the ILO, to further among the nations of the world programmes which will achieve provision for child welfare and maternity protection.

The ILO became a specialized agency of the UN in 1946.[4]

---

2 The Treaty of Peace between the Allied and Associated Powers and Germany, London, H.M. Stationery Office, 1919, Part XIII, pp. 387-411.

3 The "Declaration concerning the aims and purposes of the International Labour Organization" or "Declaration of Philadelphia" is an Annex to, and is part of, the ILO Constitution (Article 1, paragraph 1).

See UN Doc. A/72, 30 September 1946 "Draft Agreement between the United Nations and the International Labour Organization", and Res. 50 (I), 14 December 1946 "Agreements with Specialized Agencies" approving, in part, the Agreement entered by ECOSOC with the ILO.

4 See UN Doc. A/72, 30 September 1946 "Draft Agreement between the United Nations and the International Labour Organization", and Res. 50 (I), 14 December 1946 "Agreements with Specialized Agencies" approving, in part, the Agreement entered by ECOSOC with the ILO.

Structure of the ILO

The characteristic of the ILO, unique among the UN specialized agencies, is the tripartite membership of all its organs, reflected in the composition of bodies and voting rights. Governments nominate employers' and workers' representatives subject to the agreement of leading national industrial organizations of each category. The tripartite principle is complemented by the strictly observed principle of group autonomy.

The main organs of the ILO are the General Conference, the Governing Body and the International Labour Office (Constitution, Article 2). The Conference, as the supreme organ, consists of representatives of the 178 States currently Members, comprising government, employers' and workers' delegates. At the Conference and in the Governing Body, representation is made of half for Governments, and half for Employers and Workers: at the Conference, each country has two Government delegates, one Employer's delegate and one Worker's delegate. The Governing Body is made up of 28 Government representatives, ten of which come from States of chief industrial importance, 14 Employers' representatives and 14 Workers' representatives (Articles 3, 7).

The conference committees, where substantial work is done, also have tripartite membership, with a difference: in the Governing Body and in the International Labour Conference, governments have twice the voting rights of either the employers' or workers' groups, while in the committees each group enjoys an equal voting weight (Article 65 paragraph 2).

The third organ is the International Labour Office headed by a Director-General appointed by the Governing Body. The staff is appointed by the Director-General: "A certain number of these persons shall be women": no parity, but a minimum representation of women.

The Office has its headquarters in Geneva and has field offices in more than 40 countries (Article 8, 9).

Setting Standards

The main function of the ILO is to prepare and adopt international labour standards in the form of Conventions and Recommendations: there is now a corpus of 188 Conventions, five protocols and 196 Recommendations. After preparation by the Office and review by committees, the final adoption of a Convention or a Recommendation requires a two-thirds majority of the votes cast by the delegates present in the General Conference (Article 19 paragraph 2). Conventions become binding on every Member State which has ratified them in accordance with its constitutional law. Members inform the Director-General of ratification and of the measures taken "to make effective the provisions of such Convention" (Article 19 paragraph 5).

Recommendations are non-binding and hence need not be ratified.

Monitoring Standards

The ILO's monitoring system rests first with the requirement that Member States submit reports to the Office on the measures they have taken to give effect to the provisions of the Conventions to which they are a party. While Article 22 of the ILO Constitution required annual reports, they are now presented at intervals of two years for fundamental and priority Conventions, and five years for the others.[5]

Governments are required to submit copies of their reports to employers' and workers' organizations, who may comment on these reports. These organizations may also send comments on the application of Conventions directly to the ILO.

Monitoring of governments' reports is then carried out by two Committees.

The *Committee of Experts*, set up in 1926, examines Member States' reports on the Conventions they have ratified under Article 22 of the Constitution and the information and reports furnished by Member States under Articles 19 and 35.[6]

The Committee is composed of 20 eminent jurists appointed by the Governing Body for three-year terms, coming from different geographical regions, legal systems and cultures. It meets every year for two weeks in Geneva: all preparatory work is done by the Office. Decisions on comments are taken by consensus.

This Committee advises the Conference as to the facts, and it is then up to the Conference to "decide upon its attitude and upon what appropriate action it might take or indicate". The Committee's role is to give an impartial and technical evaluation of the state of application of ratified Conventions. It stresses its own independence, impartiality and objectivity. It is a technical, legal body, but it has no judicial capacity nor is it competent to give interpretations of the provisions of the Conventions. The Committee's observations are not legally binding.

The Committee makes two kinds of comments: observations and direct requests. Observations contain comments on fundamental questions raised by a State's application of a particular Convention. These observations are published in the Committee's annual report. Direct requests relate to more technical questions

---

5 There are eight 'fundamental' Conventions, including the Equal Remuneration Convention 1951 No. 100, and the Discrimination (Employment and Occupational) Convention No. 111, and four 'priority' Conventions: see *Rules of the Game, A brief introduction to International Labour Standards* (ILO, 2005), pp. 12-13.

6 The Committee of Experts was set up at the 8th Session of the International Labour Conference in 1926, first on a trial basis: for a description and evaluation of the work of the Committee and of the Conference Committee, and an assessment of ILO's role, see Alfred Wisskirchen, "The Standard-Setting and Monitoring of the ILO: Legal Questions and Practical Experience", (2005) 144 *International Labour Review*, pp. 253-289.

or requests for further information. They are not published in the report but are communicated directly to the governments concerned.

The *Committee on the Application of Conventions and Recommendations*, in brief the *Conference Committee*, also created in 1926, is one of the standing committees of the International Labour Conference. It considers the measures taken by Members to give effect to the provisions of Conventions to which they are parties and the information furnished by Members concerning the results of inspections, as well as the information and reports concerning Conventions and Recommendations communicated by Members.[7]

The two Committees have a complementary role: the Committee of Experts conducts a preliminary examination, which is followed by a treatment of the same or other cases by the Conference Committee. The reports of the Conference Committee and its conclusions as to specific cases are adopted by the International Labour Conference, thus giving them an authoritative status.

The Conference Committee, numbering between 200 and 250 full members, first discusses general questions on standard setting and monitoring raised in the General Report of the Committee of Experts. It then reviews the General Survey of the Committee of Experts, which deals with one or more Conventions on the basis of Member States' reports. Most of the Committee's work consists in dealing with individual cases. It chooses about 25 cases, on the basis of equitable geographical distribution, from the several hundred individual observations in the report of the Committee of Experts. Most of the cases discussed concern questions arising from the eight fundamental Conventions, including the Equal Remuneration Convention No. 100 1951 and the Discrimination (Employment and Occupational) Convention No. 111 1958. Most observations contain criticism of substantial deviations from the requirements of a Convention in the law or practice of a Member State.

The consideration of each case begins with a presentation by the representatives of the government of the Member State concerned, followed by spokespersons of the national employers and workers. After a general debate, the government's and the two groups' representatives speak again. Finally, the Committee adopts conclusions about shortcomings and noticeable deteriorations or improvements compared with past reviews. They ask for changes in law and practice, and may recommend that the government seek general advice or technical assistance from the ILO.

Representations and Complaints

Besides reviews by Committees, the ILO Constitution has set up a formal system of representations and complaints by which a Member State may be exposed to

---

7 Article 7 of the Standing Orders of the International Labour Conference.

public criticisms by employers' or workers' associations, other Member States, and the ILO itself.

An employer or worker association may address a representation to the Office that a Member State has failed to secure in any respect the effective observance within its jurisdiction of any Convention to which it is a party. The Governing Body may then communicate this representation to the government concerned and invite it to respond. If no statement is received within a reasonable time from the government or if the statement is not deemed satisfactory the Governing Body has the right to publish the representation and any statement made in reply (Constitution, Articles 24, 25).

Under Article 26 of the Constitution, any Member has the right to file a complaint with the International Labour Office if it is not satisfied that any other Member is securing the effective observance of any Convention which both have ratified. The Governing Body may then appoint a Commission of Inquiry to consider the complaint and report. The Governing Body may itself directly file a complaint.

The Commission of Inquiry, after a full consideration of the complaint, prepares a report which includes its findings and recommendations. The Director-General of the ILO communicates the report to the Governing Body and to each of the governments concerned and has it published. Each of these governments must inform the Director-General within three months whether or not it accepts the Commission's recommendation, and if not, whether it proposes to refer the complaint to the International Court of Justice, whose decision will be final (Articles 28, 29, 31).

If a Member fails to carry out the recommendations of the Commission of Inquiry or the Court's decision within the time specified the Governing Body may recommend to the Conference "such action as it may deem wise and expedient to secure compliance therewith" (Article 33).

Relevant ILO Conventions

The Equal Remuneration Convention No. 100 1951 adopts the principle of equal remuneration for men and women workers for work of equal value. State parties must ensure the application of this principle by the following means:

- national laws or regulations;
- legally established or recognized machinery for wage determination;
- collective agreements between employers and workers; or
- a combination of these means.

Measures should be taken to promote objective appraisal of jobs on the basis of the work to be performed (Article 3).

The Convention specifies that differential pay rates between workers corresponding to objective differences in the work to be performed, without regard to sex, are not considered contrary to the principle (Article 3).

The Discrimination (Employment and Occupation) Convention No. 111 1958 defines the term discrimination as

> "any distinction, exclusion or preference made on the basis of race, colour, sex, religion, political opinion, national extraction or social origin, which has the effect of nullifying or impairing equality of opportunity or treatment in employment or occupation."

The Convention provides that special measures or protection or assistance provided for in other ILO Conventions or Recommendations are not deemed to be discrimination, such as measures to meet particular requirements of persons who, for reasons such as sex, age, disablement, family responsibilities or social or cultural status, are generally recognized to require special protection or assistance.

The ILO Workers with Family Responsibilities Convention No. 156 1981 is inspired, in part, by the UN Convention on the Elimination of All Forms of Discrimination against Women 1979: its Preamble recalls that States Parties "are aware that a change in the traditional role of men as well as the role of women in society and in the family is needed to achieve full equality between men and women". Women are no longer alone with 'family responsibilities': the Convention applies to "men and women workers with responsibilities in relation to their dependent children, where such responsibilities restrict their possibilities of preparing for, entering, participating in or advancing in economic activity".[8] The Convention applies to all branches of economic activity and all categories of workers. A national policy should enable persons with family responsibilities who are engaged or wish to engage in employment to exercise their right to do so without being subject to discrimination and, to the extent possible, without conflict between their employment and family responsibilities. Community services, public or private, such as child-care and family services and facilities should be developed or promoted (Article 5). Information and education should be promoted (Articles 3, 6). Family responsibilities should not, as such, constitute a valid reason for termination of employment. The provisions of the Convention may be applied by stages (Articles 8, 10).

Earlier ILO Conventions and Recommendations dealt with protective measures for women at work that were revised and replaced by Conventions No. 155 and No. 171.

– Recommendation No. 4 concerning the Protection of Women and Children against Lead Poisoning 1919

8 Preamble and Article 1 (1).

- Recommendation No. 13 concerning Night Work of Women in Agriculture 1921
- Convention No. 45 concerning the Employment of Women on Underground Work of Mines of All Kinds 1935
- ILO Night Work (Women) Convention No. 89 Revised 1948
- Employment (Women with Family Responsibilities) Recommendation No. 123 1965
- Night Work Convention No. 171 1990
- Protocol of 1990 to the Night Work (Women) Convention Revised 1948.
- Others concern specifically the protection of maternity:
- Maternity Protection Convention No. 3 1919
- Maternity Protection Convention No. 103 Revised 1952
- Recommendation No. 95 concerning Maternity Protection 1952.

Other instruments also focus on equality of men and women at work. Recommendation No. 90 concerning Equal Remuneration for Men and Women Workers for Work of Equal Value, also adopted in 1951, supplements the Equal Remuneration Convention. It provides procedures for the progressive application of the principles of the Convention, to be applied to all employees in government departments or agencies, and to those whose rates of remuneration are subject to statutory regulation or public control. After consultation with the workers' and employers' associations concerned, differences between rates of remuneration for men and rates for women should be decreased and, where a system of increments is in force, equal increments for men and women workers performing work of equal value should be provided. Furthermore, action should be taken, as necessary, to raise the productive efficiency of women workers by providing facilities for vocational guidance or employment counselling, and for placement; by providing welfare and social services which meet the needs of women workers, particularly those with family responsibilities; and by protecting the health and welfare of women.

Recommendation No. 165 concerning Equal Opportunities and Equal Treatment for Men and Women Workers: Workers with Family Responsibilities 1981 recalls the basis and principles set in Convention No. 156. It gives details on measures to be taken by State Parties to implement a national policy, special measures recommended for a transitional period, and measures to be taken to promote information, education and research. Vocational guidance, counselling, information and placement services should be provided. Workers with family responsibilities should enjoy equality of opportunity and treatment with other workers in relation to preparation for and access to employment, advancement and employment security. Marital status, family status or family responsibilities should not constitute valid reasons for refusal or termination of employment. Terms of employment should enable these workers to reconcile their employment and family responsibilities. Details are given on measures to be taken on child care and family services and facilities, social security benefits, tax relief and other appropriate measures. This Recommendation has superseded the Employment (Women and Family Responsibilities) Recommendation of 1965.

The 1998 Declaration

As an approach aside from the ILO Conventions/Recommendations system, the ILO Declaration on Fundamental Principles and Rights at Work and the Follow-up to this Declaration were adopted at the 86th Session of the International Labour Conference in 1998. The Declaration binds all Member States to respect, promote and realize a select set of principles:

- freedom of association and the effective recognition of the right to collective bargaining;
- the elimination of all forms of forced or compulsory labour;
- the effective abolition of child labour; and
- the elimination of discrimination in respect of employment and occupation.

The Declaration is not a Convention, but its principles are found in relevant Conventions and basic ILO texts. The follow-up measures to this Declaration emphasize the purely promotional value of this instrument and are not subject to the ILO monitoring system.

In 1999, the Director-General of ILO declared that "The primary goal of the ILO today is to promote opportunities for women and men to obtain decent and productive work, in conditions of freedom, equity, security and human dignity". 'Decent work' sums up the aspirations of people in their working lives. It involves opportunities for work that is productive and delivers a fair income, security in the workplace and social protection for families, better prospects for personal development and social integration, freedom for people to express their concerns, organize and participate in the decisions that affect their lives, and equality of opportunity and treatment for all women and men. The ILO has also put in place a systematic policy on gender equality and gender mainstreaming which was discussed by the Governing Body in March 2000.[9]

---

9 ILO: *Decent Work*, Report of the Director-General, International Labour Conference, 87th

Conclusion

The ILO Conventions and Recommendations constitute the basis of labour law at the global level. Since 1919, the ILO has acted as a pioneer and developer in this field. It has helped to build up workers' rights, to protect women at work, and since 1951 to promote the equality of men and women at work. ILO standards reflect international endorsement of universal objectives and minimum rules of conduct in the world of work. Its tripartite structure and work methods are unique among global intergovernmental organizations: while governments are still the final deciders, employers' and workers' groups have a voice in debates and an influence in votes in internal Committees, the Governing Body and the Conference.

While the ILO has no effective enforcement power, the effect of the ILO monitoring system rests on the cumulative impact of reviews of states' annual reports by the Committee of Experts and the Conference Committee, the Governing Body and the General Conference, followed by findings, comments and recommendations. The repeated public scrutiny of a Member State's observance of ILO standards may exert a degree of political and moral pressure on governments.

Most of the ILO Conventions and Recommendations apply to both men and women. Thus women are granted the same rights as men in the fields covered by ILO instruments, such as fundamental human rights, employment and training, working conditions and occupational health and safety. Additionally, the ILO has adopted standards aimed specifically at women workers.

The most far-reaching instruments dealing with discrimination are the Discrimination (Employment and Occupation) Convention No. 111 and its supplementary Recommendation No. 111. Since their adoption in 1958, the Committee of Experts on the Application of Conventions and Recommendations has noted a great variety of legislative and practical measures taken in a number of countries to eliminate discrimination and promote equality of opportunity and treatment, particularly for women workers. Most countries have now formulated anti-discrimination policies, most often as legislation. Many have set up institutional bodies that are empowered to spur the national effort to ensure and promote equality. There is greater public awareness of the ways in which direct and indirect discrimination manifest themselves, and perhaps more sensitivity and tolerance.

However, in spite of the evidence of progress, the gap between policy and practice remains significant. The impressive quantitative increases in women's economic participation have not been matched by qualitative improvements or better working conditions. Women are still vulnerable to various forms of labour

Session, Geneva, 1989, Governing Body doc. GB.277/5/2, 277th Session, Geneva, Mar. 2000 and Circular No. 564 of Dec. 1999.

market instability. Comprehensive long-term national efforts must combine legislation with recourse procedures at the enterprise, industry and national levels and judicial enforcement. Equality, as a basic human right, should be placed firmly on the political agenda, a pre-condition for real progress.[10]

10 Christine Elstob, "The International Labour Organization Perspective", in *The Status of Women at the Dawn of the Twenty-first Century* (Proceedings published by UNESCO, 2001), pp. 21-30.

Part II
The Role of European Organizations

Chapter 3

THE COUNCIL OF EUROPE

The Council of Europe was created in 1949 to achieve greater unity between European States. It is the guardian of democracy, human rights and the rule of law. It is Europe's oldest political organization formed after World War II and, in 2007, included 47 countries. It is distinct from the European Union, an intergovernmental organization with federalist objectives and supranational powers. The Council is a traditional intergovernmental organisation, promoting cooperation among its members. Its normative activity has produced, among other instruments, the European Convention on Human Rights and its Protocols. However, the European Court of Human Rights has jurisdiction only in civil and political issues, and, in principle, not over social matters.

The Origins

On 19 September 1946, at the University of Zurich, Sir Winston Churchill gave a vibrant speech in favour of creating a regional structure, a kind of United States of Europe, starting with a partnership between France and Germany. He spoke about the tragedy of Europe, the series of frightful nationalistic quarrels: "We must all turn our backs upon the horrors of the past. We must look to the future". The first practical step would be to form a Council of Europe, in parallel to the British Commonwealth of Nations, 'mighty America' and Soviet Russia. Like other groupings, a regional grouping of Europe would not conflict with the United Nations,; it would strengthen the world organization.

Uniting parts of Europe was not a new idea. Charlemagne's Holy Roman Empire grouped large areas under a loose administration for hundreds of years, and then disintegrated. Union by military force was attempted by Napoleon Bonaparte in the 1800s, and proposed by German economists and industrialists in the 1940s during World War II.

Earlier writers, philosophers and politicians have proposed various forms of European union: the Abbot Charles de Saint-Pierre in 1728, French socialists Saint-Simon and Augustin Thierry in 1814, Italian writer and politician Giuseppe

Mazzini in 1843. After the long and bloody First World War, Austrian Count Richard Coudenhove-Kalergi founded the Pan-European movement in 1923 and hosted the first Pan European Congress in 1926. In 1930, French Prime Minister Aristide Briand presented to the League of Nations a Memorandum on the Organization of a System of European Federal Union. In a 1929 session of the League Assembly he proposed the creation of a federation of European nations based on solidarity, the pursuit of economic prosperity, and political and social cooperation. In 1931, the French politician Edouard Herriot published a book titled *The United States of Europe.*

However, it took the destructions of another World War, its immense loss of lives, the Holocaust, and the suffering and painful displacement of millions of civilians for the movement towards European unification to finally create common institutions. The emerging Cold War was an additional incentive for establishing a political solidarity among Western European countries.

In May 1948, more than a thousand delegates from some twenty countries attended the Congress of Europe in The Hague. Resolutions were adopted calling for the creation of an economic and political union to guarantee European security, economic independence and social progress; the establishment of a consultative assembly elected by national parliaments; the drafting of a European Convention on Human Rights; and the setting up of a Court to enforce its decisions. The Congress also reflected divisions between those who supported European federalism (France and Belgium) from those who favoured simple intergovernmental cooperation, such as the UK, Ireland and the Scandinavian countries.

On 5 May 1949, in St James's Palace, London, the Statute creating the Council of Europe was signed by ten 'cooperationist' countries: Belgium, Denmark, France, Ireland, Italy, Luxembourg, the Netherlands, Norway, Sweden and the United Kingdom. On 9 May 1951, the 'federalists' – Belgium, France, Italy, Luxemburg, the Netherlands and the Federal Republic of Germany – signed the Treaty of Paris, establishing the European Coal and Steel Community that preceded the European Economic Community (EEC) created by the Treaty of Rome in 1957 (see Chapter 4).

Aims of the Council of Europe

The Council now has 47 Member States and has granted observer status to the Holy See, the US, Canada, Japan and Mexico. It is headquartered in Strasbourg.

It was set up to achieve a greater unity between members. Its aims were to defend human rights, parliamentary democracy, and the rule of law; to develop continent-wide agreements standardizing member countries' social and legal practices; and to promote awareness of a European identity based on shared values that cut across different cultures.

Since the end of the Cold War in 1989, the Council has served as a political anchor and human rights watchdog for Europe's post communist democracies. It has assisted these countries in carrying out and consolidating political, legal and constitutional reform in parallel with economic reform, and it has provided know-how in areas such as human rights, local democracy, education, culture and the environment.

At its third Summit of Heads of State and Government, held in Warsaw in May 2005, the Council defined its principal tasks for the coming years as:

- promoting the common fundamental values of human rights, the rule of law and democracy;
- strengthening the security of European citizens, in particular by combating terrorism, organized crime and trafficking in human beings;
- fostering cooperation with other international and European organizations.

The Council has adopted 200 legally binding European treaties or conventions ranging from human rights to the fight against organized crime and from the prevention of torture to data protection and cultural cooperation. It also issues recommendations to governments setting out policy guidelines on legal matters, health, education, culture and sport.

Structure

The Council of Europe has four main components:

- The Committee of Ministers is the organization's decision-making body, composed of the 47 foreign ministers or their Strasbourg-based deputies (ambassadors/permanent representatives).
- The Parliamentary Assembly groups 630 members (315 representatives and 315 substitutes) from the 47 national parliaments.
- The Congress of Local and Regional Authorities is composed of a Chamber of Local Authorities and a Chamber of Regions.
- The 1800-strong secretariat.

The European Convention on Human Rights

The Convention for the Protection of Human Rights and Fundamental Freedoms, called in short the European Convention on Human Rights (ECHR), is the Council's most significant achievement. It was adopted on 4 November 1950 and came into force in 1953. It sets out a number of civil and political rights and freedoms which states are under an obligation to guarantee to everyone within their jurisdiction, among them the right to life; to protection against torture and inhuman treatment; to freedom and safety; to a fair trial; to respect for one's private and family life and correspondence; and to freedom of expression, thought, conscience, religion and assembly.

Article 14 of the Convention does prohibit discrimination in the enjoyment of all rights and freedoms set forth in it, including sex discrimination:

> "The enjoyment of the rights and freedoms set forth in this Convention shall be secured without discrimination on any ground such as sex, race, colour, language, religion, political or other opinion, national or social origin, association with a national minority, property, birth or other status."

However, Article 14 is not an independent provision of non-discrimination. A claimant to the European Court on Human Rights may only add a reference to it to his main complaint in relation to an alleged violation of one of the civil or political rights listed in the ECHR.

In keeping with the fundamental principle that all persons are equal before the law and are entitled to the equal protection of the law, Member States of the Council added Protocol No. 12 to the Convention on 4 November 2000. Under Article 1 "General prohibition of discrimination", paragraph 2 of the Protocol specifies that "No one shall be discriminated against by any public authority on any ground such as those mentioned in paragraph 1": the latter repeats the text of Article 14 of the Convention. The Protocol entered into force on 1 April 2005.

The European Court on Human Rights

The Court has been set up under Section II of the Convention. States and individuals, regardless of their nationality, may refer to the Court alleged violations by contracting states of the rights guaranteed by the Convention.

The Court's jurisdiction is compulsory for all contracting parties, and it extends to all matters concerning the interpretation and application of the Convention and Protocols. It deals with such matters only after all domestic remedies have been exhausted. Established in Strasbourg, also the site of the Council, it sits on a permanent basis. Judgments are final under certain conditions, and State Parties undertake to abide by the final judgments. Execution of the judgments is supervised by the Committee of Ministers.

The European Social Charter

The initial European Social Charter, the counterpart of the European Convention on Human Rights in the social domain, was signed on 18 October 1961 in Rome and came into force on 26 February 1965. The Charter was revised in 1996 in order to take account of the fundamental social changes which had occurred since the text was adopted. All of the 47 Member States have signed either the 1961 Charter or the 1996 revision, and in 2007, 39 have ratified either of these instruments.[1]

The Parties accept as the aim of their policy, to be pursued by all appropriate means both national and international in character, the attainment of conditions in which specific rights and principles may be effectively realised. Those pertaining to the employment of women at work include the right of employed women to protection of maternity (Article 8) and the right to equal opportunities and equal treatment in matters of employment and occupation without discrimination on the grounds of sex (Article 20). The non-discrimination obligation is repeated in Part V, Article E of the revised Charter.

Under the Appendix to the revised Charter provisions concerning the protection of women, particularly as regards pregnancy, confinement and the post-natal period, are not deemed to be discrimination under Article 20. In the same Appendix, a differential treatment of men and women based on an objective and reasonable justification is also not deemed discriminatory (Article E).

Article 26 affirms the right of all workers to protection of their dignity at work: the Parties undertake, in consultation with employers' and workers' organizations, to promote awareness, information and the prevention of sexual harassment and of recurrent, reprehensible, or distinctly negative and offensive actions against individual workers. Article 27 affirms the right of workers with family responsibilities to equal opportunities.

State Parties undertake to consider themselves bound by at least six of nine articles, which include the non-discrimination Article 20. Additionally, States should consider themselves bound by not less that sixteen articles or sixty-three numbered paragraphs.

---

1 The European Social Charter should not be confused with the Community Charter on Fundamental Social Rights of Workers 1989. Having been ratified by only 11 Member States, it is not in force and not binding. See B. Hepple, "The Implementation of the Community Charter of Fundamental Social Rights" in (1990) 53 *Modern Law Review* 643-654.

Implementation and Monitoring of the Undertakings

The provisions of the Charter should be implemented by national laws or regulations, agreements between employers or employers' organizations and workers' organizations, a combination of these two methods or other means (Article I).

Every year State Parties report on their implementation of the Charter in law and in practice. Each report concerns some of the accepted provisions of the Charter. On the basis of these reports, the European Committee of Social Rights – composed of fifteen members elected by the Council of Europe's Committee of Ministers – decides, in 'Conclusions', whether or not the States complied with their obligations. If they have not, and if a State takes no action on a decision of non-conformity, the Committee of Ministers addresses a recommendation to the State asking it to change the situation.

Complaints Procedure

The Additional Protocol to the Charter opened for signature in 1995 (ETS No. 158) and came into force on 1 July 1998. It provides a system of collective complaints as one of the measures designed to improve the effective enforcement of the social rights guaranteed by the Charter.

The Protocol entitles social partners and non-governmental organizations[2] to lodge collective complaints of violations of the Charter in States which have ratified it. The complaint is examined by the European Committee of Social Rights which rules on its admissibility. The Committee then takes a decision on the merits of the complaint, which it forwards to the parties concerned and to the Committee of Ministers in a report which is made public within four months of its being forwarded.

On the basis of the report of the European Committee of Social Rights, the Committee of Ministers adopts a resolution. If appropriate, it may recommend that the state concerned take specific measures to bring the situation into line with the Charter.

The Steering Committee for Equality between Women and Men

This Committee is the intergovernmental body responsible for defending, stimulating and conducting the Council of Europe's actions to promote equality between

[2] These are international organizations of employers and trade unions listed in the Charter, other international NGOs which have consultative status with the Council of Europe, and representative national organizations of employers and trade unions within the jurisdiction of the Contracting Party against which they have lodged a complaint (Article 1 of the Protocol).

women and men. It is answerable to the Committee of Ministers from which it receives its instructions and to which it addresses its reports and proposals.

Appointed by each of the Council's Member States, its members are "persons with high-level responsibility for policies in favour of equality between women and men, or other highly qualified specialists".

The Committee's main terms of reference are:

- to examine the situation as regards equality between women and men in European society and consider its progress;
- to promote cooperation between Member States with a view to achieve real equality between women and men as a *sine qua non* of genuine democracy and to stimulate action at both national and Council of Europe level;
- to prepare the European Ministerial Conferences on this subject.

Following the Committee's report on gender mainstreaming, the Committee of Ministers adopted Recommendation No. 98 on gender mainstreaming in October 1998. It recommends that governments disseminate the report widely and encourage its use as a tool for implementing the strategy in their programmes and activities.[3]

At the 6th European Ministerial Conference on Equality between Women and Men, held in Stockholm on 8-9 June 2006, it was reported that violations of women's human rights are increasing. Women are still marginalized in political and public life, paid less for work of equal value and find themselves victims of poverty and unemployment more often than men. These inequalities cause long-term damage to the economy. In a resolution and action plan on Achieving Gender Equality in All Spheres of Society, the European Ministers asked the Committee of Ministers to actively assess the costs (personal, social and economic) of continuing gender inequality in its 47 Member States. They also called on all Member States to make full use of tools such as gender analysis and sex-disaggregated data when planning, developing and implementing national policies, as well as to integrate a gender perspective into the budgetary process in order to achieve *de facto* gender equality.

Conclusion

The European Social Charter affirms basic rights in the area of women's protection, equal opportunities and equal treatment of employed women, and non-discrimination on the ground of sex. The Appendix to the Charter

---

3 See also Recommendation 148 (2004) and 176 (2004) on gender mainstreaming at local and regional levels.

establishes that provisions for the protection of women, particularly as regards pregnancy, are not deemed to be discriminatory, and legitimizes a justified differential treatment.

The Charter confirms the international law principle of national implementation of international conventions. The obligations of State Parties include annual reporting and review by the European Committee of Social Rights. Further action is limited to a possible recommendation from the Committee of Ministers to a State to change the situation.

The 1995 Protocol goes further by allowing collective complaints of alleged violations of the Charter by states. However, individual complaints are not allowed, and the final outcome of a complaint is also limited to a resolution or a recommendation by the Committee of Minister to the State found in violation of the Charter.

The European Social Charter has not created any international judicial mechanism to enforce and sanction violations of rights guaranteed by the Charter.

The European Convention on Human Rights has one article (Article 14) on sex discrimination, supplemented by Protocol No. 12. These do not refer specifically to women at work, while the European Social Charter has precise provisions on the protection of women at work and their rights in employment.

The only effective machinery of judicial control for discrimination at work today exists within the EU, which covers claims by individuals via the procedure of preliminary rulings requested by national courts of the Member States, as explained in Chapter 4. One wonders whether Protocol No. 12 would open up in practice an alternative judicial control mechanism on the European level to redress discrimination at work. It would possibly provide a remedy to citizens of Non-Member States of the EU.

Chapter 4

THE EUROPEAN UNION

Background

The devastation of the war and the necessity to rebuild Europe inspired statesmen like Konrad Adenauer, Winston Churchill, Alcide de Gasperi, Robert Schuman, Jean Monnet and Paul-Henri Spaak to set about creating a new order for Western Europe.

The implementation of this new regime started modestly with the Schuman Declaration of 9 May 1950. He proposed a European Coal and Steel Community (ECSC) transferring sovereignty to a supra-national 'High Authority' to share the production of these two basic war industries and prevent the reoccurrence of war between the two arch-enemies, France and Germany. The Treaty of Paris 1951 laid the foundations and created this first European Community. The founding Member States, besides France and Germany, were Italy, Belgium, the Netherlands and Luxembourg.

The success of the High Authority, under Jean Monnet, encouraged the founders to create two more European Communities. In 1957 two treaties were adopted in Rome. One set up the European Economic Community (EEC), the other created the European Atomic Energy Community (EURATOM).

The Preamble of the EEC Treaty of Rome discloses the long-term aim of "laying the foundations of an ever closer union of the peoples of Europe". Indeed, fifty years after 1957, a much closer union has been achieved and the dream of an almost federalist Europe has been crystallized step by step. The principle of uniting peoples, not States, contributed to a progressive evolution towards integration of the peoples of Europe, transferring the sovereignty of states in certain domains gradually to the organs of the EEC, the European Community (EC) the European Union (EU).

The creation of a harmonised legal regime contributed to the uniformity of the social and labour laws in the Member States that are relevant to our study.

The evolution of the integration of Europe can be surveyed *ratione personae* and *ratione materiae.*

The Scope of European Integration Ratione Personae

The six founding Member States of the three Communities were joined in 1973 by the UK, Ireland and Denmark. In 1981 Greece became the tenth Member. In 1986 Spain and Portugal joined and in 1995 Sweden, Finland and Austria became Members. The EC of fifteen members was enlarged in 2004 by ten new members: Cyprus, the Czech Republic, Estonia, Hungary, Latvia, Lithuania, Malta, Poland, Slovakia and Slovenia. In January 2007 Bulgaria and Romania joined, increasing the membership of the EC to twenty seven States, almost doubling the number of Member States as of the beginning of the century. The population of the EU reaches almost 500 million people who are governed by the same legal system and by the same norms.

The Scope of European Integration Ratione Materiae

The sources of EU law deserve special attention. However, at this stage only the basic Treaties progressively adopted during the last five decades will be enumerated:

- The Treaty of Rome (EEC) 1957
- The Single European Act (SEA) 1986
- The Treaty on European Union (TEU) (The Treaty of Maastricht) 1992
- The Treaty of Amsterdam (ToA) 1997
- The Treaty of Nice 2000
- The Treaty on the EU Constitution, was rejected by the referendum in France and the Netherlands in spring 2005.
- The Treaty of Lisbon 2007.

These are the primary sources of law of the EC/EU. The Constitution has not yet been adopted and is not binding. The Reform Treaty launched by the Brussels European Council and the Lisbon European Council 2007 revived the EU Charter on Fundamental Rights to endow it with legal force, and it is hoped that the revised instruments will be ready for ratification before 2009.

The Treaty of Rome 1957, the founding Treaty, launched the economic aims of the EEC by creating a barrier-free area where four freedoms dominate: freedom of circulation of persons, freedom of circulation of goods, freedom of circulation of services, and freedom of circulation of capital. These freedoms were implemented by 1992, the date stipulated in the Single European Act (SEA) 1986 for the completion of the single internal market. The aims of the EEC are enshrined in Article 3 of the Treaty of Rome. The SEA amended the Treaty of Rome, accelerating integration and enlarging the scope of activity of the EC to include environmental and consumer protection. The SEA amendments also empowered the European Parliament and added a Court of First Instance to alleviate the overburdened Court of Justice (ECJ).

In addition to the institutional changes, the SEA's Preamble mentions the EC's commitment to human rights for the first time.

The Treaty on European Union (TEU) 1992 (The Treaty of Maastricht) has transformed the EC into a political and monetary Union. It enlarged the scope of competence of the EU and established a single currency for the majority of the then Member States. The EU is now composed of three pillars. The first pillar holds those domains covered hitherto by the three European Communities, where integration has taken place and where the EC/EU has exclusive powers, such as the customs union, the single market, trade and agricultural policy, the four above-mentioned freedoms, social policy and freedom of competition. In addition some new policies introduced by the Maastricht Treaty itself, such as EU Citizenship, research, environment, immigration, and asylum also come under the first pillar. The policies and laws in these domains are all harmonized and integrated within the Union forming part of the *aquis communautaire.*

The second pillar carries cooperation (not integration) in common foreign and security policy, such as common positions and measures for peacekeeping, human rights, democracy and aid to non-member countries as well as disarmament and the financial aspects of defence.

The third pillar deals with cooperation (not integration) in justice and home affairs, including cooperation between judicial authorities in civil and criminal law, police cooperation, combating racism and xenophobia, fighting drugs, the arms trade and organised crime as well as terrorism and trafficking in human beings.

The Principle of Subsidiarity

The new pillars have extended the scope of activity of the Union to such a degree as to justify the principle of subsidiarity enshrined in Article 3b of the Maastricht Treaty now Article 5 EC:

> "The Community shall act within the limits of the powers conferred upon it by this Treaty and of the objectives assigned to it therein.
>
> In areas which do not fall within its exclusive competence, the Community shall take action, in accordance with the principle of subsidiarity, only if and in so far as the objectives of the proposed action cannot be sufficiently achieved by the Member States and can therefore, by reason of the scale or effects of the proposed action, be better achieved by the Community."

The principle is inspired by Roman Catholic social doctrine. It has two facets: the affirmative duty to act when the objectives to be pursued can be better attained at Community level, and the negative duty not to act where the objectives can be satisfactorily attained by the Member States.

The principle is not to be applied where the Community has exclusive powers, such as some of the domains included in the first pillar. It is to be applied where the Community and the Member States have concurrent powers. In the field of social law, including gender equality, the competences are within the concurrent powers of the Member States and the Community. As we shall see, activity on this issue is growing on the European level.

We shall come back to this principle when dealing with the social law of the EU, and the relationship between Community law and state laws governing equality of men and women.

The Unique Legal Character of the EC/EU

Regardless of the debate between a federalist versus a non-federalist approach to European integration, it is clear that the legal order of the EC/EU is *sui generis.* The legal nature of the EC cannot be described as pertaining to International Law nor to national law. EC norms are a fusion of both.

The ECJ formulated two pivotal precedents that established the true nature of the EC in the early sixties. The first precedent coined the principle of direct effect of Community law in the domestic laws of the Member States, and the second precedent created the principle of supremacy of community law over domestic laws in case of conflict between them. Both principles demonstrate the similarity of Community law to federal law.

The Van Gend & Loos *Case 1963*[1] *and the Direct Effect of Community Law*

The Dutch company *Van Gend & Loos* brought an action in a Dutch administrative court against the Dutch customs authorities for raising an import duty on a chemical product exported from Germany. The company considered the increase of import duty in trade between two Member States a violation of Article 12 of the Treaty of Rome now Article 25 which prohibits "... introducing between themselves any new customs duties on imports or exports or any charges having equivalent effect". The Dutch Court suspended the proceedings and referred the matter to the ECJ in Luxembourg for a preliminary ruling, according to the procedure laid down in Article 177 of the Treaty of Rome now Article 234.

The Court found that the Dutch company's claim was justified and ruled that Article 12 can be invoked directly by a private individual against the state authorities before a national court, although the provision has not been transformed into domestic law. The ECJ stated in its ruling that:

---

[1] Case 26/62 (1963) ECR 1.

> "the objective of the EEC Treaty, which is to establish a common market, the functioning of which is of direct concern to interested parties in the Community, implies that this Treaty is more than an agreement which merely creates mutual obligations between the States. This view is confirmed by the preamble to the Treaty, which refers not only to governments but to peoples. It is also confirmed more specifically by the establishment of institutions endowed with sovereign rights the exercise of which affects Member States and also their citizens. The conclusion to be drawn from this is that the Community constitutes a new legal order of international law for the benefit of which the States have limited their sovereign rights, albeit within limited fields, and the subjects of which comprise not only Member States but also their nationals."

The Costa v. ENEL *Case 1964*[2] *and the Supremacy of Community Law*

The principle of direct effect of Community law opened the door for the next principle, that Community law prevails over national law in case of incompatibility between the two, regardless of whether the national law is prior or posterior to Community law.

The facts of this case were as follows: In 1962 Italy nationalised the production and distribution of electricity and transferred the assets of the electricity undertakings to the National Electricity Board (ENEL) that represents a state monopoly in violation of Article 37 and other provisions of the Treaty of Rome. Mr Costa, a shareholder of Edison Volta, one of the nationalised undertakings, considered himself deprived of his dividend and consequently refused to pay an electricity bill for a negligible sum of money. In proceedings before a small claims court in Milan Mr Costa argued that the nationalisation infringed the provisions of the Treaty and that the action against him should fail. The Milan court suspended the proceedings and referred the matter to the ECJ for a preliminary ruling. The Luxembourg Court used the opportunity to elaborate on the unique legal nature of the EC and stated as follows:

> "By contrast with ordinary international treaties, the EEC treaty has created its own legal system which ... became an integral part of the legal systems of the Member States and which their courts are bound to apply. By creating a Community of unlimited duration, having its own institutions, its own personality, its own legal capacity and capacity of representation on the international plane and, more particularly, real powers stemming from a limitation of sovereignty or a transfer of powers from the States to the Community, the Member States have limited their

[2] Case 6/64 (1964) ECR 585.

> sovereign rights ... and have thus created a body of law which binds both their nationals and themselves."

The Court developed the doctrine laid down in the *Van Gend & Loos* Case and came to the following conclusion:

> "It follows from all these observations that the law stemming from the Treaty, an independent source of law, could not, because of its special and original nature, be overridden by domestic legal provisions, however framed, without being deprived of its character as Community law and without the legal basis of the Community itself being called into question. The transfer by the States from their domestic legal system to the Community legal system of the rights and obligations arising under the Treaty carries with it a permanent limitation of their sovereign rights, against which a subsequent unilateral act incompatible with the concept of the Community cannot prevail."

No future unilateral State legislation can prevail over the Treaty of Rome. The Italian nationalisation, although adopted by a posterior Italian law, cannot prevail over the prior law that implemented in Italy in 1958 the Treaty of Rome 1957. The maxim *lex posteriori derogat lex priori*, which usually resolves situations of conflict between two laws, simply does not apply in the context of the relationship between Community law and domestic law. Community law always prevails, like a federal law in relation to a state law, even if the state law is the later law. This principle of supremacy of Community law has impacted and shaped the progress of equality in the EC and influenced the *acquis communautaire* in this domain.

The Institutions of the EC/EU

Four major institutions have served the EC from the beginning:

- The European Parliament
- The Council of Ministers
- The European Commission
- The Court of Justice.

There is no separation of powers in the EC and the all important legislative powers are shared by the first three institutions. Even today after it acquired more standing in the legislative process, the European Parliament is not a true legislative body, but co-operates or co-decides together with the Council and the Commission.

The European Parliament

As of 1979 the European Parliament, the representative of the peoples of Europe, is elected by direct elections for four years. After the 2007 enlargement it numbers 786 delegates who sit according to political parties and do not represent national parliaments. The Parliament has advisory, supervisory and budgetary functions. Since 1993 it has had a say in the process of legislation, including the more recent gender equality directives.

The Council

The Council represents the governments of the Member States. Each Member State has one Minister. As of January 2007 there are twenty seven Ministers, after the accession of Bulgaria and Romania. The Council is the executive institution of the EC and has the decision-making power to finalise legislation, to conduct foreign relations and conclude treaties. It is assisted by the Permanent Representatives Committee of Ambassadors of the Member States accredited to the EC (the COREPER).

The European Commission

The powers of the Commission are diverse and wide. This institution is an integrated organ of the Community. It operates through twenty seven Commissioners. Although each of them comes from a Member State, they do not represent the States, but have solely the interests of the Community at heart. The Commission is often called the 'Watchdog of the Community', because one of its major tasks is to control the implementation of Community law by the Member States. The Commission can bring a Member State to the ECJ for infringement of Community Law under Article 169 now Article 226. The Court may impose daily fines on a Member State if the violation is proven. This may qualify the Commission as a quasi-judicial body, for it also has the power to impose fines on individuals and enterprises for violation of the Community provisions on freedom of competition according to Regulation 17/62. These decisions are subject to review by the Court of First Instance (CFI) in accordance with Article 173 now Article 230.

The Commission is also an initiator of Community legislation in the form of Regulations and Directives. Since 1992 it shares this power with the European Parliament.

It can act as an executive, administrating and implementing legislation. It also administers the funds of the Community. At the same time one can say that the legal personality of the Community is vested in the Commission, as it represents the Community internationally and also negotiates agreements on the Community's behalf.

The Commission is headed by a President, who is assisted by two Vice Presidents. The Commissioners are appointed by common accord of the governments of the Member States for a renewable term of five years.

The Court Of Justice

The Court is composed of a number of judges equivalent to the number of Member States and of nine Advocates General (AG). One Advocate General is appointed to assist the Court in each case before it. The Opinions of the Advocate General are very important in summing up the existing law, yet they are not binding on the Court.

The judges and Advocates General are nominated for six years and their term may be renewed.

The jurisdiction and competence of the Court is diverse and is exclusive in the application and interpretation of Community law in accordance with Article 219 now Article 292. The ECJ is the EU's supreme judicial body in charge of respect of the law under Article 164 now Article 220.

The Court has international jurisdiction in cases of disputes between States. This jurisdiction was exercised in very few cases for in most of the cases where a Member State violates Community Law it is the European Commission that brings an action against Member States before the Court of Justice in accordance with Article 169 now Article 226. The latter decides on the existence of an infringement and may also impose fines in case of non-respect of the judgment of the Court according to Article 171 now Article 228.

The Court is also a Constitutional Court that can review and annul acts by the Council, the Commission or the Parliament in accordance with Article 173 now Article 230. This type of action was inspired by French administrative law, as developed by the *Conseil d'Etat*. Member States and, under certain conditions individuals, may ask the Court to review the acts of the institutions because of the following grounds: 1. acts without authority, namely, abuse of power. 2. disregard of an important procedural rule. 3. disregard of a Treaty provision or 4. misuse of powers.

For our study, the most important role of the Court is the judicial authority to hand down preliminary rulings requested by the national courts when a question of validity, application or interpretation of Community law arises in cases pending before them in accordance with Article 177 now Article 234.

This provision lays down that:

> "The Court of Justice shall have jurisdiction to give preliminary rulings concerning (a) the interpretation of this Treaty, (b) the validity and interpretation of acts of the institutions of the Community ... Where such a question is raised before any court or tribunal of a Member State, that court or tribunal may, if it considers that a decision on the question

is necessary to enable it to give judgment, request the Court of justice to give a ruling thereon."

Where any such question is raised in a case pending before a court or tribunal of a Member State, against whose decisions there is no judicial remedy under national law, that court or tribunal shall bring the matter before the Court of Justice.

It is under this jurisdiction that the law governing equality was developed and enriched. The national courts and tribunals of all instances, as well as the highest courts, referred cases to the ECJ involving the interpretation of the various directives as well as of the primary law provisions enshrined in the Treaties. The national courts were left with their discretion over the facts of the cases while the ECJ was concerned with the law. The final decision in this procedure of preliminary rulings is rendered by the national courts. The division of competences between the national courts and the Luxembourg Court was mentioned in many cases and was more recently elaborated in the *Alabaster* Case 2004.[3]

In addition to these diverse roles the Court also functioned for some years as an administrative court to hear staff cases against the institutions of the EC in accordance with Article 179 now Article 236. When the Court of First Instance (CFI) was created to alleviate the ECJ of its overload of cases in 1989, the staff cases were transferred to the CFI. In 2005 a separate Tribunal was created to decide staff cases, the EU Civil Service Tribunal. The decisions of the Court in staff cases, as we shall see, have enriched the case law on equality of men and women at work, especially in the early years.

The Court's competences do not end here. Besides the Court's jurisdiction in the field of settlement of disputes, including actions for damages resulting from contractual or non-contractual liability in accordance with Articles 235 and 288 (1) and (2), the ECJ has also jurisdiction to deliver binding advisory opinions in the context of the external relations of the Community, when the compatibility of new Community agreements with the basic Treaties is questioned.

The Legislative Powers of the EC/EU

The written sources of the law of the Community can be divided into primary sources embodied in the various basic Treaties, enumerated above, and into secondary legislation, adopted by the Community itself within its competences under Article 189 now Article 249.

These provisions empower the Community to create laws. Article 189 provided that:

---

3 Case C-147/02 (2005) ECR I-3101.

- In order to carry out their task the Council and the Commission shall, in accordance with the provisions of this Treaty, make regulations, issue directives, take decisions, make recommendations or deliver opinions.
- A regulation shall have general application. It shall be binding in its entirety and directly applicable in all Member States.
- A directive shall be binding, as to the result to be achieved, upon each Member State to which it is addressed, but shall leave to the national authorities the choice of form and methods.
- A decision shall be binding in its entirety upon those to whom it is addressed.
- Recommendations and opinions shall have no binding force.

Article 189 was amended by the Treaty of European Union to take into account Parliament's increased legislative power of co-decision and is now formulated in Article 249.

The acts enumerated in Article 249 are divided into binding and non-binding measures. In the domain that interests us only directives and recommendations are relevant, as the *corpus juris* of the Community on equality of men and women at work was developed through the adoption of directives and recommendations.

As we have seen, recommendations are not binding upon the Member States, but are promotional in character and have an impact on harmonisation of the laws of the Member States. Directives are binding as to the results to be achieved upon Member States. The law on equality of men and women in the workplace is embodied in fourteen Directives, and a word of explanation is required about their impact on national law and the nature of their direct effect domestically.

Directives usually provide for a period of implementation to allow the Member States to choose the forms and methods of adaptation of their laws to the new requirements. Once this period expires the Member States are bound by the Directive. A violation of a directive by the Member State may engage the procedure of infringement, and the Commission may bring an action against the Member State as provided for in Article 226 discussed above.

A Directive also has a direct effect in domestic law wherever an action is brought against the State by an individual who invokes a directive before a national court, provided the directive is self-executory. Namely, if the directive is clear, precise and unconditional, the national court has no reason to overlook its binding force upon the Member State. This was termed as the *direct vertical effect of directives* as illustrated in the *Van Duyn* Case in 1974.[4]

4 Case 41/74 (1974) ECR 1337.

Where a directive is not self-executory, it will, nevertheless, have an *indirect vertical effect* in that an individual is entitled to bring an action against a Member State in a national court for causing him damage through the violation of the directive by lack of implementation. This was the issue of the landmark decision in *Francovich* v. *Italy 1991*,[5] and this precedent was confirmed in future cases (e.g. in the case of *Dori* v. *Recreb Srl 1993*[6]).

Mrs Marshall's Case 1986

The *direct or indirect vertical effect* has now to be distinguished from what is termed *the horizontal effect*. The ECJ was faced with this distinction for the first time in the much discussed case of *Mrs Marshall* v. *Southampton & South West Hampshire Area Health Authority (Teaching)*.[7] The directive invoked in this case is at the centre of our study and we shall, therefore, consider this preliminary ruling in detail.

Mrs Marshall was dismissed from her job with the Health Authority at the age of 62. Under national law the age of compulsory retirement for women was 60 whereas the age for men was 65. Mrs Marshall challenged the legality of her dismissal as being discriminatory and incompatible with the Equal Treatment Directive 76/207 of 1976 which prohibits discrimination in all conditions of work, including dismissal. The difference in age of retirement for men and women in England was permissible under the Sex Discrimination Act 1975, which was then in force, and which expressly excluded "provisions relating to death or retirement" from its ambit.

The case went up to the Court of Appeal and the Court referred two questions to the ECJ asking for a preliminary ruling in accordance with Article 177 now Article 234:

1. Whether a different retirement age for men and women was in breach of Directive 76/207?
2. If so, whether Directive 76/207 could be relied on by Mrs Marshall in the circumstances of the case?

The relevant circumstances were that the Health Authority, though a 'public body', was acting in its capacity as employer. The question of vertical and horizontal effects was fully argued, and the ECJ followed the submissions of Advocate General Slynn, holding (a) that the compulsory different retirement age for men and women was in breach of the Equal Treatment Directive (76/207)

---

[5] Cases C-6&9/90 (1991) ECR I-5357.

[6] Case C-91/92, (1993) ECR I-3325.

[7] Case 152/84, (1986) ECR 737.

of 1976, and, (b) that the Directive could be invoked against a public body such as the Health Authority. Namely,

> "... where a person involved in legal proceedings is able to rely on a Directive as against the State he may do so regardless of the capacity in which the latter is acting, whether employer or public authority."

By reasoning *a contrario,* in an action brought between individuals and not against the State authorities, i.e. a horizontal claim, the Directive cannot be relied upon before a national court until it is duly implemented by the national legislature and becomes part of national law.

This decision was criticised as being arbitrary and artificial, but the ECJ did not reverse it in the *Dori* Case mentioned above. The law as it stands is that actions between private individuals do not benefit from the direct effect of Directives. The solution is to be found in an amendment of the national law so as to conform with the Directive. Indeed the UK Sex Discrimination Act 1975 was amended in the wake of the *Marshall* Case in 1986 and the provision excluding retirement conditions was removed. Dismissal of women because of different retirement ages for men and women is no longer permissible in the private as well as in the public sectors in England.

In practice a new discriminatory circumstance arises. Women have an option to work as long as men do. However men do not have the option of retiring at the age of retirement of women. We shall discuss this issue at a later stage.

We have enlarged the discussion over the legal effect of directives because the legislation or secondary written sources of law adopted by the Community on the subject of our study was not in the form of Regulations but Directives that have the purpose of harmonising national laws of the Member States. It is due to this mechanism that one can speak of Community law as a 'quasi -federal law' that applies in twenty seven States in Europe and governs the rights and duties of almost 500 million citizens. In that sense it is a unique legal order.

The Substantive Written Sources of Equality Law

Primary Norms

The first and only provision to be found in the Treaty of Rome 1957 governing equality of pay for men and women for equal work was enshrined in Article 119 which stated:

> Each Member State shall during the first stage ensure and subsequently maintain the application of the principle that men and women should receive equal pay for equal work.

> For the purpose of this Article 'pay' means the ordinary basic or minimum wage or salary and any other consideration, whether in cash or in kind, which the worker receives, directly or indirectly, in respect of his employment from his employer.
>
> Equal pay without discrimination based on sex means:
>
> – that pay for the same work at piece rates shall be calculated on the basis of the same unit of measurement;
>
> – that pay for work at time rates shall be the same for the same job."

At the beginning, this was the only legal text dealing with equality of the sexes at work. Article 119 is the 'European translation' of ILO Convention on Equal Remuneration No. 100 1951.[8] However, Article 119 was much more limited in scope than the ILO Convention, as the latter imposed not only equal pay for equal work, but also equal pay for work of equal value. Article 119 appears in Chapter I (social provisions) of Title III (social policy) of Part 3 (policy of the EC) of the Treaty of Rome, yet its insertion into the Treaty was not prompted by social considerations, but rather by economic reasons and was intended to ensure that competition in the Member States was not distorted by the employment of women at lower rates than men for the same work.[9] The Article has acquired a social egalitarian significance through the case law of the Court of Justice. The ECJ confirmed the dual socio-economic function of Article 119 in the following terms: "This double aim, which is at once economic and social, shows that the principle of equal pay forms part of the foundations of the Community"[10]

Article 119 speaks narrowly of "equal pay for equal work" and not of remuneration for "work of equal value", which is the term adopted by the ILO Convention. The limitation to equal work produced difficulties in comparing jobs in segregated fields, i.e. kindergarten teachers, secretaries, midwives, where there was no "male-comparison". The ILO formula covers a much wider scope including segregated jobs to which equal value may be attributed by a job classification system or otherwise.

It is through Community legislation, and especially by the adoption of the Equal Pay Directive of 1975, that Community norms were brought in line with the ILO concept. Before we discuss Community legislation and the main written source of law governing equality, as enshrined in some fourteen Directives, we

8 Per Advocate General Trabucchi in Case 43/75 *Defrenne* v. *Sabena* (No. 2) (1976) ECR 455.

9 Smit and Herzog, *The Law of the EEC* (Commentary) Vol. 3 (Mathew Bender, New York, 1976), p. 757.

10 *Defrenne* v. *Sabena* (No. 2), at paragraph 13.

have to clarify the evolution of the primary source, Article 119 of the Treaty of Rome 1957, to its successor, Article 141 of the Treaty of Amsterdam 1997. Forty years separate these two provisions and the latter Treaty reflects the progress made.

The Treaty of Amsterdam (ToA) entered into force on 1 May 1999. Women's rights are given a higher profile under the new Treaty.[11] Article F takes over the general provision on human rights already enshrined in the Treaty of Maastricht.

> "The Union is founded on the principles of liberty, democracy, respect for human rights and fundamental freedoms and the rule of law, principles that are common to the Members States. The case law of the Community Court has repeatedly declared its adherence to fundamental human rights as part of the general principles of law that it is bound to respect."

Article 2 of the ToA provides that the Community shall promote a high level of employment and social protection, equality between men and women, the raising of the standard of living and quality of life, and economic and social cohesion and solidarity among Member States.

Article 3 (2) states that in all activities referred to in this Article, which covers the totality of the tasks of the Community, the Community shall aim to eliminate inequalities and to promote equality between women and men.

The new provisions of the ToA enable women's rights to qualify as fundamental human rights, to be generally respected in the same way as race or religion. Article 3(2), which binds the Community in all activities that it undertakes to eliminate inequalities and promote equality in practice between men and women, ensures the implementation of the idea of 'mainstreaming' equality of men and women and ranking it as an individual human right.

Article 13 empowers the Council, acting unanimously on a proposal of the Commission and after consulting the European Parliament, to take "appropriate action to combat discrimination based on sex, racial or ethnic origin, religion or belief, disability, age or sexual orientation".

Article 137 now states that the Community shall support and complement the activities of the Member States to promote equality between men and women with regard to labour market opportunities and equal treatment at work.

Finally, Article 141 replacing and amending Article 119 states the legal situation today:

> "1. Each Member State shall ensure that the principle of equal pay for male and female workers for equal work or work of equal value is applied.

[11] See European Parliament, Directorate General for Research, *Working Paper on Women's Rights and the Treaty of Amsterdam* (1998).

> 2. For the purpose of this article, 'pay' means the ordinary basic or minimum wage or salary and any other consideration, whether in cash or in kind, which the worker receives directly or indirectly, in respect of his employment, from his employer.
>
> Equal pay without discrimination based on sex means:
>
> – that pay for the same work at piece rates shall be calculated on the basis of the same unit of measurement;
>
> – that pay for work at time rates shall be the same for the same job.
>
> 3. The Council, acting in accordance with the procedure referred to in Article 251, and after consulting the Economic and Social Committee, shall adopt measures to ensure the application of the principle of equal opportunities and equal treatment of men and women in matters of employment and occupation, including the principle of equal pay for equal work or work of equal value.
>
> 4. With a view to ensuring full equality in practice between men and women in working life, the principle of equal treatment shall not prevent any Member State from maintaining or adopting measures providing for specific advantages in order to make it easier for the underrepresented sex to pursue a vocational activity or to prevent or compensate for disadvantages in professional careers."

Article 141 (1) echoes the provisions of ILO Convention 100, as already adopted in the Equal Pay Directive of 1975. Now it is enshrined, however, in a primary source of law, in the consolidated EC Treaty.[12]

Article 141(2) matches the original provision of Article 119.

Article 141 (3) empowers the Community to adopt measures to implement not only the principle of equal pay but also the principle of equal opportunities and equal treatment of men and women in all conditions of work.

Article 141 (4) gives legal backing to positive action in favour of women in order to redress past discrimination and with a view to ensure full equality in practice and not merely in theory. Without going as far as promoting affirmative action, the Article does not prevent any Member State from maintaining or adopting measures providing for specific advantages in order to make it easier for the underrepresented sex to pursue a vocational activity or prevent any Member State to compensate for disadvantages in professional careers.

We shall focus on the different issues involved in the interpretation and application of Article 141 in the relevant chapters of the book.

---

12 OJ (2002) L 325/5. This consolidating Treaty adopted the numbers of Articles as modified by the ToA.

EU Legislation

The 1970s, under the impact of the UN Decade for Women (1975-1985), saw great legislative activity in the Community in the field of equality of women at work. The first directive to be adopted was the Equal Pay Directive 1975,[13] which aimed to harmonise and approximate the national laws in the implementation of the principle of equal pay for equal work and work of equal value. It grants individuals a right of action in case of discrimination and protects employees against victimisation. The Member States were bound to respect the right to equal pay and provide for remedies.

A year later the Community adopted the Equal Treatment Directive 1976[14] on the implementation of equal treatment for men and women as regards access to employment, vocational training and promotion and working conditions including dismissal. This very comprehensive Directive has impacted the employment landscape in Europe. In the domain of sex equality it echoes the ILO Convention 111 1958. Here too a right of action was bestowed on individuals to redress discrimination without fear of victimisation. This Directive served as the basis of numerous actions by individuals and enriched, as we shall see, the Community *corpus juris* in the field of equality at work.

Two years later the Directive of 1978 on the progressive implementation of the principle of equal treatment for men and women in matters of social security was adopted.[15] The Directive has left the crucial question of retirement ages to the Member States and almost thirty years later there is no approximation of the laws in Europe. Only a minority of the Member States has equal retirement ages for men and women.

The topic of social security has been addressed in several publications[16] and the ILO is very active in this domain. We desire therefore to leave this subject for experts, and the present publication will not deal with the matter.

The 1980s saw two additional directives, both in 1986. The first was the Occupational Social Security Directive on the implementation of the principle of equal treatment for men and women in occupational social security schemes, which was subsequently modified in the mid-1990s by the Directive of 1996.[17] The second, the Self Employed (Equal Treatment) Directive[18] concerns the application of the principle of equal treatment between men and women engaged in

---

13 75/117/EEC OJ (1975) L 45/19.

14 76/207/EEC OJ (1976) L 39/40.

15 79/7 OJ (1979) L 6/24.

16 E.g. E. Ellis, *EU Anti-Discrimination Law* (Oxford, 2005), chapter 8.

17 86/378/EEC OJ (1986) L 225/40.

18 86/613/EEC OJ (1986) L 359/56.

an activity, including agriculture, in a self-employed capacity, and the protection of self-employed women during pregnancy and motherhood.

In the 1990s the issue of protection during pregnancy remained on the agenda in the context of safety and health at work. The Directive of 1992 on the introduction of measures to encourage improvements in safety and health at work for pregnant workers and workers who have recently given birth or breast-feed[19] aims to protect pregnant women from inherent risks in certain jobs. Certain activities, listed in the annex to the Directive, may not be undertaken by pregnant workers, such as work in underground mines and work which entails or might entail exposing the body to high atmospheric pressure. In addition, women may not be obliged to perform night work during pregnancy and for a period following childbirth to be determined by the national authorities. In general, pregnant workers are entitled to 14 weeks continuous maternity leave which they may take before and/or after the birth, in line with national legislation.

Apart from these provisions on health protection, the directive also provides legal protection with regard to employment rights. Dismissal on the grounds of pregnancy is strictly prohibited (protection against dismissal runs from the beginning of the pregnancy to the end of maternity leave).

While the EU, unlike the ILO, is without a tripartite composition, it adopted similar practices as from the 1990s. The social partners' Agreement on Social Policy of 31 October 1991 proposed a radical change in the Community legislative process in the sphere of social policy, which had heretofore engaged only the EU institutions. At the Maastricht summit in December 1991, 11 of the, then, 12 Member States of the Community were willing to incorporate into the EC Treaty the Agreement concluded between the social partners: cross-industry, representative employers' and unions' organizations, UNICE (now the Confederation of European Business), CEEP (the European Centre of Enterprises with Public Participation and of Enterprises of General Economic Interest), and ETUC (European Trade Union Confederation). The Social Policy Protocol to the Treaty of Maastricht embodies a compromise with an "opt-out" for the UK. The same 11 Member States signed the Directives on European Works Councils (1994), parental leave (1996) and part-time work (1997). The UK terminated the opt-out clause in May 1997. By the Treaty of Amsterdam of June 1997, the Social Policy Protocol was incorporated into a revised "Social Chapter" in the EC Treaty. This Chapter, amended by the Treaties of Amsterdam and Nice (Articles 136 ff. EC) incorporates the Agreement on Social Policy. In part, it obliges the Commission to consult management and labour in the formulation of social policy thus formally establishing a role for both in the EU legislative process.

The following Directives were first formulated as Framework Agreements that were initially negotiated by the social partners and then confirmed by

19 The Pregnancy Directive 92/85, OJ (1992) L 348/1.

Community legislation. Mention should also be made of Directive 96/34/EC of 1996 concerning the Framework Agreement on Parental Leave concluded by UNICE, CEEP and the ETUC[20] and the Council Recommendation on child care of 31 March 1992.[21] Chapters 9 and 10 will deal with maternity protection, parental leave, child care and the balance of work and home responsibilities.

The 1990s also saw the adoption of the Burden of Proof Directive 1997[22] in cases of discrimination based on sex. The general principle with regard to the burden of proof, *actori incumbit probatio* (the burden lies with the plaintiff), normally presents insurmountable problems in discrimination cases. The relevant documents are generally in the possession of the employer, while some forms of indirect discrimination are by nature difficult to prove. To solve this problem it was considered appropriate to reverse the burden of proof and place it on the employer to show that objective circumstances have prompted his actions and thus to refute the claim of discrimination. According to Article 4 of the Directive, the worker has to supply evidence leading to a presumption of direct discrimination or less favourable treatment. Then the employer must prove that the presumption is without foundation and that there was no discrimination or that the discrimination was justified by objective factors that have nothing to do with the sex of the worker.

The activity of the 1990s was concluded by the adoption of the important Directive concerning the Framework Agreement on Part-time Work by UNICE, CEEP and the ETNC,[23] which was transposed into national law two years later and implemented by collective agreements a year after that. The purpose of the agreement is, in general, to remove discrimination against part-time workers. As the majority (70%-90%) of part-time workers are women, this directive will improve working conditions for women and will have an important impact on the employment of women. Chapter 11 will deal with part-time work and atypical work with special reference to indirect discrimination.

Article 13 of the Treaty of Amsterdam gave legal backing to the 2000 General Framework Directive on Equal Treatment.[24] This Directive established a general framework for equal treatment and occupation and enlarged the scope of protection against discrimination beyond the 1958 ILO Convention 111 to cover grounds of discrimination other than sex, including age, disability and sexual orientation. Its Preamble refers expressly to ILO Convention No. 111 among the international instruments that inspired the Directive.

---

20 OJ (1996) L 145/4.

21 92/241/EEC OJ (1992) L 123/1.

22 Directive 97/80, OJ (1998) L 14/6.

23 97/81/EC OJ (1998) L 14/9.

24 2000/78 OJ (2000) L 303/16.

The Equal Treatment Directive of 1976 was amended in 2002 by Directive 2002/73,[25] and its provisions entered into force in 2005. The amended directive takes stock of the case law of the ECJ and incorporates the rulings of the Court over the years, reflecting the evolution of the law.

In 2006 a consolidating Equal Treatment Directive was adopted, Directive 2006/54/EC of the European Parliament and of the Council of 5 July 2006 on the implementation of the principle of equal opportunities and equal treatment of men and women in matters of employment and occupation (recast).[26] This Directive updates the former directives and takes account of the case law of the ECJ.

The recital (36) of the Preamble justifies the legitimacy of this legislation and its compatibility with the principle of subsidiarity:

> "Since the objectives of the Directive cannot be sufficiently achieved by the Member States and can therefore be achieved at Community level, the Community may adopt measures in accordance with the principle of subsidiarity as set out in Article 5 of the Treaty. In accordance with the principle of proportionality, as set out in that Article, this Directive does not go beyond what is necessary in order to achieve those objectives."

Unwritten Sources of Community Law

Beside the written sources of law that are embodied in the basic Treaties and Community legislation, the unwritten sources of law consist of the case law of the Luxembourg Courts and of general principles of law. The case law, although not formally binding as precedents, is a *jurisprudence constante* that lends certainty and predictability to Community law. The interpretation by the ECJ has contributed to the coherence and visibility of the law. Furthermore, the Court has created law on the model of the courts in the Common Law system. The absence of a legal text sparked the creativity of the ECJ in filling gaps.

The role of the Luxembourg Court was unique in interpreting the norms of equality via the procedure of preliminary rulings which helped to harmonise the laws of all the Member States. In the absence of a written provision the Court resorted to general principles of law and gleaned from this reservoir a solution to a pending legal issue. General principles of law are a formal source of law in International Law, as expressly provided for in Article 38 of the Statute of the International Court of Justice. No such provision is to be found in Article 164 now Article 220 which defines the role of the ECJ. Nevertheless, the Community

25 OJ (2002) L 269/15.

26 OJ (2006) L 204/23.

Court constantly filled gaps in the written law by introducing general principles of law into the Community legal order. For example, the domain of protection of human rights has been 'received' into Community law through the adoption of general principles of law, for the basic legal instruments of the Community had initially no independent provision governing human rights. The first written reference to the European Convention on Human Rights is to be found in the Preamble of the 1986 Single European Act. From that date all Treaties refer to human rights as part of the general principles of law that the Community is bound to respect.

The Court declared as early as the 1970s that it was bound to protect human rights as part of the general principles of law. Reference to human rights as part of Community law was first made in *Stauder* v. *The City of Ulm* 1969.[27] In 1970 in the *Internationale Handelsgesellschaft* Case[28] the Court clearly stated that "respect for fundamental rights forms an integral part of the general principles of law of which the Court of Justice ensures respect". Through the Court's precedents, human rights, including concepts of equality, have become part of the unwritten Community law, inspired on the one hand by international conventions which were binding on the States, and on the other hand by the Constitutions of the Member States. The inspiration from international conventions leads us straight into the aim of this study, which is to unveil the impact of ILO conventions on the development of EC/EU norms in the field of equality of men and women at work.

27 Case 29/69 (1969) ECR 419.

28 Case 11/70 (1970) ECR 1125.

Chapter 5

The ILO and the EU – The Interface

Background

The ILO has been setting universal labour standards since 1919. It addresses them globally to humanity at large. Its universal standards are therefore not ultimate ideals, but rather minimum standards that both developed and developing countries can assume. It should be noted that according to Article 19(8) of the ILO Constitution:

> "in no case shall the adoption of any Convention or Recommendation by the Conference, or the ratification of any Convention by any Member, be deemed to affect any law, award, custom or agreement which ensures more favourable conditions to the workers concerned than those provided for in the Convention or Recommendation."

Often ILO standards are a compromise or allow for supervised derogations in order to satisfy developing countries or to encourage more ratifications, especially as reservations to ILO Conventions are not an option.

This study deals with core equality standards that derive their legitimacy from the ILO Constitution and the Declaration of Philadelphia 1944 as well as the Post WWII Conventions, such as the 1951 Convention No. 100 on Equal Remuneration, Convention No. 111 on Discrimination (Employment and Occupation) 1958 and the complementary Convention No. 156 on Workers with Family Responsibilities 1981. Many of the ILO's universally accepted standards have been replicated into EU law. In the words of Advocate General Trabucchi, "Article 119 and the 1975 Directive on Equal Pay are the 'European translation' of the ILO Convention No. 100 on Equal Remuneration 1951."

Unlike the ILO standards, EU Directives are binding. Enforced through an infrastructure of control by the European Commission and by the powerful ECJ, they protect 500 million people in the 27 Member States of the EU.

Comparison of the substantive provisions of the ILO standards and EU law discloses a remarkable similarity of definitions, scope, and exceptions. Significantly, the early ILO Conventions predated the EU Directives by twenty years. The EU had no part in the creation of these legal norms. Until recently, the EU harvested its basic rules from ILO Conventions and complemented them with more details. To use a metaphor created by Professor Blanpain the Community was a "trailer" rather than a "locomotive" when it comes to social law and fundamental principles of equality.[1]

A Non-Formal Relationship between the ILO and the EU

Today, both the ILO and the EU aim to coin rules for fair conditions of work, social justice and equality. However, this was not always the case. The encounters between the ILO and the EU were not formalised and their relationship took place in isolated instances. We shall illustrate seven of these *ad hoc* instances, five involving decisions of the Community Court, in the following pages.

1. The Defrenne *Case 1976*

In the *Defrenne (No. 2)* Case[2] the ECJ referred to ILO Convention No. 111 as part of the general principles of law that the Court respects where there is a gap in EU written law. While it did not apply the Convention to the case, it mentioned the Convention as a possible inspiration for the future. As we shall see, at that time Community law recognised the principle of equal pay but the 1976 Directive on Equal Treatment was not yet adopted.

2. The Levy *Case 1993*

In 1993 The ECJ referred to the ILO Convention No. 89 on Night Work 1948 when it decided the *Levy* Case,[3] ruling that the ban of night work for women was incompatible with the Equal Treatment Directive

> "unless the application of such a provision (prohibiting night work) is necessary to ensure the performance by the Member State concerned of obligations arising under an agreement concluded with non-member countries prior to the entry into force of the EEC Treaty."

This Court ruling assumed that France had not yet denounced ILO Convention No. 89 and was bound by it. As we shall see in Chapter 8, the Court thus attributed supremacy to the ILO Convention. In fact France had denounced Convention No. 89 on 26 February 1993, some six months before the Court's ruling on 2

1 R. Blanpain, *European Labour Law* (10th rev. edn, 2006, Kluwer Law International), pp. 232 *et seq.*

2 Case 43/75 (1976) ECR 455.

3 Case C-158/91 (1993) ECR I-4287. See also *Commission* v. *France* 1988 and 1997, *Commission* v. *Italy* 1997 *et al.* to be dealt with in Chapter 8.

August 1993. France had ceased to have any obligation under this Convention at the date of the ruling.

3. Commission *v.* Austria *2004*

In the 2004 case of the *Commission* v. *Austria,*[4] also discussed in Chapter 8, the ECJ was confronted with the ILO Convention No. 45 concerning Underground Work (Women) 1935, which prohibited the employment of women in underground mines. Austria had ratified this Convention and was bound by it before it joined the EU in 1995. The Commission held that Austria was violating the Equal Treatment Directive of 1976, which promotes equal treatment for men and women at work, including access to jobs. The exclusion of women from underground work in mines was seen as a violation of the principle of equality. As in the *Levy* Case, the question arose of how to overcome the conflict between a prior international obligation binding Austria and its new obligation to respect Community law.

Article 307 (3) (ex Article 234 EEC) of the EC Treaty provides that the obligations arising from international agreements concluded by Member States with non-Member States before they join the EU are not affected by the provisions of the EC Treaty. This was the *ratio decidendi* in the *Levy* ruling.

In *Commission* v. *Austria,* however, the ECJ ruled that Article 307 (2) provides that Member States should take all appropriate measures to eliminate the incompatibilities between the prior engagements and EU law, including, *inter alia,* the denunciation of ILO Convention No. 45. So in this case, more recent EU law was given supremacy over an older ILO standard.

4. Convention No. 153 on Hours of Work and Rest Periods (Road Transport) 1979

The EU is not a member of the ILO, but has Observer status. The question of how the Community could participate in negotiations on ILO conventions first arose in connection with Convention No. 153 on Working Hours and Rest Periods in Road Transport 1977-1979, an area which at that time was covered by EEC Regulation No. 543/69 of the Council of 25 March 1969 on the harmonization of certain social legislation relating to road transport.[5] In order to facilitate the Community's participation in the various negotiations, the ILO had drafted a working document for the Conference. However, the solutions outlined in that document were not endorsed by a number of Member States because some employers and workers feared that their own influence in the Conference would thereby be reduced.

---

4 Case C-203/03 (2004) ECR I-935.

5 OJ (1969) L 77/49.

The document, drawn up by the Governing Body of the ILO on 12 February 1981,[6] was supplemented by another dated 31 May 1989. In essence, the two documents provided, with regard to negotiations, that Community Member States could authorize the EU Commission to propose amendments on their behalf, that the "authority" referred to in Article 19 of the ILO Constitution might be the EU Council and finally that the Community could ratify the Convention by means of a statement, provided that prior notification from all the Twelve Member States at the time confirmed that such a statement constituted ratification.

These two documents also refer to the commitments undertaken by Member States which have ratified a convention. They point out in this connection that Member States alone can be held liable for failure to comply with those undertakings, even if the breach of the provisions of such a convention is attributable to a Community measure adopted by majority decision.

5. *Convention No. 162 concerning Asbestos 1986*

The problem of the Community's competence in relation to the ILO arose again during the preparation of Convention No. 162 concerning Safety in the Use of Asbestos 1983-1986, an area which had been covered by four Community Directives. Because a number of states took the view that the ILO Constitution did not allow the Community to take part in the Conference, the Council decided that the Community and its Member States would present the Community's position on the basis of the relevant Community Directives. The EU Commission brought an action for annulment against this Council decision on the grounds that it breached Article 228 of the EEC Treaty. However, it withdrew its action following the Council's adoption on 22 December 1986 of a generally satisfactory solution (in the Commission's view) to the problem of Community participation in ILO negotiations.

This solution is confined to cases coming within the exclusive competence of the Community. It imposes full compliance with the tripartite consultation procedure provided for in Convention No. 144 and maintains the autonomy of both sides of industry: employers and workers. It also stipulates that the Community's replies to the ILO questionnaire must be adopted by the Council following a proposal from the Commission, and that they must take account of consultations with employers' organizations and trade unions. For the preparation of the first reading of a draft convention, the Commission must propose that the Council adopt a decision authorizing it to negotiate and giving it a negotiating brief. When the Conference considers the draft convention, the Commission speaks on behalf of the Community and acts in close consultation with the

6 ILO Governing Body, "The Relationship of Rights and Obligations under the Constitution of the ILO to Rights and Obligations under Treaties establishing regional Groupings", 215th session, February-March, 1981.

Member States. The delegates of the Member States retain their right to speak during the plenary session of the Conference.

6. The ECJ's Opinion 2/91 of 1992, relating to Convention No. 170 concerning Chemicals 1990

In July 1988 the Commission, pursuant to the above Council decision of 22 December 1986, requested the Member States to reply to the ILO questionnaire relating to Convention No. 170. Several Member States contested the Community's exclusive competence to act in the matter. As a result, the Member States sent their replies directly to the ILO, thereby preventing transmission of replies at Community level. The Commission took the view that the exclusive competence of the Community was not a matter on which there was any doubt and it wrote to the Council on 12 May 1989 requesting that it be given powers of negotiation in respect of Convention No. 170.

On 30 November 1989 the Council adopted a decision which enabled the Commission to present the Community point of view during the negotiations in question, subject to close consultation with the Member States. The latter retained their right to express views on aspects which fell within the areas of national competence. This Council decision set out a procedure by which differences over EU competence could be resolved. In the decision the Council also agreed to re-examine its decision of 22 December 1986 and, if necessary, with the agreement of the Commission, to supplement that decision with provisions covering cases of joint competence of the Community and the Member States, as well as with provisions designed to avoid difficulties arising from the Constitution of the ILO or its practices as an institution.

After Convention No. 170 was adopted in 1990, the EU Commission wrote the ILO stating its view that all the Member States were under an obligation to inform the Director-General of the ILO that the competent authorities, within the meaning of Article 19 (5) (c) of the ILO Constitution, were in the case of Convention No. 170 the Community institutions. At this point, several national delegations to the Council indicated their refusal to accept that the Community had exclusive competence to conclude the Convention. The Commission therefore asked the ECJ to give an Opinion according to Article 228, now Article 300 EC.

In 1993 the ECJ rendered *Opinion 2/91*,[7] clarifying its position on the compatibility of ILO Convention No. 170 with EU law. The issue of the competence of the Community to conclude this Convention in its own name and the resulting binding force on the Member States was also addressed.

While the *Defrenne* and *Levy* Cases as well as *the Commission* v. *Austria* Case are treated in this study as forming part of the substantive law (*Defrenne* in Chapter

---

[7] (1993) ECR I 1061.

6 in the context of equal pay and the other two cases in Chapter 8 in the context of protective measures and the banning of night work or work in underground mines for women), the ECJ's *Opinion 2/91* deals with the relationship between the EU and the ILO in the field of social law in general. This Opinion throws some light on the possibility of collaboration between the EU and the ILO in the elaboration of standards where the competences of the EU *ratione materiae* converge with the ambit of the ILO Convention.

The Court's Opinion stated:

"2. If the conditions of participation in an international convention exclude conclusion by the Community itself but the area covered by that convention comes within the external competence of the Community, that external competence may be exercised through the medium of the Member States acting jointly in the Community's interest.

3. The Community's competence to enter into international commitments may arise from an express attribution by the Treaty or flow implicitly from its provisions. Whenever Community law has created for the institutions of the Community powers within its internal system for the purpose of attaining a specific objective, the Community has competence to enter into the international commitments necessary for the attainment of that objective, even in the absence of an express provision to that effect.

4. The conclusion of Convention No. 170 of the International Labour Organization concerning safety in the use of chemicals at work is a matter which falls within the joint competence of the Member States and the Community.

The field which it covers falls within the social provisions of the Treaty, which constitute Chapter 1 of Title III on social policy. The fact that the Convention sets out rules in an area in which the Community enjoys an internal legislative competence does not, however, confer exclusive competence on the Community, since Article 118a of the Treaty envisages the introduction of directives only in order to lay down minimum requirements, with the result that Member States may apply the rules of the Convention, assuming that they are more stringent, on the basis of the freedom which they have to go beyond the requirements of the directives, the opposite being equally possible, since the rules of the Convention are also only minimum rules. The same applies with regard to the directives adopted on the basis of Article 100 of the Treaty, since they also lay down minimum requirements.

In contrast, certain requirements of the Convention, although not contradictory to existing directives, relate to an area, that of classification, packaging and labelling of dangerous substances, in which, given the development of the Community's legislative activity, which has not

> been limited to fixing minimum requirements, it must be considered that the Member States are no longer competent to undertake international commitments outside the framework of the Community institutions.
>
> Finally, with regard to the general principles which the Convention contains for its implementation, in particular the consultation of the most representative organizations of employers and workers, it must be considered that, in so far as the substantive provisions of the Convention come within the Community's sphere of competence, the Community is also competent to undertake commitments with regard to the implementation of those provisions *despite the fact that social policy is a matter which at present falls predominantly within the competence of the Member States.*" [*Emphasis added.*]

The Court further stated that:

> "6. When it appears that the subject-matter of an international convention falls partly within the competence of the Community and partly within that of the Member States, the requirement of unity in the international representation of the Community makes it necessary to ensure close cooperation between the Community institutions and the Member States both in the process of negotiation and conclusion and in the fulfilment of the obligations entered into."

The ECJ's Opinion declared that "the conclusion of ILO Convention No. 170 is a matter which falls within the joint competence of the Member States and the Community".

Can the EU ratify an ILO Convention? The Court's Opinion does not give an answer to this question, saying: "It is not for the Court to assess any obstacles which the Community may encounter in the exercise of its competence because of constitutional rules of the ILO."

The answer to the ratification question depends on two considerations: obstacles from the point of view of international law, namely whether ILO Conventions are open to non-Member States and to regional entities, and obstacles from the point of view of EU Law, such as situations where the Community has no external competence to conclude international agreements in the domain at issue.

The Court's answer to the first consideration acknowledged that, from the point of view of the ILO, the Community has simple observer status. Although it may participate in deliberations, the ILO Constitution does not confer on it a right to vote (Article 12(2)). In addition, Article 15(5)(d) of the Constitution makes it clear that Member States alone may ratify an ILO convention.

On the second consideration, the Court fully examined the substantive competence of the Community in social matters governing conditions of work, which although not exclusive, is concurrent to the competence of the Member

States. It came to the conclusion that the Community has a joint competence with the Member States in the domain of Convention No. 170.

Is this Opinion valid today, fourteen years later?

The landscape of social and employment policy has changed in the 1990s. Social policy no longer falls predominantly within the competence of the Member States. Formally the turning point came with the 1997 Treaty of Amsterdam.

Since the ECJ's 1993 Opinion the Community has expanded its scope in the field of social law, especially in the domain of equality at work. A number of important Directives were adopted both before the Treaty of Amsterdam (e.g. the Pregnancy Directive 1992, the Framework Directive on Parental Leave 1996, and the Directive on Part-Time Work 1997) and after that Treaty (e.g. the General Framework Directive on Equal Treatment 2000, the Equal Treatment Directive 2002, and the consolidating Directive of 2006). The primary laws, as formulated in the Treaty of Amsterdam as well as Community legislation, have covered the domain of equality in the internal law of the Community in detail. Social policy and equality at work have become a fundamental task and aim of the EU.

Moreover, the old argument that the tripartite system of the ILO is an obstacle to the exercise of exclusive competence by the Community cannot apply in cases where Community legislation itself has been adopted in the framework of agreements with the three social partners, such as the Directives on Parental Leave, Part-Time Work, Fixed-Term Employees, and the Equal Treatment General Framework Directive. The removal of this obstacle is confirmed in specific provisions that call for continued collaboration with the social partners, such as the Recital (11) of the Preamble of the 2006 consolidating Directive on Equal Treatment:

> "The Member States, *in collaboration with the social partners*, should continue to address the problem of the continuing gender-based wage differentials and marked gender segregation on the labour market by means such as flexible working time arrangements which enable both men and women to combine family and work commitments more successfully. This could also include appropriate parental leave arrangements which could be taken up by either parent as well as the provision of accessible and affordable child-care facilities and care for dependent persons." [*Emphasis added.*]

In a sense, EU legislation has adopted the ILO model of the tripartite system. Starting in the 1990s, the EU developed Framework Agreements between the main employer associations and the European trade unions and subsequently gave these agreements legislative backing in the form of Directives. Blanpain's statement that:

> "the ILO is really tripartite and national delegations to the ILO Conference are equally tripartite ... The same is not true at the European level. Within

> the framework of the European Community, the social partners have at most an advisory status and have often only a very marginal input"[8]

does not reflect the situation today.

We conclude that there are now fewer obstacles for the Community to be a party to ILO Conventions, at least from the aspect of EU competence regardless of its being concurrent or exclusive.

7. Preamble of the General Framework Equal Treatment Directive 2000

The seventh instance in the development of the EU-ILO relationship is found in the Preamble of the General Framework Equal Treatment Directive 2000. The Recital (4) expressly refers to various international instruments dealing with equality and abolishing discrimination, and among them we find reference to ILO Convention No. 111, which prohibits discrimination in the field of employment and occupation. In none of the previous Directives is there any mention of the ILO, although acknowledgment was due.

The Present Working Relationship between the ILO and the EU

The working relationship between the ILO and the EU has nevertheless become closer. Meaningful cooperation between them has expanded, particularly in the field of working conditions, equal opportunities and equal treatment, which is the subject of this study.

In March 2000 it was agreed to step up the collaboration between the two organisations and new modalities were worked out:

> "1. the Commission, representing the Community, shall attend the meetings of the ILO and the Governing Body.
>
> 2. the Commission shall ensure that where appropriate, representatives of the ILO are invited to attend meetings of EU bodies dealing with social and labour matters, which by their nature are of interest to the ILO.
>
> 3. the President of the Commission and the Director-General of the ILO or their representatives shall consult each other at the appropriate stage on any development within their organisation that might have a bearing on the cooperation between the two parties.

---

8 Blanpain, *supra*, note 1 at p. 105.

4. a high-level meeting shall be held once a year, alternately in Brussels and Geneva, to review cooperation during the year and to determine the direction of future activities.[9]

5. The Commission and the ILO have established contact points to ensure an effective follow up of their meetings. These contact points will also report to the annual high-level meeting."[10]

These modalities of cooperation establish a new agenda of priorities responding to the profound changes and the new challenges facing both organisations.

The impact of the ILO on EU law is evidenced not only in the EU Directives' mirroring of ILO Conventions. ILO promotional initiatives also find an echo in EU policies.

For example, in the Declaration on Fundamental Principles and Rights at Work 1998 the ILO identified four strategic objectives as crucial to its mandate in the context of globalisation:

1. fundamental principles and rights at work,
2. the promotion of employment for women and men,
3. the enhancement of social protection, and
4. the promotion of social dialogue.

Together these constitute the essence of 'Decent Work'.

The European Council of Ministers of December 2006 decided to co-operate more closely with the ILO and promote the Decent Work Agenda of the Organisation: "A stronger partnership between the EU and the ILO is critical to making decent work a global reality."[11]

In summary, over the years the EU not only incorporated substantive ILO standards into its own law, but was also inspired by the tripartite method as of the 1990s and the Decent Work Agenda in 2006.

While in the past the EU has not acknowledged the rich legacy it drew from the ILO, we hope that this study will clarify the powerful impact of ILO standards on EU laws and thus fill a gap as to the historic sources of law in the EU.

---

9 Exchange of Letters with the Commission of the EC, 245th Session, sixth item on the Agenda, February-March, 1990, updated on 14th May 2001.

10 European Commission and ILO cooperate on Social Issues <www.eurofound.ie>.

11 See the *Report of the Director General on Decent Work*, 1999, and also *World of Work*, No. 59, April 2007, p. 36.

Part III
Selected Issues

Chapter 6

EQUAL PAY

Background

The ILO Global Report under the follow-up to the ILO Declaration on Fundamental Principles and Rights at Work 2007 dealing with *Equality at Work: Tackling the Challenges*[1] provides the following summary:

> "Despite advances, in particular the considerable progress in women's educational attainments, women continue to earn less than men everywhere, and the unequal burden of family responsibilities places them at a disadvantage in finding full time employment."

Nine out of ten ILO Member States have ratified the Equal Remuneration Convention No. 100 1951. The condemnation of discrimination at work is today almost universal and the legal norms are well established and yet there is still a gap in pay in practice between men and women. The problem is the enforcement of the principles and the standards and increasing judicial control.

The EU, as we have seen, possesses more efficient measures of control and enforcement than does the ILO, yet even the EU knows a gender pay gap in practice, half a century after the adoption of the principle of equal pay for equal work, as enshrined in Article 119 of the Treaty of Rome 1957.

What do we mean by a gender pay gap? This question was asked at the EU Copenhagen Conference on Equal Pay,[2] organized for EU Candidate Countries pending their accession in 2004.

The Conference concluded that the issue of gender pay gap is a complex one which is caused by an accumulation of many factors. One can look at the pay gap both as an issue related to the structure of the labour market and as an issue of discrimination. As a structural issue, the focus is on the fact that labour markets are segregated and women often work in sectors with lower pay, such

1 ILO Conference 96th Session 2007, p. ix.

2 Copenhagen Conference on Gender Equality for EU Candidate Countries, 29 November 2002.

as social services. As an issue of discrimination, the attention is centered on payrolls that are gender biased, as women are paid less for jobs of equal or even higher value. Both aspects need to be addressed.

The gender segregation of the labour market contributes possibly more than other factors, to the disparity in pay.

Eurostat[3] published in 2005 the percentage difference in pay between men and women in the Member States. The pay gap varies between 5% to 25%. The gap in the U.K. and Germany amounts to almost 25%, while Belgium, Greece and Portugal show a pay gap of 5% to 10%.

More recent data provided by official EU publications after the 2004 enlargement disclose that:

> "Women still outnumber men in education. The percentage of women graduates (tertiary level) increased to 58% in 2003, due to the higher level of education in the new Member States. Women now also represent 41% of PhD graduates."

Yet this fact does not in itself contribute to the narrowing of the pay gap. The fact is that:

> "the share of part-time employment is on average 30.4 % for women compared to only 6.6 % for men and the gap has slightly increased since 1998. This is one among many factors, which explains the gender pay gap. The new Member States have a much lower proportion of part-time jobs, partly due to labour market rigidity and partly due to the lower wage level, which makes this option less available."[4]

This shows the complexity of the causes of the pay gap and the challenge to overcome the injustice.

These figures indeed speak for themselves and portray the interaction between many factors that stand in the way of a solution for Europe of the twenty seven.

The ILO Standards

The ILO Convention concerning Equal Remuneration for Men and Women Workers for Work of Equal Value No. 100 and Recommendation No. 90 were adopted in 1951. Observance of the principle of equal remuneration has been an objective of the ILO since its foundation. The original text of the ILO Constitution already

3 <epp.eurostat.ec.europa.eu> Eurostat, *The Labour Force Survey*, 2005.

4 European Commission Report on Equality between Women and Men COM(2006)71 Final.

recognised in its Article 41 (Article 427 of the Treaty of Versailles 1919) among the general principles "of special and urgent importance" the principle that men and women should receive "equal remuneration for work of equal value". The principle is again enshrined in the Preamble of the present Constitution. The Philadelphia Declaration 1944 (which was subsequently incorporated into the Constitution) reaffirmed that:

> "all human beings, irrespective of race, creed and sex, have the right to pursue both their material well-being and their spiritual development in conditions of freedom and dignity, of economic security and equal opportunity."

A number of Conventions and Recommendations adopted by the International Labour Conference prior to the 1951 instruments already contain specific reference to the principle, such as the Employment (Transition from War to Peace) Recommendation No. 71 1944.

Convention No. 100 is now ratified by 163 States and has universal recognition and is considered a core Convention amongst the ILO human rights conventions. Equality is a concept linked with social justice and with the principle that labour is not a commodity – the first principle of the Philadelphia Declaration. The ILO Convention No. 100 is ratified by all Member States of the EU.

The Convention promotes the implementation of the principle with the collaboration of the three social partners – employers, employees and Governments – "to ensure the application to all workers of the principle of equal remuneration for men and women workers for work of equal value". The principle covers the public and the private sector and manual as well as non-manual workers.

One of the important contributions of this Convention is the wide definition of remuneration that has been taken over by Article 119 of the Treaty of Rome 1957 now Article 141 and adopted by EU law, as we shall see later on. Article 1 of the Convention lays down that:

> "the term 'remuneration' includes the ordinary, basic or minimum wage or salary and any additional emoluments whatsoever payable directly or indirectly, whether in cash or in kind, by the employer to the worker and arising out of the worker's employment."

Equality of pay is not limited to the basic or ordinary wage. It embraces additional emoluments, such as, allowances based on seniority, marital status, housing, bonuses, etc. The term "whether in cash or in kind" opens the door wide open to include benefits and perks within the ambit of remuneration and to subject those benefits to equal treatment.

The ILO realised already in 1951 the importance of extending equal pay beyond the same or equal work to work of equal value. The EU has incorporated this concept in 1975 in secondary legislation and subsequently in primary law in the 1997 Treaty of Amsterdam. The ILO faces a difficult implementation of the concept even today, fifty six years after its adoption. The ILO Committee of Experts published in 2007 a General Observation concerning Convention No. 100:

> "The Committee notes that difficulties in applying the Convention in law and in practice result in particular from a lack of understanding of the scope and implications of the concept of 'work of equal value'. This concept is a cornerstone of the Convention and lies in the heart of the fundamental right of equal remuneration for men and women for work of equal value and the promotion of equality. The Committee, therefore, considers it necessary to underscore the importance and clarify the meaning of 'work of equal value'."

The Committee noted that historical attitudes towards the role of women in society, along with stereotypical assumptions regarding women's aspirations, preferences, capabilities and 'suitability' for certain jobs, have contributed to occupational sex segregation in the labour market. This resulted in the undervaluation of jobs predominantly performed by women, such as kindergarten teachers and nurses that are remunerated relatively less than jobs of equal value performed by men.

The concept of work of equal value is essential in order to redress the results of occupational segregation and permits a wider scope of comparison between jobs performed by men and women in different places or enterprises, or between different employers.

In its examination of reports submitted by governments under the Convention, the Committee has been pleased to note cases in which the principle has been applied to compare remuneration received by men and women engaged in different occupations, such as wardens in sheltered accommodation for the elderly (predominantly women) and security guards in office premises (predominantly men), or school meal supervisors (predominantly women) and garden and park supervisors (predominantly men) Comparing the value of the work done in such occupations, which may involve different types of qualifications, skills, responsibilities or working conditions but which is nevertheless work of equal value overall, is essential in order to eliminate pay discrimination which results from the failure to recognize the value of work performed by men and women free from sex bias.

The Committee of Experts recommended the following measures:

> "5. In order to establish whether different jobs are of equal value, there has to be an examination of the respective tasks involved. This examination must be undertaken on the basis of entirely objective and non-discriminatory criteria ... While the Convention does not prescribe any specific method for such an examination, it does presuppose the

use of appropriate techniques for objective job evaluation (Article 3) ... Analytical methods of job evaluation have been found to be the most effective. Such methods analyse and classify jobs on the basis of objective factors relating to the jobs to be compared such as skill, effort and responsibilities or working conditions (see paragraph 141 of the 1986 General Survey on equal remuneration) ... it is important to ensure that the selection of factors for comparison, the weighing of such factors and the actual comparison carried out, are not inherently discriminatory. Often skills considered to be 'female', such as manual dexterity and those require in caring professions, are undervalued or even overlooked, in comparison with traditional 'male' skills, such as heavy lifting."

The Committee further urged that:

"7. ... Measures for the objective evaluation of jobs can be taken at the enterprise, sectoral or national level, in the context of collective bargaining as well as through national wage-fixing mechanisms."[5]

EU Legislation

The definition of 'pay' according to Article 119 of the Treaty of Rome now Article 141 echoes the ILO definition of 'remuneration':

"'Pay' means the ordinary basic or minimum wage or salary and any other consideration, whether in cash or in kind, which the worker receives, directly or indirectly, in respect of his employment from his employer."

The difference between the two versions is only in style and not in substance. "Pay" and "any other consideration" replace "remuneration" and "any additional emoluments whatsoever".

The ILO Convention provides in Article 1 (b) that the term "equal remuneration for men and women workers for work of equal value" refers to rates of remuneration established without discrimination based on sex. Article 119 is more explicit, in the sense that the provision specifies that equal pay without discrimination based on sex means that pay for the same work at piece rates shall be calculated on the basis of the same unit of measurement and that pay for work at time rates shall be the same for the same job. The limitation of the comparison "to the same work" and "the same job" in the EC excluded at the beginning discrimination for work of equal value covered by the ILO.

5 ILO Committee of Experts Observation on Convention No. 100 2007.

It is the 1975 Directive on Equal Pay that brought EC law in line with the ILO. The Directive widened the scope of Article 119 to cover the comparison beyond the same work or the same job. The Directive specifies that:

> "In particular when a job classification system is used in determining pay, it must be based on the same criteria for both men and women and so drawn up as to exclude any discrimination on grounds of sex."

As we shall see later on, the extension of equal pay to work of equal value has occasioned some difficulty in practice.

The Directive prescribes "the elimination of all discrimination on grounds of sex with regard to all aspects and conditions of remuneration".

Article 2 of the Directive imposes a duty upon Member States to:

> "introduce into their national legal system such measures as are necessary to enable all employees who consider themselves wronged by failure to apply the principle of equal pay to pursue their claims by judicial process after possible recourse to other competent authorities."

All Member States (and all new Member States that joined subsequently) were under an obligation to "abolish all discrimination between the pay of men and women arising from their laws, regulations and administrative provisions". States were also bound to ensure that any discrimination embodied in collective agreements or individual contracts of employment were declared null and void or amended.

The ambit of the Directive covers both the private sector and the public sector. The widening of the scope of equal pay to work to which equal value is attributed has made it possible to introduce equality also in segregated fields of employment. It is here that the impact of the ILO standard is most relevant, as we shall see when we deal with the case law of the ECJ. The principle of equal pay for work of equal value is since 1997 also enshrined in a primary written source of EU Law, namely in Article 141 of the Treaty of Amsterdam that amended and replaces Article 119.

The implementation of the EU law on Equal Pay is naturally left to the Member States, but unlike the control of the standards by the ILO globally, within the EU the effective control is entrusted to the Commission and the Community Court of Justice.[6]

---

6 As to enforcement mechanisms, see Constantinos Kombos and Maria Hadjisolomou, "The Mechanisms Used by the ILO and the EU in Combating Employment Discrimination in Pay: Converging Divergence?", vol 11.2 *Electronic Journal of Comparative Law*, (September 2007), <www.ejcl.org/112/art112-1.pdf>.

EU Case Law

It is the role of the Court of Justice from early times, in accordance with Article 164 of the Rome Treaty now Article 220, to ensure compliance with the law: "The Court of Justice shall ensure that in the interpretation and application of the Treaty the law is observed". In the field of equality the Court in addition contributed in elaborating rules and in filling gaps. The precedents of the Court are an independent source of law that complemented the written law of the Community.

The Court was empowered to give decisions in three types of actions subject to different procedures. We shall follow this procedural classification to give a clearer picture of its contribution to the substantive law.

A. Actions brought by the Commission – the 'watchdog' of the Community – against Member States for infringement of Community Law in accordance of Articles 169 and 171 of the Rome Treaty now Articles 226 and 228.

B. Preliminary rulings requested by national courts and tribunals concerning the interpretation of Community law in accordance with Article 177 of the Rome Treaty now Article 234.

C. Actions brought by officials of the Community against the organs of the EC, namely in staff cases within the internal law of the Community, in accordance with Article 179 of the Rome Treaty now Article 236. The jurisdiction of the Court in staff cases was delegated in 1989 to the Court of First Instance and in 2005 it was further transferred to a special Staff Administrative Tribunal. We shall follow these decisions as to substance regardless of the nature of the Court or Tribunal.

Actions Brought by the Commission against Member States

As we have seen, the European Commission was empowered by Article 169 of the Rome Treaty now Article 226 to bring actions against defaulting states for violations of Community law. This coercive measure is not available for the enforcement of ILO standards. In addition, by virtue of Article 171 now Article 228:

> "If the Court of Justice finds that a Member State has failed to fulfil an obligation under this Treaty, the State shall be required to take the necessary measures to comply with the judgment of the Court of Justice."

The Treaty of Maastricht has added a penal sanction to infringements by states. Article 171 (2) was added to provide that:

> "If the Commission considers that the Member State concerned has not taken such measures it shall, after giving that State the opportunity to

> submit its observations, issue a reasoned opinion specifying the points on which the Member State concerned has not complied with the judgment of the Court of Justice."

If the Member State concerned fails to take the necessary measures to comply with the Court's judgment within the time-limit laid down by the Commission, the latter may bring the case before the Court of Justice. In so doing it shall specify the amount of the lump sum or penalty payment to be paid by the Member State concerned which it considers appropriate in the circumstances.

If the Court of Justice finds that the Member State concerned has not complied with its judgment it may impose a lump sum or penalty payment on it.

The enforcement of EU law is thus effectively controlled by the Commission and by the Court of Justice. In the early 1980s alone three actions were brought by the *Commission* v. *The Grand Duchy of Luxembourg,*[7] *Commission* v. *U.K.*,[8] and *Commission* v. *Denmark.*[9] In the Luxembourg case the Court found in its judgment of 9 June 1982 that Luxembourg was violating the Community Directive on Equal Pay. It declared:

> "by not adopting within the period prescribed ... the measures necessary to eliminate discrimination in the conditions for the grant of head of household allowances to civil servants, the Grand Duchy of Luxembourg has failed to fulfil one of the obligations under the EEC Treaty."

The granting of allowances to head of the household as part of pay and denying such allowances to women, who are usually not head of the household, is highly discriminatory. The institution of *chef de famille* is incompatible with equality of men and women. Consequently, on 20 April 1983 Luxembourg passed a new law, abolishing the discriminatory provision relating to *allocations de famille.*

The *Commission* v. *U.K.* Case has its origin in the fact that there was no provision in the Equal Pay Act 1970 for a woman to claim equal pay for work of equal value if a job evaluation scheme had not been carried out. Furthermore, there was no obligation on the employer to carry out a job evaluation, and, where it had been done, it was held by the courts not to be binding unless accepted by both parties. In addition it was not possible under the law then in force to challenge a job evaluation scheme on the grounds that it contained hidden or indirect discrimination. The Commission maintained that the above deficiencies in the Act constituted an infringement of the U.K.'s obligations to give full effect to the provisions of Article 119 and the Equal pay Directive that widened the scope of equal pay to cover work of equal value. The Court sided with the Commission

7 Case 58/81 (1982) ECR 2175.

8 Case 61/81 (1982) ECR 2601

9 Case 143/83 (1985) ECR 427.

and held in its judgment of 6 July 1982 that the U.K. failed to fulfil its obligations under Community law.

An amendment to the Equal Pay Act 1970 was passed by Parliament in 1983 in the form of the Equal Pay (Amendment) Regulations. The rule of equal pay for equal work was extended to cover work of equal value, the assessment of which does not depend exclusively upon a job evaluation study but upon more individualised criteria such as "the demands made on her for instance in terms of effort, skill, decision".

The *Commission* v. *Denmark* Case also involved the infringement of the Equal Pay Directive 1975 in that the Danish Equal Pay Law of 4 February 1976 referred only to equal pay "for the same work", which entailed a restriction of the principle of equal pay for work to which equal value is attributed under the Equal Pay Directive 75/117/EEC. The Court gave judgment against Denmark on 30 January 1985.

The ILO standard of equal pay for work of equal value, as laid down in Convention No. 100, has thus become law through the ECJ's effectiveness of implementation, as evidenced in the cases against Luxembourg, the U.K. and Denmark.

In 1993 the Court sided with the Commission in *Commission* v. *Belgium* 1993.[10] Belgium failed to implement the Equal pay Directive as regards additional redundancy payments.

The ECJ declared that

> "(1) ... by retaining legislation which excludes female workers over the age of 60 from eligibility for the additional redundancy payments provided for by Collective Agreement No. 17, rendered compulsory by the Royal Decree of 16 January 1975, the Kingdom of Belgium has failed to fulfil its obligations under Article 119 of the Treaty;"

The reasoning of the ECJ was as follows:

> "It is necessary to begin by examining the plea in law as to infringement of Article 119 of the Treaty. As is apparent from the case law of the Court, the concept of pay within the meaning of the second paragraph of Article 119 comprises any other consideration, whether in cash or in kind, whether immediate or future, provided that the worker receives it, albeit indirectly, in respect of his employment from his employer. The fact that certain benefits are paid after the termination of the employment relationship does not prevent them from being in the nature of pay within the meaning of Article 119 of the Treaty.[11]

---

10 Case C-173/91 (1993) ECR 673.

11 See, in particular, the ruling in the *Barber* Case C-262/88 [1990] ECR I-1889, para. 12.

> On the other hand, that definition of 'pay' cannot cover social security schemes or benefits such as, for example, retirement pensions, which are governed by statute without any element of negotiation within the undertaking or branch of activity concerned, and which apply compulsorily to general categories of workers. Such schemes provide workers with the benefit of a statutory system to the financing of which the workers, the employers and, in some cases, the public authorities contribute to an extent determined less by the employment relationship between the employer and the worker than by considerations of social policy.[12] Having regard to the criteria thus elicited by the Court, the additional payment at issue, although *sui generis* in certain respects, must be deemed to constitute 'pay' within the meaning of Article 119 of the Treaty."

In 1999 the Commission instituted an action against Greece, *Commission* v. *The Hellenic Republic* 1999,[13] for failure to fulfil its obligation to implement fully the principle of Equal Pay for men and women and to abolish discriminatory family and marriage allowances retroactively.

The contribution of the Court of Justice to the development of the principle of equal pay and the elucidation of what constitutes pay is best evidenced by the numerous decisions rendered through the procedure of preliminary rulings.

Preliminary Rulings

Very early in the history of equal pay in the Community and even before the entry into force of the Equal Pay Directive 1975, the first three preliminary rulings of the ECJ concerned the air hostess Gabrielle Defrenne in three separate actions she brought before the Belgian courts.

Article 119 on Equal Pay came up for interpretation before the ECJ for the first time in 1971. The Belgian *Conseil d'Etat*, faced with problems of interpretation of Community law in the first *Defrenne* v. *The Belgian State* Case,[14] referred certain questions to the Community Court.

Gabrielle Defrenne worked as an air hostess with the Sabena Airlines from 19 December 1951. She was compulsorily retired on February 1968 upon attaining the age of 40 years. Under the collective agreement with the airline air hostesses retire at that age, whereas no age limit was fixed for men. Miss Defrenne commenced two actions in Belgian courts, one in the *Tribunal de Travail* in Brussels against the airline for unjust dismissal. The other action was before the *Conseil*

[12] See Case 80/70 *Defrenne* (1971) ECR 445, paras 7 and 8.

[13] Case C-187/98 (1999) ECR I-7713.

[14] See *supra*, note 8.

d'Etat against the Belgian State demanding the annulment of the Royal Decree of 13 December 1969 which set up a pension scheme in a detrimental way to women civil aircrews. Her argument in the Labour Tribunal was based on the infringement by the airline of Article 119 of the Rome Treaty concerning salary, severance pay and pension. She claimed damages for an unlawful dismissal. The *Tribunal de Travail* dismissed her claim. In the action before the *Conseil d'Etat* her action was based on the fact that the Royal Decree unlawfully discriminated between male and female employees as regards pension entitlements, in violation of Article 119 of the Treaty.

The Belgian *Conseil d'Etat* availed itself of the procedure of preliminary rulings from the Community Court and referred the following questions:

> "Is the retirement pension granted under a social security scheme financed by workers' and employers' contributions, as well as by State grants, an emolument indirectly paid by the employer to the worker and arising out of the latter's employment?
>
> Can the regulations prescribe different age limits in respect of male and female members of aircrews and civil aircraft?
>
> Do air hostesses and stewards employed in civil aviation do the same work?"

The Court in its ruling of 25 May 1971 replied to the first question in the negative so that it was not necessary to answer the two other questions.

While emphasizing that "consideration in the nature of social security benefits is not in principle alien to the concept of pay" the Court ruled that this concept, as defined in Article 119, could not be extended to:

> "social security schemes or benefits, in particular retirement pensions, directly governed by the legislation without any element of agreement within the undertaking or the occupational branch concerned, which are obligatorily applicable to general categories of workers."

The Court decided:

> "A retirement pension instituted within the framework of a legal social security scheme, does not constitute an emolument indirectly paid by the employer to the worker and arising out of the latter's employment, within the meaning of Article 119(2) of the Treaty."

The Court decided that the pension schemes were statutory rather than contractual for although the schemes were financed by contributions of employees, employers and the state, the employee was entitled to the benefits by fulfilling the requirements of national law and not by reason of the employers' contributions.

The nature of the statutory obligations took them outside the scope of Article 119.

Miss Defrenne appealed meanwhile against the decision of the *Tribunal de Travail* to the *Cour de Travail* in 1971. This time the Labour Appeal Court in *Defrenne* v. *Sabena (No. 2)*[15] referred to the ECJ the question of direct applicability of Article 119 as regards a claim for the difference of salary received by a male cabin steward performing the same tasks as an air hostess. The Court was asked to give a preliminary ruling on the following questions:

> "Does Article 119 introduce directly into the national law of each Member State of the European Community the principle that men and women should receive equal pay for equal work and does it, therefore, independently of any provision, entitle workers to institute proceedings before national courts to ensure its observance, and if so as from what date?
>
> Has Article 119 become applicable in the internal law of the Member States by virtue of measures adopted by the European Community or must the national legislator be regarded as alone competent in this matter?"

The Court answered the questions referred to it as follows:

> "The principle that men and women should receive equal pay, which is laid down by Article 119, may be relied on before national courts. These courts have a duty to ensure the protection of the rights which that provision vests in individuals, in particular in the case of those forms of discrimination which have their origin in legislative provisions or collective labour agreements, as well as where men and women receive unequal pay for equal work which is carried out in the same establishment or service, whether private or public ...
>
> Council Directive 75/117 does not prejudice the direct effect of Article 119 ...
>
> Even in the areas which Article 119 has no direct effect, that provision cannot be interpreted as reserving to the national legislature exclusive power to implement the principle of equal pay since, to the extent to which such implementation is necessary, it may be achieved by a combination of Community and national provisions ..."

The Second Defrenne Ruling rendered on 8 April 1975 was a landmark in the development of Community Law on Equal Pay in that it settled the question of the relationship between Article 119 and national legislation. It resolved doubts as to the self-executory character of Article 119 in cases of direct discrimina-

15 Case 43/75 (1976) ECR 455.

tion. The Court ruled that individuals can rely on its provisions directly before national tribunals.

The Court drew a distinction between

> "direct and overt discrimination which may be identified solely with the aid of criteria based on equal work and equal pay referred to by the Article in question (Article 119) and, indirect discrimination and disguised discrimination which can only be identified by reference to more explicit implementing provisions of a Community or national character." (para. 19)

The Court went on to explain that direct discrimination is one which

> "has its origin in legislative provisions or in collective agreements and which may be detected on the basis of a purely legal analysis of the situation. This applied even more in cases where men and women receive unequal pay for equal work carried out in the same establishment or service, whether public or private." (paras 22-23)

The reference to the private sector surprised the Commission that assumed when drafting the Equal Pay Directive that Article 119 imposed directly duties only upon states.[16]

The ruling stresses the social and egalitarian aspects of the principle of equal pay for men and women. Following the ruling of the ECJ, the Belgian *Cour de Travail* awarded Miss Defrenne the sum of BF 12,716 by way of arrears of salary.

Miss Defrenne was, however, not satisfied with the sums awarded by the Belgian Labour Appeals Court and on 16 September 1976 lodged an appeal before the *Cour de Cassation* of Belgium against the judgment of the *Cour de Travail*. The Belgian Supreme Court referred the question[17] for a preliminary ruling to the Community Court.

The first part of the question raised by the *Cour de Cassation* sought to discover whether the principle of equal pay laid down by Article 119 may be interpreted as requiring general equality of working conditions for men and women, so that the insertion into the contract of employment of an air hostess of a clause bringing the contract to an end when she reaches the age of 40, it being established that no such limit is attached to the contract of male cabin attendants who carry out the same work, constitutes discrimination prohibited by that provision.

The second part of the question focused on whether, apart from the specific provisions of Article 119, Community law contains any general principle pro-

---

16 See Eve C. Landau, *The Rights of Working Women in the European Community* (Commission of the European Communities, Brussels, 1985), p. 25.

17 *Defrenne* v. *Sabena* (No. 3) Case 149/77 (1979) ECR 1365.

hibiting discrimination based on sex as regards the conditions of employment and working conditions of men and women.

The Court answered in the following manner:

> "The Court has repeatedly stated that respect for fundamental personal human rights is one of the general principles of Community Law. There can be no doubt that the elimination of discrimination based on sex forms part of those fundamental rights. Moreover, the same concepts are recognised by the European Social Charter of 18 November 1961 and by Convention 111 of the International Labour Organisation of 25 June 1958 concerning discrimination in respect of employment and occupation."

The Court referred to the ILO standard enshrined in Convention 111 prohibiting discrimination in all conditions of employment, but regretfully did not apply it to the present case. Although the EC Directive on Equal Treatment in all conditions of work, which echoes the ILO Convention, was meanwhile adopted on 9th February 1976, it had not at that time entered into force. It did enter into force by 12 August 1978 – too late for Miss Defrenne.

The Court ruled on June 1978 that:

> "the Community had not at the time of the events [now] before the Belgian Court, assumed any responsibility for supervising and guaranteeing the observance of the principle of equality between men and women in working conditions other than remuneration."

Had Miss Defrenne brought her third case after the implementation of the Equal Treatment Directive she would have won her case.

The *Defrenne Rulings* evidence the shortcomings of EU law of the time. They do not reflect the legal position today. We shall deal with equality in all conditions of work when we discuss the Equal Treatment Directive 1976 including its amendment in 2002, and the consolidating 2006 Directive, in Chapter 7.

The rulings in the *Defrenne* cases were initiated on the basis of the principle of equal pay for equal work laid down in Article 119. We shall return now to the interpretation of the ECJ of this provision. The *ratio decidendi* of the rulings, as far as the scope of pay is concerned, is that statutory pension schemes governed by legislation without any element of a contractual basis between the employer and the employee do not come under 'pay'. As we shall see, this ruling was followed in a long line of precedents. We now have to focus on the positive elements of what constitutes 'pay' and to address the preliminary question of the legal nature of the entitlement to equal pay.

The Legal Nature of the Principle of Equal Pay

Is the principle of equal pay for men and women in the nature of a *jus cogens* from which there is no derogation, or can the parties contract out of the legal requirement of equality of remuneration?

The clearest answer is given by the Danish Act respecting equal wages for men and women 1976 Section 5 provides that "No employee may waive his rights under this Act".

Article 4 of the Equal Pay Directive provides that:

> "Member States shall take the necessary measures to ensure that provisions appearing in collective agreements, wage scales, wage agreements or individual contracts of employment which are contrary to the principle of equal pay shall be, or may be declared, null and void or may be amended."

National legislation in some Member States confers a right to equal pay without leaving any discretion in the matter to the contracting parties (e.g. France, Belgium). In the U.K. and Ireland, the legal formula is that an equality clause is implicit in any contract of employment. In other terms, it appears that the parties have no autonomous will in the matter and 'lose' their right to freedom of contract and hence forfeit the possibility to contract out of the basic principle of equal pay for equal work or work of equal value.

An interesting Irish Case of *PMPA* v. *Kathleen Keenan & Other Insurance Officials* 1983[18] illustrates the *jus cogens* quality of the principle of equal pay. Kathleen Keenan and 14 co-workers signed an agreement with their employer not to pursue an equal pay claim. When they changed their mind and their claim came to the Supreme Court, the Court declared that: "any compromise of the female employees present claim for less than the entitlement under the (Equal Pay) 1974 Act would of course be unlawful" (per J. Henchy). According to this judgment the principle of equal pay tolerates no derogations.

A somewhat similar approach was manifested five years earlier by Lord Denning in the UK case of *Clay Cross (Quarry Services) Ltd* v. *Fletcher 1978*.[19]

In this case a woman sales clerk claimed equality of pay with a man who had been recruited later than she to do like work. She introduced him and showed him how to do his work. He was paid at a higher weekly rate than she was because, when the vacancy that he filled had arisen, he had been the only suitable applicant for it and had required to be paid the same wage as he had earned in his previous job. The employers had been indifferent whether they

---

18 The Irish Supreme Court, (1983) No. 34, *Irish Law Times* Vol. I No. 5 (September 1983).

19 (1978) IRLR 361.

recruited a man or a woman and contended, under Section 1 (3) of the Equal Pay Act 1970 (as amended), that the difference between the woman's and the man's contract was due to a material difference other than the difference of sex, between her case and his. The Court of Appeal rejected that contention on the grounds expressed by Lord Denning, Master of the Rolls:

> "An employer cannot avoid his obligations under the Act by saying 'I paid him more because he asked for more' or 'I paid her less because she was willing to come for less!' If any such excuse were permitted the Act would be a dead letter. Those are the very reasons why there was unequal pay before the statute. They are the very circumstances in which the statute was intended to operate."

The ECJ expressed the same idea that the principle of Equal Pay enshrined in Article 119 is of "a mandatory nature" in the case of *Helga Nimz* v. *Hambourg* 1991[20] and no derogation is allowed in a collective agreement. The Court declared that:

> "Since Article 119 is mandatory in nature, the prohibition of discrimination between male and female workers not only applies to the action of public authorities, but also extends to all collective agreements designed to regulate employment relationships and to contracts between individuals."[21]

The Court stated in its ruling that:

> "(1) Article 119 of the EEC Treaty must be interpreted as precluding a collective agreement, entered into within the national public service, from providing for the period of service of employees working at least three-quarters of normal working time to be fully taken into account for reclassification in a higher salary grade, where only one-half of such period of service is taken into account in the case of employees whose working hours are between one-half and three-quarters of those normal working hours and the latter group of employees comprises a considerably smaller percentage of men than women, unless the employer can prove that such a provision is justified by factors whose objectivity depends in particular on the relationship between the nature of the duties performed and the experience afforded by the performance of those duties after a certain number of working hours have been completed.

[20] Case C-184/89 (1991) ECR 297.

[21] See also the ruling of 27 June 1990 in Case C-33/89 *Kowalska* v. *Freie und Hansestadt Hamburg* (1990) ECR I-2591.

> (2) Where there is indirect discrimination in a provision of a collective agreement, the national court is required to set aside that provision, without requesting or awaiting its prior removal by collective bargaining or any other procedure, and to apply to members of the group disadvantaged by that discrimination the same arrangements as are applied to other employees, arrangements which, failing the correct application of Article 119 of the EEC Treaty in national law, remain the only valid system of reference."

The Royal Copenhagen Case 1995[22] follows the previous precedent in its preliminary ruling. The case involved the Danish Union of Semi-skilled Workers and the Confederation of Danish Industry acting for Denmark's porcelain manufacturer, the Royal Copenhagen Company. The remuneration of women workers paid on a piecework basis, employed in the process of the "blue pattern painters", was substantially lower than that of men workers employed as automatic machine operators. The Union claimed that there was a flagrant violation of the equal pay principle. The Company rejected the claim on the basis that the difference in pay had been fixed by a collective agreement.

The Court held that the Company's argument was unacceptable on the grounds that Article 119 of the EC Treaty establishes a mandatory duty and that the discrimination against women workers is therefore strictly prohibited regardless of whether the rates of pay are fixed by a public authority, an individual contract or a collective agreement.

The general principle gleaned from these illustrations is that equal pay for equal work or work of equal value is a *jus cogens* and constitutes a fundamental right that tolerates no consensual derogation.

What is Pay?

The case law of the ECJ is rich in illustrations of the scope of pay. Chronologically, mention should be made of the *Sabbatini-Bertoni* v. *European Parliament* and *Chollait-Baudin* v. *Commission* Cases 1972[23] where an expatriation allowance was considered part of pay.[24] These are staff cases to which we shall refer separately later on. In these cases the discrepancy in pay involved the payment of an expatriation allowance. The legality of the termination upon marriage of

---

22 Case C-400/93 (1995) ECR I-1275.

23 Case 32/71 (1972) ECR 345.

24 Not only expatriation allowances were considered pay, family allowances to *chefs de famille* were also considered 'pay' in the *Commission* v. *The Grand Duchy of Luxembourg* Case, *supra*, note 3.

an expatriation allowance, payable as part of pay, was questioned in circumstances discriminatory to women. The Court treated this entitlement as part of pay and annulled a decision discriminatory to women which was based on the discriminatory Staff Regulations.

In *Worringham and Humphreys* v. *Lloyds Bank* 1981[25] the facts were as follows: Lloyds Bank required both men and women clerks to join the bank's pension scheme. However for employees under 25 years of age the schemes for men and women were different. Before the age of 25 women were not expected to contribute to the pension fund. The men's scheme was contributory throughout and they were required to pay 5% of their salary by way of contribution. In order to make up for this difference, men under 25 received a 5% addition to their gross pay. This meant, firstly, that if a man left the bank his contributions were returned whatever his age, whereas a women leaving before the age of 25 received no payment by way of pension contributions. Secondly, the 5% addition to the salaries of men under 25 was counted in their gross pay and thus gave them a higher calculation base in respect of certain benefits and social advantages such as redundancy payments and unemployment benefits as well as mortgage and credit facilities. When the case was referred to the ECJ for a preliminary ruling from the UK Court of Appeal, the ECJ ruled that:

> "1. A contribution to a retirement benefits scheme which is paid by the employer in the name of the employees by means of an addition to the gross salary and which therefore helps to determine the amount of that salary constitutes 'pay' within the meaning of the second paragraph of Article 119 of the EEC Treaty.
>
> 2. Article 119 of the Treaty may be relied upon before the national courts and these courts have a duty to ensure the protection of the rights which this provision vests in individuals, in particular in a case where, because of the requirement imposed on men only or only on women to contribute to a retirement benefits scheme, the contributions in question are paid by the employer in the name of the employee and deduced from the gross salary whose amount they determine."

The ruling was most important for the 14,000 women employed by Lloyds Bank receiving less gross pay than men employed in like work. Under the U.K. legislation at that time the U.K. courts would have had to reject the claim, because Section 6 (I)(A)(b) of the Equal Pay Act 1970 excluded from its ambit 'terms related to death or retirement'. Now that the Community Court decided that contributions to a retirement benefits scheme which were paid by the employer are 'pay', the

25 Case 69/80 (1981) ECR 767; See also *Liefting* v. *The University of Amsterdam*, 1984, Case 23/83 (1984) ECR 3225.

Court of Appeal could make the appropriate declaration without applying the exclusion clause imposed by the national statute. The U.K. judges interpreted the ruling of the Community Court in a way

> "to demonstrate the proposition that a pension scheme which has its origin in some legislative act and operates without reference to any contractual arrangement in that regard between the employer and employees does not fall within the scope of Article 119 ... On the other hand, where the benefit arising from the pension scheme is derived from ... the terms of a contract of employment ... then the benefit arising *ex consensu* is within the concept of pay as defined by Article 119."

The clear distinction provided by the Court was followed subsequently in the *Bilka-Kaufhaus GmbH* v. *Weber von Harz* Case 1986,[26] where part-time women employees were discriminated in that they had no access to an occupational pension scheme. The case involved many legal issues, e.g. indirect discrimination, in addition to the question as to the nature of the scheme as 'pay'. Darmon AG submitted that each pension scheme has to be examined individually in order to test whether it fell within the scope of Article 119 now Article 141. The Court found that the occupational pension scheme in this case was based on an agreement between Bilka and the staff Committee representing its employees and was entirely financed by the employer.

Benefits paid to the employees under the scheme therefore constitute consideration received by the worker from the employer in respect of the employment, as referred to in the second paragraph of Article 119.

One may add, it also falls within the definition of 'remuneration' under ILO Convention No. 100, reproduced earlier on.

The scope of what is covered under pay was in issue also more recently. The Grand Chamber of the Court delivered a ruling in June 2004 in a case referred to it by the Austrian Supreme Court in *Austrian Trade Unions* v. *Austrian Wirtschsftskammer* 2004[27] concerning termination payments. There is no doubt that termination payments normally advanced by the employer and calculated on the basis of the length of the employment are surely part of pay and are covered by Article 141 as to equality of men and women. However, including in the calculation periods of military service as part of the length of service and excluding periods of parental leave is not very clear.

The Court stated that:

> "2. Article 141 EC and Council Directive 75/117/EEC of 10 February 1975 on the approximation of the laws of the Member States relating

[26] Case 170/84 (1986) ECR 1607.

[27] Case C-220/02 (2004) ECR I-5907.

to the application of the principle of equal pay for men and women do not preclude the calculation of a termination payment from taking into account, as length of service, the duration of periods of military service or the civilian equivalent performed mainly by men but not of parental leave taken most often by women."

Part-time Work and Pay

The issue of part-time work has preoccupied the ECJ in numerous cases, as we shall see in Chapter 11. The concept of treating part-time work as the same work as full time work, but different from it only quantitatively, and meriting a *pro rata* evaluation, was not automatically accepted by the Court. The first case before the ECJ dealing with equal pay for part-time work was that of *Jenkins* v. *Kingsgate (Clothing Productions) Ltd* 1981.[28] It concerned disparity in the hourly pay. Full time employees (40 hours per week) received 10% more per hour than did part-time workers (working 30 hours per week). This was a *prima facie* violation of Article 119 that specifies that "pay for work at time rates shall be the same for the same job".

The Court ruled on 31 March 1981 as follows:

> "1. A difference in pay between full time workers and part-time workers does not amount to discrimination prohibited by Article 119 of the Treaty unless it is in reality merely an indirect way of reducing the pay of part-time workers on the ground that that group of workers is composed exclusively or predominantly of women.
>
> 2. Where the national court is able, using the criteria of equal work and equal pay without the operation of Community or national measures, to establish that the payment of lower hourly rates of remuneration for part-time work than for full time work represents discrimination on the basis of difference of sex the provisions of Article 119 of the Treaty apply directly to such a situation."

The *ratio decidendi* of the ruling, although much criticised[29] is a positive contribution, however, to the law of equality. First, it confirmed the direct effect of Article 119 in a situation where the payment of lower hourly rates of pay for part-time work represented discrimination based on sex. Secondly, although a discrimination

---

28 Case 96/80 (1981) ECR 911.

29 See R. Plender, "Equal Pay for Men and Women; Two Recent Decisions of the European Court", (1982) *American Journal of Comparative Law* pp. 627-653 at p. 650; Erika Szyszczak, "Differences in Pay for Part-Time Work" (1981) 44 *Modern Law Review* 672-682.

between full time workers and part-time workers was not considered as indirect discrimination based on sex *per se*, the Court ruled that the discrimination must be justified on objective grounds by an employer. The onus of proof is thus shifted to the employer. The Court did not, however, define the term 'objectively justified' nor the term 'indirect discrimination' so that many elements remained to be decided by national courts and Community law had to wait for the subsequent interpretation by the ECJ and subsequent legislative reforms.

Once the objective grounds for the difference in pay are established, the ILO criteria for a valid exemption from the principle of equal pay are satisfied, as will be elaborated later on.

The problem of part-time work is now dealt with within the framework of the Directive on Part-Time Work, 97/81/EC of 15 December 1997[30] and the question of Burden of proof is likewise now regulated by Directive 97/80/EC of 1997 amended by Directive 98/52.[31]

Some five years later the ECJ had to render a preliminary ruling in *Bilka-Kaufhhaus GmbH* v. *Weber von Harz 1986*[32] dealing with indirect discrimination to part-time workers, who were excluded from an occupational pension scheme. The Court considered this scheme as part of 'pay' as it was "based on an agreement between Bilka and the Staff Committee representing its employees ... financed entirely by the employer". The discrimination thus fell under Article 119 now Article 141.

Are Perks and Other Emoluments in Cash or in Kind 'Pay'?

The leading case on the scope of emoluments in kind is no doubt the *Garland* v. *British Rail Engineering Ltd.* 1982.[33] This case was referred to the ECJ by the House of Lords on a point which at first sight would appear to be related to retirement benefits, namely, travel facilities for former employees to enjoy after retirement which discriminate against former female employees. Mrs Garland alleged in the Industrial Tribunal that she had suffered discrimination in that female employees of British Rail no longer enjoyed free travel facilities for their families upon retirement although male employees continued to do so. Her claim failed because the Tribunal considered that the matter fell within the exclusion of Section 6 (4) of the Sex Discrimination Act 1975 in that it was a provision relating to retirement. The Employment Appeal Tribunal allowed an appeal but this decision was subsequently overruled by the Court of Appeal. When

30 OJ (1998) L 14/6.

31 OJ (1998) L 205/66.

32 Case 170/84 (1986) ECR 1607.

33 Case 12/81 (1982) ECR 359.

the case came to the House of Lords the question of the relevance of European Community Law was raised. The House of Lords referred the matter to the ECJ for a preliminary ruling.

The Community Court, after investigating the legal nature of the special travel facility to former employees and their families, which the British Rail granted *ex gratia* although not contractually bound to do so, came to the conclusion that free travel was in the nature of a grant in kind to the employees and their dependents directly or indirectly in respect of their employment and as such constituted 'pay' within the meaning of Article 119.

The 1982 ruling was generous to consider a non-contractual benefit in retirement as 'pay'. The House of Lords accepted the ruling with a sigh of relief. This construction avoided the conflict between Community law that does not exclude terms relating to retirement and the Sex Discrimination Act 1975 that did exclude such terms before its amendment in 1986. The House of Lords could consider the free travel granted to retired employees as a 'deferred pay' and the conflict between EC law and national law was thus avoided.

In *Lewen* v. *Denda*[34] the ECJ ruled that an *ex gratia* Christmas bonus paid by an employer to all employees constituted 'pay'. Depriving a women on maternity leave of her Christmas bonus is discrimination and a violation of Article 119 now 141.

In *Andrea Kruger* v. *Kreiskrankenhaus Ebersberg* 1999,[35] concerning end of year bonuses, the ECJ ruled that:

> "Article 119 of the EC Treaty ... must be interpreted as meaning that exclusion by a collective agreement from entitlement to a special annual bonus provided for by that collective agreement of persons in employment which involves a normal working week of less than 15 hours and normal pay not exceeding a fraction of the monthly baseline and is, on that basis, exempt from compulsory social insurance constitutes indirect discrimination based on sex, where that exclusion applies independently of the sex of the worker but actually affects a considerably higher percentage of women than men."

In *Gabriel Gruber* v. *Silhouette International Schmied GmbH & Co. KG* 1999[36] the ECJ was asked by an Austrian court to deliver a preliminary ruling on the compatibility with EU law of an indirectly discriminatory payment on termination of an employment by a woman who resigned for maternity reasons.

In this regard, two different arguments have been put forward. According to the first, put forward by Mrs Gruber and the Commission, the groups to be

34 Case C-333/97 (1999) ECR I-7243.

35 Case C-281/97 (1999) ECR 5127.

36 Case C-249/97 (1999) ECR I-5295.

compared are workers who resign from employment for reasons of maternity and workers who resign for important reasons. When this comparison is made, a disadvantage exists, since the first group receives only one half of the termination payment granted to the second group. In this argument, therefore, resigning from employment for reasons of maternity is considered to be equivalent to an important reason within the meaning of Paragraph 26 of the Personnel Law giving rise to entitlement to the full termination payment provided for in Paragraph 23(1) of that Law.

Silhouette and the Austrian Government, on the other hand, argue that the groups to be compared are workers who resign for reasons of maternity and workers who resign from employment without any important reason or who voluntarily end their employment relationship for reasons of personal convenience. Here, the argument runs, there is no disadvantage, since the first group is entitled to a termination payment, whilst the second receives none. It follows that Paragraph 23a (3) of the Personnel Law, providing for entitlement to a limited termination payment, constitutes a special provision granting preferential treatment for the workers concerned.

The Court ruled that the reduced termination payment in the circumstances of the case is a violation of Article 119 and incompatible with the principle of equal pay and constitutes indirect discrimination.

In *Gillespie* v. *Northern Health and Social Services Board* 1996[37] a maternity benefit based upon contract paid by the employer to the employee constitutes 'pay' because it was based upon the employment relationship.

Severance pay was also considered by the ECJ as part of 'pay' in *Kowalska* v. *Freie Hansastadt Hambourg* 1990[38] and redundancy payments and contractual occupational pension schemes were also considered as part of 'pay' in *Barber* v. *Guardian Royal Exchange Assurance Group* 1990[39] and subject to the Equal Pay Principle. Sick pay was considered 'pay' in *Rinner-Kuhn* v. *FWW* 1989.[40]

In *Levez* v. *Jennings (Harlow Pools) Ltd.* 1998[41] the question of remedies arose regarding breach of equal pay. Even unfair dismissal compensation was considered 'pay' in *R.* v. *Secretary of State for Employment ex parte Seymour Smith and Perez* 1999.[42]

From this rather empirical case law certain broader principles could be gleaned as to the scope of 'pay'. The general tendency was to enlarge the scope

37 Case C-342/93 (1996) ECR I-475.

38 Case 33/89 (1990) ECR I-2591.

39 Case C-262/88 (1990) ECR I-1889.

40 Case 171/88 (1989) ECR 2743.

41 Case C-326/96 (1998) ECR 7835.

42 Case C-167/99 (1999) ECR I-623. See also *Botel's* Case 1992 (Case C-360/90 (1992) ECR I-3589) re paid time off to attend courses and conferences.

of elements of pay so as to subject all types of discrimination in remuneration and emoluments, in cash or in kind, to the principle of equality. Indeed the definition of what is 'remuneration' under the ILO Convention No. 100 is not an exhaustive definition. it states: "the term remuneration includes ... any additional emoluments whatsoever ... arising out of the worker's employment." The above cases fall within the ILO conception.

What Is 'Equal Work'?

The Community Court not only construed 'pay' in a liberal manner, it also interpreted 'work' and gave it a wider significance in *Macarthy* v. *Smith* 1980.[43] It ruled that the principle of equal pay for equal work is not confined to situations in which men and women are contemporaneously doing equal work for the same employer. It held that the principle enshrined in Article 119 applies to the case where it is established that, having regard to the nature of her services, a woman had received less pay than a man who was employed prior to the woman's period of employment and who did equal work for the employer.

Does the Principle of Equal Pay Have Exceptions?

Where there is an objective justification for the disparity of pay which is not based on sex and the employer can prove it, the principle of equal pay will not apply. Article 3 (3) of Convention No. 100 on Equal Remuneration for Work of Equal Value 1951 expressly states that:

> "Differential rates between workers which correspond, without regard to sex, to differences, as determined by such objective appraisal, in the work to be performed, shall not be considered as being contrary to the principle of equal remuneration for men and women workers for work of equal value."

The first case dealing with an objective reason for disparity in pay between men and women workers related to the difference between part-time and full time workers is, as we have seen, that of *Jenkins* v. *Kingsgate* 1981 discussed above. The ECJ opened the door to the possibility of proving that differences in pay may be justified by an objective appraisal, which is not based on grounds of sex, e.g. in the case of a differentiation of pay between full time and part-time workers. The fact that mainly women were part-time workers and the allegations that Ms Jenkins suffered indirect discrimination based on sex did not outweigh the

---

43 Case 129/79 (1980) ECR 1275.

possibility that the employer could prove objective reasons as an exception to the principle of equal pay.

The facts of the case were as follows: Kingsgate Clothing Productions Ltd, manufacturers of ladies' clothing, employed 89 persons of whom 35 were men and 54 women. All the men except one worked full time (i.e. 40 hours per week). Of the women employees, five worked part-time. In November 1975, shortly before the entry into force of the Equal Pay Act 1970, Kingsgate fixed the hourly pay for full time work at the same rate for both men and women. It considered, however, that there was a fundamental difference between part-time and full time work, independently of the sex of the worker, which justified a difference in pay. The pay for part-time work was therefore fixed at a rate 10% lower than that applicable to full time work. The difference was not based on either the characteristics of the worker or the quality of the work. it was motivated by the need (a) to discourage absenteeism; (b) to ensure that the expensive machinery in the factory was being used to its fullest extent, and (c) to encourage greater productivity.

The plaintiff, Mrs Jeanette Pauline Jenkins, who worked 30 hours per week as a special machinist, took the view that she was unfairly prejudiced by the fact that, although she was engaged to perform the same work as that performed by one of her men colleagues employed full time, she drew an hourly rate of pay lower than that drawn by her colleague in contravention of Article 119 on equal pay, which specifies "that pay for work at time rates shall be the same for the same job".

The Court did not rule on the question of indirect discrimination of part-time workers in comparison to full time workers. The Court found that: "A difference in pay between full time workers and part-time workers does not amount to discrimination prohibited by Article 119". It is for the employer to prove that the difference in pay is prompted by objective reasons other than sex discrimination.

The following case, decided some 18 years later, corroborates the existence of an exception to the principle of equal pay on objective grounds.

In *Angestelltenbetriebsrat der Wiener Gebietskrankenkasse* v. *Wiener Gebietskrankenkasse* 1999 doctors and psychologists were performing the same service of psychotherapy. The doctors were predominantly men and were paid more than the psychologists who were mainly women. The Austrian Court referred the following question for a preliminary ruling to the ECJ: Should the different qualifications of the two groups affect the character of the work performed so as to be considered non-equal work, and consequently justifying a different scale of pay? The Court concluded that, although the doctors and psychologists performed "seemingly identical activities", their "knowledge and skill (was) acquired in very different disciplines".[44] The Court ruled that the female psychologists were not discriminated on the basis of sex. "The term 'the same work' does not apply ... where the same activities are performed over a considerable length of time by persons the basis of whose qualification to exercise their profession is different. This ruling was criticised for being "self-contradictory" by some of the authors.[45]

The Court, relying upon the opinion of the Advocate General Cosmas, found that there were objective reasons for the differentiation between the doctors and the psychologists. These reasons were not based on sex.

> "Professional training is not merely one of the factors that may be an objective justification for giving different pay for doing the same work; ... it is also one of the possible criteria for determining whether or not the same work is being performed."

Such objective reasons are a valid exception to the principle of equal pay, justified as such by Article 3 (3) of the ILO Convention No. 100.

The ECJ was convinced in this case that objective reasons justified the difference in pay between the doctors and the psychologists. "Seemingly identical tasks" may not amount to "equal work" where the persons performing the work are of different professional training and qualifications.

In both these cases the justification of a differentiation in pay resulted in indirect discrimination for women employees. The *Jenkins* case related to a discrimination of part-time workers, this group consisting of a greater number of women. The second case involved two categories of persons exercising psychotherapy, the lower paid group (the psychologists) consisted of a greater number of women, the higher paid group (the doctors) consisted mainly of men. However, Article 3 (3) of ILO Convention No. 100 provides for the application of an exception to the principle of equal pay where there is a genuine objective reason for the disparity in pay, and a difference in qualification and skill may satisfy the test of a genuine objective justification.

In the case of *Cadman* v. *Health and Safety Executive* 2006[46] the Grand Chamber of the Court delivered a ruling on the question of whether disparity of pay based on different lengths of service requires proof by the employer that objective reasons and not discrimination based on sex were the justification of unequal pay. In other words does disparity in pay as a result of longer experience a genuine objective reason even without proof, or does the burden of proof shift to the

---

44 Case C-309/97 (1999) ECR I-2865 at p. 2917.

45 E. g. Evelyn Ellis, *EU Anti-Discrimination Law* (Oxford EC Law Library, 2005), at p. 163 and also Craiq and Burca, *EU Law: Text, Cases and Materials* (3rd edn, Oxford University Press, Oxford, 2003), at p. 850.

46 Case 17/05 OJ (2006) C 294/10.

employer to prove that the length of service has in fact contributed to greater experience and that the disparity in pay took account of the length of service. Doubts arose on this issue in the wake of certain decisions of the Court, which will be discussed more fully in Chapter 12 dealing with the issue of burden of proof and discrimination.

What is relevant here is the clear ruling as to the objective justification of unequal pay when it comes to the assessment of experience and length of service as a determinant of pay. The ruling states that as a general rule recourse to the criterion of length of service is appropriate to attain the legitimate objective of rewarding experience acquired which enables the worker to perform his duties better. The employer does not have to prove what is obvious, that experience *per se* is an objective reason for disparity in pay, unless the worker provides evidence of raising serious doubts in that regard.

Equal Pay for Work of Higher Value

A rather curious request for a preliminary ruling came from an Irish Court in the *Murphy* v. *Bord Telecom Eireann* case 1988[47] concerning equal pay for work of unequal value. Ms Murphy and her women colleagues were performing work of higher value than their male colleagues, yet they were paid less. According to the Irish Equal Pay Act 1974 claims could be made only in respect of the "same or like work". The Irish Court referred the case to the ECJ to rule on the position of Community Law. The ECJ had no difficulty to adopt reasoning *a fortiori* and to rule that the women were discriminated against and that paying less for work to which higher value is attributed is all the more a violation of Article 119 and the principle of equal pay.

Attention should be drawn to the European Commission Code of practice on Equal Pay. Although this Code is not binding, it may serve as a useful guidance.

Equal Pay for Work of Equal Value

The normative formula for the comparison of pay between men and women is based on the same work, similar work, work of equal value and even on work of unequal value, where the plaintiff, like in the *Murphy* case, performs work of higher value.

In practice the assessment of work for the purpose of equal pay is at the heart of the difficulty of surmounting discrimination. On the national level the

---

47 Case 157/86 (1988) ECR I-673.

process of harmonisation of legislation with Community law encountered a number of difficulties. In the United Kingdom, Ireland, the Federal Republic of Germany, Greece and Portugal the problem of finding a 'comparable man' in segregated types of employments posed difficulties. "Frequently ... the applicant must find a man working in the same establishment, employed by the same employer and doing comparable work".[48] Even where a 'comparable man' is found he is sometimes paid more for the same work "because he would not come for less". Is this a good defence for an employer to a discrimination case?[49] In the majority of cases however the crucial point is the adoption of a valid and non-discriminatory job evaluation scheme in conformity with Article 1 (2) of the Equal Pay Directive 1975:

> "In particular where a job classification system is used for determining pay, it must be based on the same criteria for both men and women and so drawn up so as to exclude any discrimination on grounds of sex."

In segregated professions (e.g. nurses) there is a general undervaluation of work performed by women which leads to discrimination. National courts and tribunals hearing complaints may need to reconsider the means by which they assess job evaluation techniques on a case-to-case basis, in the light of the ruling of the ECJ in the case of *Gisela Rummler* v. *Dato-Druck 1986.*[50] The Court ruled that the 1975 Directive does not prohibit the use, in a job classification system for the purpose of determining rates of pay, of the criterion of muscular effort or that of the heaviness of the work if, in view of the nature of the tasks involved, the work to be performed does require the use of a certain degree of physical strength, so long as the system as a whole, by taking into account other criteria, such as the degree of knowledge, concentration and responsibility, precludes any discrimination on grounds of sex. A job classification system must take into account criteria for which workers of each sex may show particular aptitude.

In the case of *Dr Pamela Mary Enderby* v. *Secretary of State for Health* 1993,[51] the question of disparity of pay between jobs of equal value was raised and

---

48 See *Network of Experts on the Implementation of the Equality Directives, Final Consolidated Report 1987* (V/1987/88/EN p. 16. See also *Eve C. Landau* "International Labour Standards: The Case of Equal Pay-European Community Perspective" in Gladstone *et al.* (eds) *Labour Relations in a Changing Environment* (Walter de Gruyter, Berlin. N.Y., 1992), at pp. 390-391).

49 See Sir Anthony Lester, "Equal Pay and Equal Treatment without Sex Discrimination: Community and United Kingdom Law", in *Records of the Proceedings of the European Conference, Brussels, May 1985* (Louvain, 1986) p. 407.

50 Case 237/85 (1986) ECR 2101.

51 Case C-127/92 (1993) ECR I-5535.

the question of objective justification came up and in its wake also the issue of burden of proof. The Court gave the following ruling:

> "1. Where significant statistics disclose an appreciable difference in pay between two jobs of equal value, one of which is carried out almost exclusively by women (Speech therapists) and the other predominantly by men (Pharmacists), Article 119 of the Treaty requires the employer to show that that difference is based on objectively justified factors unrelated to any discrimination on grounds of sex.
>
> 2. The fact that the respective rates of pay of two jobs of equal value, one carried out almost exclusively by women and the other predominantly by men, were arrived at by collective bargaining processes which, although carried out by the same parties, are distinct, and, taken separately, have in themselves no discriminatory effect, is not sufficient objective justification for the difference in pay between those two jobs.
>
> 3. It is for the national court to determine, if necessary by applying the principle of proportionality, whether and to what extent the shortage of candidates for a job and the need to attract them by higher pay constitutes an objectively justified economic ground for the difference in pay between the jobs in question."

The following case also concerned work of equal value. The comparison was made between midwifes' pay and pay of a male clinical technician as regards a supplement and a reduction in working time for inconvenient working hours. A Swedish Labour Court requested the ECJ to give a preliminary ruling in the case *Jamstalldhetsombudsmannen* v. *Orebro Ians landsting* 2000.[52] The ECJ ruled that:

> "If a difference in pay between two groups compared is found to exist, and if the available statistical data indicate that there is a substantially higher proportion of women than men in the advantaged group (enjoying reduction of working time), Article 141 of the Treaty requires the employer to justify the difference by objective factors which are unrelated to any discrimination on grounds of sex."

The Court went on to state that:

> "Neither the reduction in working time, by reference to the standard normal working time for day-work, awarded in respect of work performed according to a three-shift roster, nor the value of such a reduction, are to be taken into consideration for the purpose of calculating the salary used as the basis for a pay comparison for the purposes of Article 141 of the Treaty and Directive 75/117. However, such a reduction may constitute

52 Case C-236/98 (2000) ECR 2189.

> an objective reason unrelated to any discrimination on grounds of sex such as to justify a difference in pay. It is for the employer to show that this is the case."

The difficulty in applying the ILO principle of equal pay for work of equal value in practice may have eased slightly over the years by its implementation within the EU in the wake of the 1975 Directive, i.e. in over thirty years. Globally however the 56 years that elapsed since the adoption of ILO Convention No. 100 have not improved substantially the application of the concept of 'work of equal value' as we have seen above in the General Observation of the ILO Committee of Experts published in 2007.

Actions Brought by Officials of the Community against the Institutions

Returning to the EU and the contribution of the ECJ case law we find that within the internal application of the principle of equal pay to officials of the Community there were cases of discrimination which the Court addressed and redressed.

The principle of equal pay and the issue of indirect discrimination arose in the cases of *Sabbatini-Bertoni* v. *European Parliament* and *Chollet-Baudain* v. *Commission* 1972 mentioned above. The legality of the termination of an expatriation allowance upon marriage, in circumstances discriminatory to women, was questioned in these cases. The applicants maintained that Article 4 (3) of Annex VII to the Staff Regulations that provided that a staff member "loses entitlement to the allowance if ... he/she does not become the head of the family" upon marriage, was illegal because it was contrary, first to the general principle of law of equality of men and women, and, second, to Article 119 which enshrines the principle of equal pay for men and women. According to Article 1 (3) of the same Annex the term 'head of household' normally refers to a married male official, whereas a married female official is considered to be 'head of household' in exceptional circumstances, in particular in cases of invalidity or serious illness of the husband.

The Court found that the Staff Regulations were arbitrary.

They cannot treat officials differently according as to whether they are male or female, since the termination of the status of expatriate must be dependent for both male and female officials on uniform criteria, irrespective of sex.

The Court annulled the discriminatory decisions by which the applicants' expatriate allowance was withdrawn upon marriage. The Court's judgment was rendered in the spirit of 'equality begins at home'.[53] The ECJ recognized the need to ensure equality in the matter of pay and working conditions for men and women employed by the Community itself, within the context of the

53 See E.C. Landau, "The Rights of Working Women in the European Community", in *European Perspectives* (Commission of the EC, Brussels, 1985), at p. 22.

Staff Regulations. The Court refrained however from doing so, as we may recall, in the *Defrenne* Case. It merely applied Article 119 which only dealt with pay and not with equality in other conditions of work, which is now included in the amendment in Article 141 of the Treaty of Amsterdam 1997. The Court thus made at that time a distinction between employees of the Community and employees in the Member States. This artificial distinction could be set aside after the adoption and implementation of the Equal Treatment Directive 1976, which will be the subject of Chapter 7.

Other staff cases that deserve a mention are *Airola* v. *Commission* 1975[54] and *Razzouk and Beydoun* v. *Commission* 1984.[55] In the latter case the issue was sex discrimination contained in the Community's Staff Regulations as regards the provision of survivors' benefits to the relatives of deceased employees. In his submissions Advocate General Sir Gordon Slynn was of the opinion that a retirement pension received by a civil servant of the Community, and also a survivor's pension received by the latter's widow or widower was 'pay' and subject to the principle 'analogous' to Article 119 now Article 141.

The ECJ's judgment was rather based on the general principle of equal treatment of men and women officials in the Community and emphasized that the relationship of the institutions of the Community and their employees is "by no means limited ... [to] Article 119".

Conclusion

EU Equal Pay law: i.e. Article 119 now 141 and the Equal Pay Directive 1975 are the 'European translation' of ILO Convention No. 100.

The extension of equal pay for equal work to cover work of equal value (The 1975 Directive) was adopted to bring EU law in line with the ILO standard. The implementation of the principle of equal pay for work of equal value was proved, however, to be more complicated than envisaged. In the cases brought before the ECJ for a preliminary ruling, the Court sometimes found difficulty in applying the principle with clarity, i.e. in the Austrian case involving graduate psychologists and psychotherapists that were doing the same job or at least performing a task of equal value.

The wide definition of pay under EU law is inspired by the ILO definition of 'remuneration'. The ECJ was generous to extend the concept of 'pay' to cover a wide range of emoluments and equality consequently applies to gratuities and perks, even to those that are granted *ex gratia* and after retirement as we have seen in the *Garland* case.

---

54 Case 21/74 (1975) ECR 221.

55 Cases 75 &117/82 (1984) ECR 1509.

The exception to the principle of equal pay elaborated by the ECJ's case law, where the employer can prove objective reasons unrelated to sex, is already justified expressly by ILO Convention No. 100 in Article 3 (3). Although the ECJ mentioned more than once that it is up to the national court to establish the existence of such an objective reason in each case, it tried nevertheless to elaborate certain general criteria.

Whilst there are no express references to the ILO standards and the ECJ is silent as to the impact of ILO Convention NO. 100, the influence of the universal norms of equality is evident and the provisions of the Convention are followed and given effective application in the Member States via the ECJ's case law and its control powers. Unlike Convention No. 100, ILO Convention No. 111 was referred to on one occasion, but unfortunately not followed, in *Defrenne* v. *Sabena (No. 2)*, prior to the 1976 Equal Treatment Directive's entry into force. It is to the Equal Treatment Directive that we turn in the next Chapter.

Chapter 7

EQUAL TREATMENT

Background

The massive participation of women in the workforce after the Second World War has changed the role of women in society, and the new perception of women as equal partners resulted in the shaping of equality of treatment. Three elements characterise this change and are interwoven as both cause and effect:

First, the participation of women in the work force during the war years established a new social pattern, where women replaced the fighting men by necessity. After the war this pattern became irreversible for economic reasons. Women mostly became joint breadwinners with their husbands or heads of family.

Second, with the advent of decolonisation after the War, many women assumed important roles in building and shaping independence in newly emerging countries. This was the case in India, Israel, Sri-Lanka, etc., that appointed women as their Heads of Government, like Indira Ghandi, Golda Meir and Chandrika Bandaranaike, to mention just the more famous ones.

Third, the appearance of family planning and the pill meant that women could control reproduction, facilitating their active role outside the home.

These three elements contributed to the greater participation of women in working life outside the home, but their role in the home was not taken over by the community or by any other institution. Women simply acquired a dual role and have had to cope with both as best they can. The changes created by the emancipation of women still require fair adjustment through measures promoting child care and a balance between home responsibilities and work.[1]

As we have seen in the previous chapter, the ILO tackled the issue of equal remuneration for men and women workers as early as 1951. The problem of discrimination in employment and occupation and equal treatment in all

[1] See opening address "Equality and Human Rights", to the Conference on the Status of Women at the Dawn of the Twenty-first century, by Eve. C. Landau, Proceedings published by UNESCO, 2001, at p. 10.

conditions of work, which is the subject of this chapter, was addressed by the ILO soon after in 1958, fifty years ago.

Some statistical data published by the EU in 2003 may be interesting in this connection. Women outnumber men in education. The percentage of women graduates in the 25 Member States increased to 58% due to the higher level of education in the new Member States. Women also represent 41% of the PhD graduates. The gender gap in employment decreased by 0.5 percentage points to 15.8 % between 2002 and 2003 in the EU of 25. 30.4% of women in the work force worked part-time, compared to only 6.6% of men, and the gap has slightly increased since 1998. This is one among many factors which explains the gender pay gap. The new Member States have a much lower proportion of part-time jobs, partly due to labour market rigidity and partly due to the lower wage level, which makes this option less attractive.

ILO Standards

The Discrimination (Employment and Occupation) Convention No. 111 and the supplementary Recommendation No. 111 were adopted in 1958 to deal with the overall problem of discrimination on grounds of race, colour, sex, religion, political opinion, national extraction or social origin. The Convention has a wide scope and defines discrimination as including any distinction, exclusion or preference on any of the grounds specified in education, vocational guidance and training, access to employment and in all conditions of work.

Both these instruments apply to all persons and all forms of employment, whether in the private or the public sector, salaried or independent.

It is not open for ratifying Member States to enter reservations. Convention No. 111 has to date been ratified by 165 states, including all the 27 EU Member States. With the ratification of Convention No. 111 by China in 2006, the number of people covered worldwide by this Convention has expanded considerably.

States bound by the Convention undertake to declare and pursue a national policy aimed at eliminating all forms of discrimination in respect of employment and occupation. They must repeal any statutory provisions and modify any administrative instructions or practices which are inconsistent with this policy, and are under a duty to enact legislation and promote educational programmes that favour its acceptance and implementation, in cooperation with national employers' and workers' organisations.

Recommendation No. 111 spells out in more detail the measures which should be taken in pursuance of policies governing equality of opportunity and treatment. It suggests that appropriate agencies should be set up to foster public understanding and acceptance of the principles of non-discrimination and also to examine complaints when the policy is not being observed.

EU Legislation

The *corpus juris* on EU equality at work is to be found in the Directive on Equal Treatment 1976 that was inspired by ILO Convention No. 111 concerning Discrimination (Employment and Occupation) 1958. The Directive was amended in 2002 by Council Directive 2002/73/EC[2] and entered into force in 2005. A further consolidating Directive was adopted in 2006, bringing together five existing directives in a single text. However, this Directive is not yet in force.[3]

The ILO Convention is wider in scope than the 1976 Directive in that it prohibits discrimination in the work place on grounds based on race, colour, sex, religion, political opinion, national extraction or social origin. The 1976 Directive deals exclusively with equality of men and women workers. The latter does not speak of the negative aspect of discrimination as does the Convention, but rather uses a positive approach of equal treatment of men and women.

The protection of other underprivileged groups in the Community was introduced at a much later stage, in 1999, when the Treaty of Amsterdam and its Article 13 entered into force and two Framework Directives were adopted in 2000: Council Directive 2000/78/EC Establishing a General Framework for Equal Treatment in Employment and Occupation,[4] and Council Directive 2000/43/EC Implementing the Principle of Equal Treatment between Persons Irrespective of Racial or Ethnic Origin.[5]

Article 13 of the Treaty of Amsterdam empowers the Community to take appropriate action to combat discrimination based on sex, racial or ethnic origin, religion or belief that are covered by the ILO Convention No. 111 and further extends the prohibition of discrimination to cover also persons discriminated on the basis of disability, age and sexual orientation. Thus Community Law today has caught up with ILO Convention No. 111 and has even included protection to these three additional groups that are not covered by the ILO Convention of 1958. Over forty years separate the ILO Convention and the EU comprehensive legal instruments. These groups of underprivileged categories of persons waited for a long period to be recognised and accorded equality and positive action in the European Community.

Besides the differences in scope between the Convention and the 1976 Directive, and the positive approach of the Directive to equal treatment, the coverage of all the facets of employment is the same both under the Convention and the Directive.

---

2 OJ (2002) L-269/15.

3 Directive 2006/54/EC of the European Parliament and the Council, OJ (2006) L 204/23.

4 OJ (2000) L-303/16.

5 OJ (2000) L-180/22.

However, the Convention targeted in Article 3(b) also education, whereas the Directive aimed only at equality at work and vocational training.

The definition of "employment" and "occupation" under Article 1 (3) of the ILO Convention includes "access to vocational training, access to employment and to particular occupations, and terms and conditions of employment". In a similar manner the Directive aims to achieve equality between men and women as regards access to employment and vocational training and promotion and as regards working conditions. The Directive expressly mentions also promotion and dismissal (Article 5), which may be considered as falling implicitly under the "terms and conditions of employment" used by the Convention. However, the Directive is more explicit.

Article 1 of the Convention defines "discrimination" to include:

> "(a) any distinction, exclusion or preference made on the basis of race, colour, sex, etc., which has the effect of nullifying or impairing equality of opportunity or treatment in employment or occupation."

The Convention includes an exception or defence to discrimination in Article 1 (2) as follows: "Any distinction, exclusion or preference in respect of a particular job based on the inherent requirements thereof shall not be deemed to be discrimination". Article 2 (2) of the Directive likewise provides an exception "where the sex of the worker constitutes a determining factor". The Convention and the Directive are in complete harmony.

Protective measures for women are respected both by the Convention and by the Directive. Article 5 of the Convention provides that special measures of protection covered by ILO Conventions and Recommendations shall not be deemed to be discrimination. Article 2 (3) of the Directive provides that "This Directive shall be without prejudice to provisions concerning the protection of women, particularly as regards pregnancy and maternity".

The Directive also provides in Article 3 (2) (c) for a review of protective measures in the following manner:

> "those laws, regulations and administrative provisions contrary to the principle of equal treatment when the concern for protection which originally inspired them is no longer well founded shall be revised, and that where similar provisions are included in collective agreements labour and management shall be requested to undertake the desired revision."

The revision of protective measures for women will be dealt with in chapter 8.

Unlike the ILO Convention, the Directive provides for judicial remedies in Article 6:

> "Member States shall introduce into their national legal systems such measures as are necessary to enable all persons who consider themselves

> wronged by failure to apply to them the principle of equal treatment within the meaning of Articles 3, 4 and 5 to pursue their claims by judicial process after possible recourse to other competent authorities."

As we shall see from the abundant case law, the Directive has contributed to equal treatment of men and women in the workplace via the proliferation of actions by individuals, victims of discrimination, and the Community Court in its decisions harmonised the laws throughout the Community.

Article 2 (4) opened the door to positive action in favour of women:

> "This Directive shall be without prejudice to measures to promote equal opportunity for men and women, in particular by removing existing inequalities which affect women's opportunities in the areas referred to in Article 1 (1)."

These areas include notably access to employment, promotion, and vocational training and cover all working conditions. The issue of positive (or affirmative) action will be the subject of Chapter 14.

In 2002 in the wake of the Amsterdam Treaty, especially on the basis of Article 13, and after the adoption of the revised Article 141 to replace Article 119, the Community elaborated an amendment to the 1976 Equal Treatment Directive. This amendment takes account of the rulings of the ECJ interpreting the 1976 Directive over a span of 25 years. It opens the door slightly wider towards positive action for women, and it includes for the first time the issue of sexual harassment as part of sex discrimination, to be covered by Chapter 13. This amending Directive entered into force in 2005.

In 2006 a consolidating directive was adopted to update and to partially codify the various directives in one instrument: Directive 2006/54/EC of the European Parliament and of the Council of 5 July 2006 on the implementation of the principle of equal opportunities and equal treatment of men and women in matters of employment and occupation (recast) mentioned in Chapter 4.

The addition of "equal opportunities" to the title of the new Directive highlights the new aim of equality of opportunities to complement equality of treatment.

Professor Blanpain interprets equal opportunities in a different way. For him equal opportunities means equality at the start but not equality of outcome. He distinguishes between the provisions regarding "access to employment ... no actual job is guaranteed" and those where equality in outcome is ensured, such as equal treatment in conditions of work, including dismissal.[6]

---

6 See R. Blanpain, *European Labour Law* (10th rev. edn, Kluwer Law International, 2006), at p. 466.

The new Directive, which has not yet entered into force, refers to the EU Charter of Fundamental Rights in recital (5) of the Preamble:

> "(5) Articles 21 and 23 of the Charter of Fundamental Rights of the European Union also prohibit any discrimination on grounds of sex and enshrine the right to equal treatment between men and women in all areas, including employment, work and pay."

The Charter is granted a legally binding value like the Treaties by the European Council Meeting of June 2007 and confirmed in Lisbon in December 2007:[7]

> "5) Replacement of Article 6 on fundamental rights with a text reading as follows:
>
> 1. The Union recognises the rights, freedoms and principles set out in the Charter of Fundamental Rights of 7 December 2000."

The prohibition of discrimination and the right to equal treatment between men and women is no longer limited to the domain of work, but extends "to all areas."

EU Case Law

We shall discuss first the implementation of equality in the field of access to employment, and then deal separately with the practice of equal treatment regarding vocational training, and finally, we shall examine equality in all conditions of work, including the thorny issue of dismissal.

When the Equal Treatment Directive entered into force three decades ago there were many segregated jobs in the European Community. Certain jobs were not open to women at all e.g. armed police, the army, the church, fire services. Men, on the other hand, had, for instance, no access to vocational training as midwives and as kindergarten teachers.

The Directive in Article 2 (2) provided that:

> "This Directive shall be without prejudice to the right of Member States to exclude from its field of application those occupational activities and, where appropriate, the training leading thereto, for which, by reason of their nature of the context in which they are carried out, the sex of the worker constitutes a determining factor."

The Equal Treatment Directive tolerated these exceptions on a transitory basis as the following provision shows. Article 9 (2) laid down that:

[7] See Brussels European Council 21/22 June 2007 Presidency Conclusions, at p. 26.

> "Member States shall periodically assess the occupational activities referred to in Article 2 (2) in order to decide, in the light of social developments, whether there is justification for maintaining the exclusions concerned. They shall notify the Commission of the results of this assessment."

Directive 2002/73/EC of the European Parliament and of the Council of 23 September 2002 amending Council Directive 76/207/EEC on the implementation of the principle of equal treatment for men and women as regards access to employment, vocational training and promotion, and working conditions states in its Preamble, recital (11) that:

> "The occupational activities that Member States may exclude from the scope of Directive 76/207/EEC should be restricted to those which necessitate the employment of a person of one sex by reason of the nature of the particular occupational activities concerned, provided that the objective sought is legitimate, and subject to the principle of proportionality as laid down by the case law of the Court of Justice."

This is in the spirit of Article 1 (2) of ILO Convention No. 111, using the concept of the inherent requirements of a job.

If an opera advertises for a baritone singer and rejects the application of a woman singer, this would not be considered discrimination because of the nature of the particular occupational activity concerned, or in the terminology of ILO Convention No. 111, "[a]ny distinction, exclusion or preference in respect of a particular job based on the inherent requirements thereof shall not be deemed to be discrimination."

This exception proves the rule that access to jobs should be open regardless of sex and that equality of treatment is a fundamental human right according to the 2002 Directive.

The role of the Court of Justice was crucial in interpreting the Equal Treatment Directive 1976. Over 200 cases came up before the ECJ and over forty leading cases were decided by the ECJ between 1976 and the entry into force of the 2002 Directive in 2005.

In the domain of equal treatment of men and women as regards access to employment, the classification of the decisions of the Court into three groups of actions that we have applied to the study of the principle of Equal Pay may not prove appropriate. The greatest contribution of the ECJ is through the procedure of preliminary rulings. Some illustrations of actions brought by the Commission against Member States for failure to fulfil their obligations will nevertheless be briefly covered.

Actions Brought by the Commission against States

One of the early actions by the Commission addressed the issue of discrimination of men in the case of *Commission* v. *U.K.* 1983.[8] Men were denied access to vocational training as midwives for sociological reasons. The Court of Justice was reluctant to condemn the UK as the relationship between midwives and patients at the time was governed by personal sensitivities. The ECJ recommended a gradual change of policy. The question of access of men to the employment and vocational training as midwives arose also in Ireland and Germany and the profession was gradually opened for men.[9] It is interesting to note that in the early 1980s the concept of segregated jobs was current and men were excluded not only from midwifery, but also from work as kindergarten teachers, home-aides, etc. Women were usually excluded from the army, the police, fire brigades, prison service, etc.

Women were likewise excluded from jobs involving night-work, from underground mines, and from jobs involving manual lifting of weights. In addition, considerations of protection of health for women excluded them from hazardous occupations, such as exposure to lead, etc. This exclusion originated in ILO Conventions dealing with protective measures for women, which will be dealt with in Chapter 8.

A typical national legislation of those days is to be found in the Luxembourg Act respecting Equal Treatment 1981 which enumerates certain exceptions. Under Article 2 (2):

> "For the time being, the following shall not be regarded as conflicting with this Act:
>
> (a) laws and regulations on night work of women in industry,(b) laws and regulations on the employment of women in mines;(c) laws and regulations on the engagement of women in the army, police force and gendarmerie; (d) laws, regulations and administrative provisions on the employment of customs officers, postal workers, prison wardens, forest warders, members of military bands, process-servers and holder of religious office."

The issue of the prohibition of night work for women arose before the ECJ in an action for infringement brought by the *Commission* v. *France* 1997.[10] The ECJ declared that by maintaining in force Article L 213-1 of the *Code du Travail*,

---

8 Case 165/82 (1983) ECR 3431; See also *Commission* v. *Federal Republic of Germany* 1983, Case 248/83 (1985) ECR 1459.

9 See Eve C. Landau, *The Rights of Working Women in the European Community* (European Perspective Series, Commission of the E.C., Brussels, 1985), at pp. 40-41.

10 C-197/96 (1997) ECR I-1489.

prohibiting night work by women in industry, whereas no such prohibition exists in relation to men, the French Republic has failed to fulfil its obligations under Article 5 (1) of Council Directive 76/207/EEC of February 1976 on the implementation of the principle of equal treatment for men and women as regards access to employment, vocational training and promotion, and working conditions.

The French Government had by then denounced ILO Convention No. 89 on prohibition of night work for women. However, by retaining Article L 213-1 of the Code legal uncertainty remained as to the rights of individuals and the relationship of the Code to the Directive.

France did not comply with the ECJ's judgment, whereupon the Commission brought an action against France under Article 171 now Article 228 requesting the Court to impose a daily fine of 142,425 Euros for non-implementation of its earlier judgment of 13 March 1997 until compliance by France was established and the violating provision was removed from the Code. We shall address this case again in Chapter 8 dealing with abolition of protective measures for women.

Preliminary Rulings

Access to Jobs

The question of equality as regards access to jobs was dealt with by the ECJ in four leading cases relating to the field of 'segregated' occupations, namely work in prisons, police, the navy and the army.

The first request for a preliminary ruling came from Germany in the case of *Von Colson and Kamann* v. *Land North Rhein Westphalia* 1984.[11] Sabine von Colson and Elisabeth Kamann underwent a period of training in the Werl prison at the end of their social worker's course. They applied for vacant posts at the same prison. The governor of the prison stated that he preferred to take on a man without experience rather than women. The two social workers brought action against the prison for discrimination. The Hamm Labour Court, dealing with the case, requested a preliminary ruling from the Community Court on the question of remedies. There was no doubt here that discrimination as regards access to employment was established.

The Hamm Court asked as follows:

> "1. Does it follow from Council Directive 76/207/EEC that discrimination on grounds of sex in relation to access to employment must be sanctioned by a requirement that the discriminating employer conclude a contract of employment with the candidate discriminated against?

[11] Case 14/83 (1984) ECR 1891. See also *Harz* v. *Tradax* 1984, Case 79/83 (1984) ECR 1921.

5. In case of a negative answer to the first question, what should the legal sanction be for discrimination in relation to access to employment in violation of the Directive?"

The ruling of the Court was as follows:

"1. Council Directive 76/207/EEC does not provide that sex discrimination in relation to access to employment is to be sanctioned by a requirement that the employer conclude a contract of employment with the candidate discriminated against.

2. The directive does not contain any unconditional and sufficiently clear sanctions entitling an individual to claim reparation in case of discrimination, in the absence of implementing national legislation to that effect.

3. Although the Directive 76/207/EEC leaves to the Member States the free choice of sanctions in case of violation of the prohibition to discriminate, it implicitly requires that the reparation imposed by each State shall be effective, of a dissuasive force and adequate in relation to the prejudice suffered. it should consist of real damages beyond the purely symbolic indemnity as, for example, the reimbursement of expenses actually incurred by the candidate. It is for the national judicial authority to apply the directive within the permitted discretion and ensure that the interpretation is in conformity with the requirements of Community law."

It is noteworthy that the Labour Court of Hamm awarded the plaintiffs, von Colson and Kamann, the unprecedented sum of DM 21,000 each, as damages plus interest. German law would have awarded only the reimbursement of expenses, such as a the price of a rail ticket to come to an interview.

The impact of this ruling as well as of the rulings that followed in the cases of *Marshall (No. 2)* 1993[12] is evidenced in the amendment of the Directive of 2002. Article 6 (2) of the Directive provides:

"Member States shall introduce into their national legal systems such measures as are necessary to ensure real and effective compensation or reparation as the Member States so determine for the loss and damage sustained by a person injured as a result of discrimination contrary to Article 3, in a way which is dissuasive and proportionate to the damage suffered; such compensation or reparation may not be restricted by the fixing of a prior upper limit, except in cases where the employer

[12] Case C-271/91 (1993) ECR I-4367 and *Draehmpaehl* 1997, Case C-180/95 (1997) ECR I-2195.

can prove that the only damage suffered by an applicant as a result of discrimination within the meaning of the Directive is the refusal to take his/her job application into consideration."

In the case of *Johnston* v. *Royal Ulster Constabulary* 1986[13] the Royal Ulster Constabulary (RUC) refused to renew Ms Johnston's contract of employment since she was not trained in the use of firearms nor permitted to use them. It was argued on behalf of RUC that in view of the security situation in Northern Ireland a derogation to the Equal Treatment Directive was justified on grounds of public safety. To allow women to carry and use firearms increased the risk of their becoming targets for violence. In this case the discrimination of the plaintiff was governed by considerations of protection of public security and protection of women in situations of armed conflict. Nevertheless the ECJ ruled:

> "The differences in treatment between men and women that Article 2 (3) of Directive 76/207/EEC allows, out of concern to protect women, do not include risks and dangers, such as those to which any armed police officer is exposed in the performance of his duties in a given situation that do not affect women as such."

The Court, unlike the Chief Constable, saw no objection to training and arming women on duty in Northern Ireland. On the contrary the Court believed that the plaintiff was discriminated against by not being employed full time by RUC.

The case related also to the interpretation of Article 6 of the Directive concerning effective judicial remedies. The Court ruled that:

> "The principle of effective judicial control laid down in Article 6 of the 1976 Directive did not allow a certificate, issued by a national authority stating that the conditions for derogating from the principle of equal treatment for men and women for the purposes of protecting public safety are satisfied, to be treated as conclusive evidence so as to exclude the exercise of any power of review by the courts. The provision contained in Article 6 to the effect that all persons, who consider themselves wronged by discrimination between men and women, must have an effective judicial remedy, may be relied upon by individuals as against a Member State, which has not ensured that it is fully implemented in its internal legal system."

The ECJ stated in its ruling that such a certificate cannot be conclusive evidence, and the derogation must satisfy the criteria laid down by the Directive on Equal Treatment itself. The Directive does not expressly allow exceptions on the ground

13 Case 222/84 (1986) ECR, 1651.

of public security. Furthermore, any derogations from the fundamental principle of equal treatment must be interpreted restrictively.

In the case of *Sirdar* v. *Army Board and Secretary of Defence* 1999,[14] however, the plaintiff, a cook, was denied access to employment with the British Royal Marines on the ground that the Royal Marines have to act both in specific capacities and be qualified for combat duty. Combat duty is not usually open to women, as they may be physically unsuited for offensive hand to hand combat.

The ECJ ruled that:

> "In determining the scope of any derogation from an individual right such as the equal treatment of men and women, the principle of proportionality, one of the general principles of Community law must ... be observed ... That principle requires that derogations remain within the limits of what is appropriate and necessary in order to achieve the aim in view and requires the principle of equal treatment to be reconciled as far as possible with the requirements of public security which determine the context in which the activities in question are to be performed.
>
> However, depending on the circumstances, national authorities have a certain degree of discretion when adopting measures which they consider to be necessary in order to guarantee public security in a Member State."

The view has been expressed that the special circumstances of the operation of the Royal Marines, a small force operating in difficult and unsanitary conditions, lacking in personal privacy, was the real justification for a derogation to the principle of equal treatment, more so than the consideration of public safety.[15] One may also explain the different rulings in the Johnston and Sirdar Cases in that Johnston was not involved in offensive-combat duty, but merely in a defensive role.

In *Kreil* v. *Germany* 2000[16] the ECJ stated in its preliminary ruling that the German military law that discriminates women in that they are not allowed to be armed and that they are allowed to serve merely in the medical or musical units is unjustified on objective grounds and is not satisfying the principle of proportionality and thus it violates the Equal Treatment Directive.

Summarising the four cases, the ECJ opened the doors for women in three of them. The *Sirdar* Case was decided upon objective considerations and her exclusion from serving in the Royal Marines was justified.

---

14 Case C-273/97 (1999) ECR I 7403.

15 See "EC Law on Justification for Sex Discrimination in Working Life" in R. Blanpain (ed.), *Collective Bargaining, Discrimination, Social Security and European Integration* (Kluwer, Deventer, 2003).

16 Case C-285/98 (2000) ECR I-69.

The last three decades have seen a great change in attitudes towards stereotyped classifications of jobs as masculine or feminine in character. Jobs have become largely unisex. The ILO exception to equality as expressly provided for in Article 1 (2) of Convention 111: "Any distinction, exclusion or preference in respect of a particular job based on inherent requirement thereof shall not be deemed to be discrimination", is probably the best formulated justification for a derogation from the principle of equality and may serve as an exception that proves the rule.

Access to Vocational Training

The case that comes to mind in this context is that of *Ms Schnorbus* v. *Land Hessen* 2000[17] Ms Schnorbus applied for training as a lawyer. However, her application was rejected and postponed and priority was given to men who had completed compulsory army service. Schnorbus based her claim in the German court on sex discrimination and the German court asked the ECJ to render a preliminary ruling on the question of the compatibility of the preference of the German ex-service men to Ms Schnorbus with the Equal Treatment Directive. Was this preference justified on objective grounds or was it a measure of indirect discrimination, (as women are exempt from military service in Germany) and therefore incompatible with the Equal Treatment Directive?

The ECJ was of the opinion that the burden of proof shifts to the Land Hessen to prove that the discrimination of Ms Schnorbus was justified on objective grounds unrelated to sex. The defendants justified the preference of men on the objective ground that the military service had delayed the advancement in their careers until the completion of the service and they merited an earlier access to the vocational training as lawyers. The measure in favour of the ex-service men was thus considered compatible with the Directive on Equal Treatment.

Equal Conditions of Work, Including Dismissal

The 2002/73/EC Directive amending the Equal Treatment Directive 76/207/EEC provides in Article 3 (1) that:

> "Application of the principle of equal treatment means that there shall be no direct or indirect discrimination on the grounds of sex in the public or private sectors, including public bodies, in relation to:
>
> (c) employment and working conditions, including dismissals."

---

17 Case C-79/99 (2000) ECR I-10997.

This provision replaces Article 5 (1) of the 1976 Directive which stated that:

> "Application of the principle of equal treatment with regard to working conditions, including dismissal, means that men and women shall be guaranteed the same conditions without discrimination based on grounds of sex."

The majority of the cases decided by the ECJ were naturally based on the original Directive of 1976.

The landmark decision on dismissal is *Ms Marshall* v. *Southampton Area Health Authority (Teaching)* 1986.[18]We may recall the facts of the case that gave rise to a claim of discrimination. Ms Marshall worked as a dietician at the Health Authority and was dismissed at the age of 62. Ms Marshall wished to continue her career until the age of 65, the retirement age of men. The Authority had an implied term in their contract with the employees that they were obliged to retire at the age at which they became eligible to draw a retirement pension, namely, in England at the age of 65 for men and at the age of 60 for women. Ms Marshall complained that her discriminatory dismissal caused her loss of job satisfaction in addition to financial loss.

The ECJ made a distinction between differential retirement ages, which violate the Equal Treatment Directive and its Article 5 that prohibits discriminatory dismissals, and differential retirement pension ages that are excluded by Article 7 from the Social Security Directive 79/7/EEC. The right to work until the age of 65 should apply equally to men and women. The Court interpreted Article 5 (1) as follows:

> "Article 5 (1) of Council Directive 76/207/EEC provides that application of the principle of equal treatment with regard to working conditions, including the conditions governing dismissal, means that men and women are to be guaranteed the same conditions without discrimination on grounds of sex ... an age limit for the compulsory dismissal of workers pursuant to an employer's general policy concerning retirement falls within the term 'dismissal' used in this manner, even if the dismissal involves the grant of a retirement pension."

The operative part of the ruling states that:

> "Article 5 (1) of Council Directive 76/207/EEC must be interpreted as meaning that a general policy concerning dismissal involving the dismissal of a woman solely because she has attained the qualifying age for a state pension, which age is different under national legislation for men and for women, constitutes discrimination on grounds of sex, contrary to the Directive."

---

[18] Case 152/84 (1986) ECR 723.

Article 5 (1) is now replaced by Article 3 (1) (c) and the same interpretation would be followed today.

Ms Marshall could rely directly on the Directive as the authority she was working for was a public authority and she enforced the ruling against an organ of the state, as we have explained in Chapter 4, when dealing with the vertical direct effect of directives. When claiming the amount due to her as compensation she insisted to obtain also a certain sum as interest on the amount due. Her claim reached the House of Lords and the latter referred the case to the ECJ.

The Court, in answer to the questions referred to it by the House of Lords, ruled:

> "1. The interpretation of Article 6 of Council Directive 76/207/EEC of 9 February 1976 on the implementation of the principle of equal treatment for men and women as regards access to employment, vocational training and promotion, and working conditions must be that reparation of the loss and damage sustained by a person injured as a result of discriminatory dismissal may not be limited to an upper limit fixed *a priori* or by excluding an award of interest to compensate for the loss sustained by the recipient of the compensation as a result of the effluxion of time until the capital sum awarded is actually paid.
>
> 2. A person who has been injured as a result of discriminatory dismissal may rely on the provisions of Article 6 of the Directive as against an authority of the State acting in its capacity as an employer in order to set aside a national provision which imposes limits on the amount of compensation recoverable by way of reparation."

Ms Marshall could thus obtain full compensation damages as well as interest for the discriminatory dismissal she had suffered. Her case contributed to the development of EU law on the subject and as far as remedies are concerned the new Directive of 2002 has enshrined the ruling in the amended Article 6 (2) in the following manner:

> "Member States shall introduce into their national legal systems such measures as are necessary to ensure real and effective compensation or reparation as the Member States so determine for the loss and damage sustained by a person injured as result of discrimination contrary to Article 3, in a way which is dissuasive and proportionate to the damage suffered; such compensation or reparation may not be restricted by the fixing of a prior upper limit, except in cases where the employer can prove that the only damage suffered by an applicant as a result of discrimination within the meaning of this Directive is the refusal to take his/her job application into consideration."

As to age/sex discrimination, the 2000 General Framework Directive does not as yet foresee a single age of retirement for both men and women. Recital 14 of the Preamble leaves the door open for disparity in stating that: "This Directive shall be without prejudice to national provisions laying down retirement ages".

But the consolidating 2006 Directive, which lists examples of discrimination in Article 9, expressly includes in paragraph (f) "fixing different retirement ages" as an example of discrimination. The Member States are given little time to adjust their retirement ages by the date of entry into force of the Directive.

Indirect Discrimination

We have discussed so far cases involving direct discrimination as far as the implementation of the 1976 Equal Treatment Directive is concerned. Indirect discrimination is also prohibited by Article 2 (1) but the Directive does not provide any definition of what amounts to indirect discrimination. The first time we encounter a definition is in the 1997 Directive on the Burden of Proof. Article 2 (2) provides that:

> "For purposes of the principle of equal treatment referred to in paragraph 1, indirect discrimination shall exist where an apparently neutral provision, criterion or practice disadvantages a substantially higher proportion of the members of one sex unless that provision, criterion or practice is appropriate and necessary and can be justified by objective factors unrelated to sex."

This definition is enshrined again with a slight change in the 2006 consolidating Directive in Article 2 that provides also a definition of 'direct discrimination':

> "1. For the purposes of this Directive, the following definitions shall apply:
>
> (a) 'direct discrimination': where one person is treated less favourably on grounds of sex than another is, has been or would be treated in a comparable situation;
>
> (b) 'indirect discrimination': where an apparently neutral provision, criterion or practice would put persons of one sex at a particular disadvantage compared with persons of the other sex, unless that provision, criterion or practice is objectively justified by a legitimate aim, and the means of achieving that aim are appropriate and necessary."

Most cases of indirect discrimination that came up before the ECJ involved women part-time workers, such as the *Jenkins* v. *Kingsgate* Case, discussed in the Chapter dealing with Equal Pay. We shall therefore postpone the discussion of the topic of indirect discrimination to Chapter 11 dealing more specifically with part-time work.

Conclusion

The above survey shows advancement and improvement in equal opportunities and access to jobs. Employment has become unisex and there is a lot less job segregation. This Chapter does not deal, however, with the important issue of reconciling work and family, as Chapter 10 is devoted to the problem of workers with family responsibilities. It also does not cover the problem of protective measures and their progressive abolition. This will be dealt with in Chapter 8. The prohibition of discrimination on grounds of pregnancy and maternity will likewise be treated separately in Chapter 9.

As we have seen, the length of working life for women has been prolonged by the *Marshall Ruling of 1986* to be the same as that for men regardless as to whether the age of retirement is the same for men and women. The impact of the 2006 Directive on equality of ages of retirement is still left to be seen.

The recent issues covered by the Directive on Equal Treatment, such as sexual harassment and positive action, will be dealt with in Chapter 13 and Chapter 14 respectively.

There is no doubt that the standards of equality enshrined in the ILO Convention No. 111 have been faithfully interpreted by the ECJ and, as was summarised by the Legal Adviser to the Irish Equality Authority:

> "The scope and expression of European equality law has changed dramatically since 1957. It has moved from a side effect of the market to a more inclusive and broad-based concept of equality with an explicit human rights foundation."[19]

The social goals inspired by the ILO have impacted the economic aims that at first motivated the European Community.

However, the glass of equality at work is not yet full. In practice the conclusion at this stage, like that of the Commission's Gender Equality Report 2005,[20] is that in spite of the advances, inequality still remains.

---

19 See Eillis Barry Summer School Seminar, "EU Gender Discrimination Law", 7 June 2006, at p. 11.

20 (COM) (2005) 44 final (Brussels 14/02/2005).

Chapter 8

PROTECTIVE MEASURES FOR WOMEN

Background

The need to protect women and children at work was expressed during the last quarter of the nineteenth century, in the context of fast industrialization in Western Europe and North America, on the grounds that they were weaker than men and more susceptible to exploitation and abuse. Early legislation addressed questions of working hours, women's work in mines, weight-lifting restrictions, and work with toxic substances. For instance, the UK was the first country to prohibit women from working underground in 1842, and, in 1844, to restrict their work at night. Historically, protective legislation came to alleviate some of the extreme hardships on the weak and the exploited – women and children – in working long hours, in night work, in mining – labouring under painful and unhealthy industrial conditions.

The protection of women at work as a 'weaker' category of workers was at first considered not only legitimate but a worthy cause for governments and trade unions. However, with the rise of feminism, the promotion of human rights for all and the right to equality for women and men in the late twentieth century, protecting women at work – except for maternity provisions based on objective contingencies – became controversial as discriminatory, an obstacle for equality.

Thus, protective measures for women – again, except for maternity provisions which were and are considered as legitimate and needed – were progressively eroded, and for many, abolished at the national and international levels.

Protective measures mean national and international laws, regulations, directives, enforced by law and justice and designed to protect women workers by regulating the terms and conditions of their labour, such as regulation forbidding night work for women, protecting them against harmful work environment or products, working in mines, and limiting the weights they can lift.

This Chapter reviews the evolution of international legislation and the case law of the European Court of Justice on specific protection issues: night work for women, protection of women against substance poisoning, women's work in mines and maximum weight limits for women.

The evolution of these rules shows that protective measures for women in specific fields and circumstances, except for maternity protection, are no longer warranted, have lost their *raison d'être* and have become counter productive, besides being a violation of equality between women and men. The key breakthroughs of this evolution were the 1975 ILO Resolution and Plan of Action referring to the need to review all protective legislation applying to women in the light of 'up-to-date scientific knowledge and technical advances' and, for the EU, the Council Directive 76/207/EEC of 9 February 1976 on the implementation of the principle of equal treatment for men and women as regards access to employment, vocational training and working conditions.

In 1981, the ILO Conference adopted the Occupational Safety and Health Convention, Convention No. 155, which applied to 'all workers' without distinction of sex. The only optional exclusion from its application was 'limited categories of workers in respect of which there are particular difficulties' (Article 2(1) and (2)). The aim of the Convention is to prevent accidents and injury to health arising out of, linked with or occurring in the course of work, by minimizing, so far as is reasonably practicable, the causes of hazards inherent in the working environment. This includes, among others, chemical, physical and biological substances and agents.[1]

In 1989, Council Directive 89/391/EEC on the introduction of measures to encourage improvements in the safety and health of workers at work was adopted on 12 June 1989. Employers have the obligation, among others, to take the measures necessary for the safety and health protection of workers, including prevention of occupational risks and provision of information and training, as well as provision of the necessary organization and means. The Directive refers to 'workers' without distinction as to sex.

The ILO and EU instruments provide a legal basis to promote equality by extending protective measures to all workers.[2] The need to give protection and support to women at work during and after pregnancy has been recognized by both organizations through the principle of accommodation for differences between groups. Essentially, the concept stems from the realization that the achievement of equal treatment can only become a reality where some reasonable allowance is made for objective differences. In this instance, the difference requiring accommodation is women's reproductive functions, a basis for special arrangements to meet the needs of women in pregnancy, birth, recovery after birth and breast-feeding.

---

1 Article 4(2) and (5)(a).

2 See ILO Meeting of Experts on Special Protective Measures for Women and Equality of Opportunity and Treatment, 1989 (Doc. MEPMW/1989/7) p. 76. Report published in 1990.

The issues of pregnancy and maternity protection are examined in Chapter 9.

Night Work for Women

ILO Standards

ILO standards that prohibit or restrict women's work in arduous industrial conditions were originally hailed as major humanitarian advances for the protection of female workers. They have now become an object of controversy and division among the ILO's social partners – government, employers' and workers' representatives.

Several ILO instruments, from the 1919 Convention to a 1990 Protocol, show an evolution from the protection of women to the protection of all night workers without sex distinction.

A first Night Work (Women) Convention No. 4 was adopted on 28 November 1919. It declared that women without distinction of age were not to be employed during the night – defined as a period of at least eleven consecutive hours, including the interval between ten o'clock in the evening and five o'clock in the morning – in any public or private industrial undertaking, except in cases of force majeure. This Convention has been shelved as an outdated instrument.

A Recommendation concerning Night Work of Women in Agriculture No. 13 was adopted on 15 November 1921. Member States were to regulate the employment of women in agricultural undertakings during the night in such a way as to ensure to them a period of rest compatible with their 'physical necessities' and consisting of not less than nine consecutive hours, if possible.

Convention No. 4 was replaced in 1934 by Convention No. 41, the second Night Work (Women) Convention (Revised). It substituted, in exceptional circumstances, the period 10 p.m. to 5 p.m. to the period 11 p.m. to 6 a.m. in the definition of the term 'night', and exempted from the prohibition of night work 'women holding responsible positions of management who are not ordinarily engaged in manual work'. This Convention is also shelved as outdated.

It was replaced by Convention No. 89 adopted on 9 July 1948. 'Night' was then re-defined as a period of at least eleven consecutive hours, including an interval of at least seven consecutive hours falling between ten o'clock in the evening and seven o'clock in the morning. Different intervals could be prescribed for different areas or industries, subject to consultations with employers' and workers' organizations, before prescribing an interval beginning after eleven o'clock in the evening. The new Convention excluded from the prohibition of night work not only women holding responsible positions of a managerial or technical character, but also women employed in health and welfare services not ordinarily engaged in manual work. The night work prohibition could be suspended by the government, after consultation with the employers' and workers' associations concerned, in case of a serious emergency demanded by the national interest.

Article 5 (1) of the Maternity Protection Recommendation No. 95 1952 prohibited night work and overtime work, not for all women, but for pregnant and nursing women.

In 1958, the Discrimination (Employment and Occupation) Convention No. 111 and Recommendation No. 111 established the principle of non-discrimination on a number of grounds including sex, including access to vocational training, access to employment and to particular occupations, and terms and conditions of employment. Its Article 5 provides:

1. Special measures of protection or assistance provided for in other Conventions or Recommendations adopted by the International Labour Conference shall not be deemed to be discrimination.
2. Any Member may, after consultation with representatives employers' and workers organizations, where such exist, determine that other special measures designed to meet the particular requirements of persons who, for reasons such as sex, age, disablement, family responsibilities or social or cultural status, are generally recognized to require special protection or assistance, shall not be deemed to be discrimination.

In 1958, the ILO thus considered that protective measures were not incompatible with equality nor in any way constituted discrimination.

The First International Women's Year (1975) presented the occasion to develop a more broadly based and coherent approach to the question of equality between women and men. Following a general discussion on equality for women workers in 1975, the International Labour Conference adopted the Declaration on Equality of Opportunity and Treatment for Women Workers and two resolutions which stressed that the promotion of equality of opportunity and treatment between men and women should be the main objective of all ILO activities relating to women. The Declaration called upon the ILO to "carry out thorough and sufficiently extensive studies on matters relating to special protection for women and men as the case may be". It contained several principles including the continuous promotion and improvement of working and living conditions for all employees; the protection of women against the risks inherent in their employment and occupation on the same basis and with the same standards of protection as men, in the light of advances in scientific and technological knowledge; the limitation or the adoption of special protective measures to types of work proved to be harmful for women from the standpoint of their social function of reproduction; and the revision and periodic updating of these measures in the light of advances in scientific and technological knowledge. The Plan of Action which supplements this Declaration adds that:

> "Measures should be taken to review all protective legislation applying to women in the light of up-to-date scientific knowledge and technical advances and to revise, supplement, extend to all workers, retain or repeal such legislation according to national circumstances, these measures being aimed at the improvement of the quality of life."

The emphasis was thus changing from the protection of women to the requirement that equality implies granting equal opportunities and treatment for women and men in all employment respects including coverage by protective legislation.

By 1989, the prohibition of night work for women had become a divisive issue among the ILO social partners. The workers' organizations felt that the prohibition of night work for women in Convention No. 89 should remain as an important and necessary protection. To the employers' organizations, the Convention was discriminatory and an impediment to economic and social progress. Many of the government representatives had similar views: there was no reason for differential treatment between men and women, except in respect of maternity protection.

Faced with this dilemma, the ILO still tried to achieve both protection and equality. The General Conference adopted two instruments in 1990, which lifted the general prohibition of night work for women, limiting it to ensuring that an alternative to night work is made available to women.

The first was the Night Work Convention No. 171 1990 adopted on 26 June 1990. This Convention makes no distinction among sexes: it applies to both men and women, except for maternity protection. Night work was now defined as all work performed during a period of not less that seven consecutive hours (instead of 11 in the 1989 Convention) including the interval from midnight to 5 a.m. (instead of 11 p.m. to 6 a.m. in the 1989 Convention). The 1990 Convention applies to all employed persons except those employed in agriculture, stock raising, fishing, maritime transport and inland navigation (Article 2). Specific measures required by the nature of night work should be taken for night workers in order to protect their health and safety, assist them to meet their family and social responsibilities, provide opportunities for occupational advancement, and provide appropriate compensation (Article 3). Article 7 requires that "Measures shall be taken to ensure that an alternative to night work is available to women workers who would otherwise be called upon to perform such work" for a period of at least sixteen weeks before and after childbirth, of which at least eight weeks are before the expected date of childbirth, and for additional periods in respect of which a medical certificate is produced stating that it is necessary for the health of the mother or child. During these periods, a woman worker is not to be dismissed or given notice of dismissal, except for justifiable reasons not connected with pregnancy or childbirth, her income should be maintained at a level sufficient for the upkeep of herself and her child in accordance with a suitable standard of living, she is not to lose the benefits regarding status, seniority and access to promotion attached to her regular night work position, and there should be no reduction in the protection and benefits connected with maternity leave. Compensation for night work in the form of working time, pay or similar benefits applies to "night workers", i.e. both men and women.

This preference is therefore strictly limited to pregnancy and childbirth conditions of women.

The other instrument is the Protocol of 1990 to the Night Work (Women) Convention (Revised), also adopted on 26 June 1990, confirming the policies set in the Convention. It further states that national laws or regulations may provide that variations in the duration of the night period as defined in Article 2 of the Convention and exemptions from the prohibition of night work contained in Article 3 may be introduced by decision of the competent authority after consulting the most representative organizations of employers and workers. However, this requires that the national authority has satisfied itself that adequate safeguards exist in the establishment as regards occupational safety and health, social services, equality of opportunity and treatment for women workers, and only for a specified, renewable, period of time.

EU Legislation

The EU policy on night work for women has been based consistently on the 1976 Council Directive, revised in 2002, and several ECJ rulings.

The Council Directive 76/207/EEC of 9 February 1976, dealt with in Chapter 7, refers in Article 1 to the implementation "of the principle of equal treatment for men and women as regards access to employment, vocational training and promotion, and working conditions". Its broad scope applies implicitly to night work for women, as part of working conditions.

It firmly established "the principle of equal treatment", meaning "that there shall be no discrimination whatsoever on grounds of sex either directly or indirectly by reference in particular to marital or family status". The Directive is without prejudice to the right of Member States to exclude from its field of application those occupational activities and, where appropriate, the training leading thereto, for which, by reason of their nature or the context in which they are carried out, the sex of the worker constitutes a determining factor. It is also without prejudice to provisions concerning the protection of women, particularly as regards pregnancy and maternity.

Article 5 (2) of the Directive imposes on Member States the duty to take the measures necessary to ensure that any laws, regulations and administrative provisions contrary to the principle of equal treatment "shall be abolished". And Article 5 (2) (c) addresses the issue of revision of protective measures for women "when the concern for protection which originally inspired them is no longer well founded". Furthermore, Article 9 (2) requires Member States to periodically assess the occupational activities referred to above in order to decide, in the light of social developments, whether there is justification for maintaining the exclusions concerned.

This Directive was amended by Directive 2002/73/EC of 23 September 2002. Preamble Recital (11) states that equality between women and men is a fundamental principle under Article 2 and Article 3 (2) of the EC Treaty and the case law of the Court of Justice. It makes clear that the occupational activities that Member States may exclude from the scope of Directive 76/207/EEC should be restricted to those which necessitate the employment of a person of one sex by reason of the nature of the particular occupational activities concerned, provided that the objective sought is legitimate, and subject to the principle of proportionality as laid down in the ECJ case law. Protective measures for women have become progressively redundant. Both the ILO and the EU eventually saw in them only temporary provisions to yield eventually to the fundamental principle of equality of men and women.

EU Case Law

In the case of *Ministère Public* v. *Stoeckel (1991)* of 4 October 1989[3], the *Tribunal de Police* of Illkirch (France) requested a preliminary ruling from the ECJ on the compatibility of the French Labour Code with Council Directive 76/207/EEC. This case was decided on the basis of French law only, without reference to the relevant ILO Convention.

The Court replied to the *Tribunal*'s question on the interpretation of the Directive 76/207/EEC on the implementation of the principle of equal treatment for men and women as regards access to employment, vocational training and promotion, and working conditions. It recalled that under Article L 213-1 of the French *Code du Travail*, women may not be employed for any nightwork, in particular in plants, factories or workshops of any kind whatsoever. However, the same Article provides for a number of exceptions, relating for example to management posts or executive technical posts and to situations where, because of particularly serious circumstances, provision must be made for the prohibition of nightwork by women employees working in successive shifts to be suspended when the national interest so requires, under the conditions and in the circumstances envisaged in the *Code du Travail*. As a result of economic difficulties brought about by foreign competition, the Suma firm found that the number of necessary redundancies could be limited if a continuous shift-work were adopted, involving nightwork for all the workforce. An agreement, negotiated with the unions, stipulated that recourse to nightwork was an exceptional measure and that Suma would revert to day-work only as soon as the economic constraints had ceased. As the female workers in the company had the necessary

3 Case C-345 (1989) ECR I-4047.

skills for the posts that had been retained, the parties, wishing to ensure that women were given the same opportunities as men, agreed to make all posts available to both men and women. Approved by a majority vote of the female workers, the system was introduced on 1 October 1988.

Before the *Tribunal de Police*, Mr Stoeckel contended that Article L 213 of the *Code du Travail* was contrary to Article 5 of the Directive 76/207.

The *Tribunal de Police* then stayed the proceedings pending a ruling by the Court on the following question:

> "Is Article 5 of the Directive of 9 February 1976 sufficiently precise to impose on a Member State an obligation not to lay down in its legislation the principle that nightwork by women is prohibited, as in Article L. 213-1 of the *Code du Travail?*"

The Court recalled that the purpose of the Directive is to implement in the Member States the principle of equal treatment for men and women with regard, *inter alia*, to access to employment and working conditions. To that end, the Directive requires the abolition or the revision of national provisions that are contrary to that principle where the concern for protection which originally inspired is no longer well founded.

The French and Italian governments submitted that the prohibition of nightwork for women, which is any case subject to numerous exceptions, is in conformity with the general aims of protecting female workers and with particular considerations of a social nature relating, for example, to the risks of attack and the heavier domestic workload borne by women.

The Court replied that, whatever the disadvantages of nightwork may be, it did not seem that, except in the case of pregnancy or maternity, the risks to which women are exposed when working at night are, in general, inherently different from those to which men are exposed. Concerning the risks of attack, if assumed that they are greater at night than during the day, appropriate measures can be adopted to deal with them without undermining the fundamental principle of equal treatment for men and women.

As far as family responsibilities are concerned, the Court had already held that the Directive is not designed to settle questions concerned with the organization of the family or to alter the division of responsibility between parents. The Court concluded that the concern for protection, by which the general prohibition of nightwork by women was originally inspired, no longer appears to be well founded and the maintenance of that prohibition, by reasons of risks that are not peculiar to women or preoccupations unconnected with the purpose of Directive 76/207, cannot be justified by the provisions of Article 2 (3) of the Directive.

In reply to the question of the *Tribunal de Police*, the Court stated that Article 5 of Directive 76/207 was sufficiently precise to impose on the Member States the obligation not to lay down by legislation that principle that nightwork by women is prohibited, even if that is subject to exceptions, where nightwork for men is not prohibited.

In another case, *Ministère public* v. *Levy*,[4] in its ruling of 2 August 1993, the Court referred to the *Stoeckel* case in which it held that Article 5 of Directive 76/207/EEC is sufficiently precise to impose on the Member States the obligation not to lay down by legislation the principle that night work by women is prohibited, even if that is subject to exceptions where night work for men is not prohibited. It follows that, in principle, a national court is under a duty to give full effect to that rule, refusing to apply any conflicting provision of national legislation. In the *Levy* ruling, the Court again affirmed that the national court was under an obligation to ensure that Article 5 of the Directive was fully complied with by refraining from applying any conflicting provision of national legislation, but added the qualification:

> "unless the application of such a provision is necessary in order to ensure the performance by the Member State concerned of obligations arising under an agreement concluded with non-member countries prior to the entry into force of the EEC Treaty."[5]

This referred to ILO Convention 89.

In two cases heard three years later, in 1997, the Court followed the *Stoeckel* ruling.

In the case of *Commission* v. *France*,[6] on 10 June 1996, the Commission brought an action under Article 169, now Article 226, of the EC Treaty for a declaration that by maintaining in force Article L 213-1 of the *Code du Travail* prohibiting nightwork by women in industry whereas no such prohibition exists in relation to men, the French Republic has failed to fulfil its obligations under Article 5 (1) of Council Directive 76/207/EEC of 9 February 1976.

Under Article 9 (1) of the Directive, Member States were required to put into force the laws, regulations and administrative provisions necessary in order to comply with the Directive within a period of 30 months of its notification and, with respect of Article 5 (2) (c), within a period of four years. The latter period expired on 14 February 1980.

---

4 Case C-158/91 (1993) ECR I-4287.

5 The first paragraph of Article 234 of the EEC Treaty provides that the rights and obligations arising from agreements concluded before the entry into force of the Treaty between one or more Member States on the one hand, and one or more non-member countries on the other, are not affected by the provisions of the Treaty. Nonetheless, the second paragraph obliges the Member States to take all appropriate steps to eliminate any incompatibilities between such an agreement and the Treaty. Article 234 is of general scope and applies to any international agreement, irrespective of subject matter, which is capable of affecting the application of the Treaty.

6 Case C-197/96 (1997) ECR I-1489.

The provisions in Article L 213-1 of the *Code du Travail* were adopted in order to implement ILO Convention No. 89 of 9 July 1948, which France ratified by law of 7 July 1953. Following the *Stoeckel* judgment, France denounced Convention No. 89, with effect from 26 February 1993. As we have seen, the ECJ must have overlooked this fact when it decided the *Levy* ruling some six months later, on 2 August 1993.

In view of the *Stoeckel* judgment and France's denunciation of Convention No. 89, the Commission took the view that the French legislation was incompatible with Article 5 of the Directive and that the French government was therefore bound to remedy that incompatibility. By letter of 2 March 1994, the Commission put the French government on notice to submit observations within two months pursuant to the first paragraph of Article 169 now 226 of the Treaty.

Not satisfied with the French government's response on 10 May 1994, the Commission sent it a reasoned opinion on 9 November 1994 in which it requested the government to take the necessary measures to make its legislation consistent with Article 5 of the Directive within two months. As the government failed to comply with the reasoned opinion within the prescribed period, the Commission brought these proceedings in accordance with Article 171 now 228 of the Treaty imposing sanctions on States for non-fulfilment of the ECJ's rulings.

In its defence, the French government submitted that, at present, there is no longer any discrimination in law or in fact in France between nightwork by men or women. Since ILO Convention No. 89 was denounced, Article L 213-1 of the *Code du Travail* has no longer been applicable in France because Article 5 of the Directive has direct effect and consequently individuals are entitled to rely on it before national courts in order to have the contested provision set aside. It also referred, on one hand, to a ministerial answer to a parliamentary question of 13 December 1993, which explained the significance of the Community case law with regard to Article L 213-1 of the *Code du Travail* and national's courts obligations to set aside the application of that provision in the event of a dispute and, on the other, to the existence of agreements organizing night work by women in those sectors where it is most widespread. For the French government, the practice followed in this matter confirmed that Article L 213-1 of the *Code du Travail* is in fact no longer applied.

The Court was not satisfied with these arguments. It found that, following the French government's denunciation of Convention No. 89, French legislation was incompatible with Article 5 of the Directive.

> "The Court has consistently held that the incompatibility of national legislation with Community provisions, even provisions which are directly applicable, can be finally remedied only by means of national provisions of a binding nature which have the same legal force as those which must be amended. Mere administrative practices, which by their nature are alterable at will by the authorities and are not given the appropriate

> publicity, cannot be regarded as constituting the proper fulfilment of obligations under the Treaty."[7]

The Court noted that, because the *Code du Travail* Article has been retained, individuals are in a position of uncertainty as to their legal situation and exposed to unwarranted criminal proceedings. In conclusion, the Court declared that, by maintaining in force Article L 213-1 of the *Code du Travail*, the French Republic had failed to fulfil its obligations under Article 5 (1) of Directive 76/207/EEC of 9 February 1976 on the implementation of the principle of equal treatment for men and women as regards access to employment, vocational training and promotion, and working conditions.

In a further confirmation of *Stoeckel*, the case of *Commission* v. *Italy*[8] heard similar arguments, *mutatis mutandis*, and ended with a similar judgment: Italy's position was the same as France, and its arguments were also rejected by the Court. The Commission brought an action under Article 169 now 226 of the EC Treaty for a declaration that, by not adopting within the prescribed period the laws, regulations and administrative provisions necessary in order to comply with Council Directive 76/207/EEC of 9 February 1976, and by retaining in national law rules prohibiting nightwork by women contrary to Article 5 of the Directive, the Italian Republic had failed to fulfil its obligations under Community law.

Following the *Stoeckel* ruling, Italy, like France, had denounced ILO Convention No. 89 but had not abrogated the prohibition of nightwork by women contained in Article 5 (1) of Italian Law No. 903 of 9 December 1977 on Equal Treatment for Men and Women at Work. The Court's ruling of 4 December 1997 adopted the declaration sought by the Commission.

On 21 April 1999, the European Commission asked the ECJ to impose a financial sanction of €142,425 per day on France for failure to implement the judgment of the Court of 13 March 1997, in which the Court had found that France was infringing the principle of equal treatment between men and women by retaining within its legislation a prohibition on nightwork for women and not for men, pursuant to Article 171 now 228 of the EC Treaty. The Commission's action was in accordance with Article 171 now 228 imposing sanctions on States for non-fulfilment of an ECJ ruling.

After an initial rejection by the French Senate caused in part by the opposition of French trade unions, France's National Assembly finally adopted, on 29 November 2000, a law lifting the ban on nightwork for women, ending the conflict with the EU.

---

7 See *Commission* v. *France*, Case C-334/94 (1996) ECR I-1307, paragraph 30.

8 Case C-207/96 (1997) ECR I-6869.

Furthermore, following the adoption of ILO Convention No. 171, there is now compatibility between EU law and the ILO on equality of treatment of men and women regarding night work.

Women's Protection against Substance Poisoning

ILO Standards

One Recommendation and several Conventions have been adopted by the ILO General Conference giving protection to women and, for some, children, against work in contact with poisonous or dangerous substances in various situations.

The General Conference of the ILO adopted a Recommendation No. 4 concerning the Protection of Women and Children against Lead Poisoning on 29 November 1919. In view of the "danger involved to the function of maternity and to the physical development of children", their exclusion from employment in specific processes involving lead treatment was recommended to Member States, under set conditions. The ILO status of this Recommendation is that this instrument is "to be revised".

This Recommendation was followed by the adoption by the Conference on 25 October 1921 of the C13 White Lead (Painting) Convention, No. 13 1921. It entered into force on 31 August 1923. Its Article 3 prohibits the employment of males under eighteen years of age and of all females in any painting of an industrial character involving the use of white lead or sulphate of lead or other products containing these pigments, with exceptions for painters' apprentices. Sixty-two countries have ratified the Convention. It is to be revised, presumably because of the protective measures for women it includes.

Women's Underground Work in Mines

ILO Standards

Convention No. 45 concerning the Employment of Women on Underground Work in Mines of All Kinds was adopted by the Conference on 21 June 1935. It entered into force on 30 May 1937. Article 2 forbids the employment of women, whatever their age, on underground work in any mine. National laws may exempt from this prohibition females holding positions of management, who do not perform manual work, females employed in health and welfare services, female trainees and other females who may occasionally have to enter the underground part of a mine for the: purpose of an non-manual occupation.

Ninety-seven countries have ratified this Convention. Its status is that of "Other instrument subject to a request for information".

Convention No. 176 of 22 June 1995 on safety and health in mines does not refer to women only but lays down rules on safety and health irrespective of the worker's sex. It replaced, de facto, Convention No. 45 in abolishing the total prohibition of the employment of women in mines.

EU Legislation

As in the previous section on night work for women, the basic EU legislation is to be found in Council Directive 76/207/EEC of 1976 and Directive 2002/73/ EC of 2002.

EU Case Law

In the case of *Commission* v. *Austria*,[9] the ruling, delivered on 1 February 2005, referred to the prohibition of the employment of women on underground work in mines of all kinds in ILO Convention No. 45. The Convention was ratified by Austria on 3 July 1937.

As noted above, Convention No. 176 of 22 June 1995 makes no reference to men and women, but only to 'workers'. Austria ratified this Convention but, at the time of the judgment, had not denounced Convention No. 45.[10]

In its judgment, the Court recalled that, in the case of *Brown* v. *Rentokil Ltd.*[11] by reserving to Member States the right to retain or introduce provisions which are intended to protect women in connection with 'pregnancy and maternity', Article 2 (3) of Directive 76/207 recognized the legitimacy, in terms of the principle of equal treatment, first, of protecting a woman's biological condition during and after pregnancy and, second, of protecting the special relationship between a woman and her child during the period which follows pregnancy and childbirth. However, this Directive:

> "... does not allow women to be excluded from a certain type of employment solely on the ground that they ought to be given greater protection than men against risks which affect men and women in the same way and which are distinct from women's specific needs of protection, such as those expressly mentioned ... Nor may women be excluded from a certain type of employment solely because they are on average smaller and less

9 Case C-203/03 (2005) ECR I-935. See Chapter 5.

10 Among EU Members, Finland (19.9.1997), Ireland (27.5.1988), Luxemburg (3.3.1958), the Netherlands (29.2.1937) and the UK (18.7.1936) have denounced Convention No. 45.

11 Case C-394-96 (1998) ECR I-4185, para. 17.

> strong than average men, while men with similar physical features are accepted for that employment.
>
> ... the general prohibition of the employment of women in the underground mining industry laid down in Article 2 (1) of the [Austrian] regulation of 2001 ... does not constitute a difference in treatment permissible under Article 2 (3) of Directive 76/207."

The obligations imposed on the Republic of Austria by Convention No. 45 of the ILO are incompatible with Articles 2 and 3 of Directive 76/207. Article 7 of Convention No. 45 of the ILO contains a denunciation clause. The appropriate steps for the elimination of this incompatibility include the denunciation of the Convention. However, as the next opportunity for Austria to denounce the Convention will only occur on the expiry of a period of ten years starting on 30 May 1997, the Court ruled that, by maintaining in force national provisions such as those contained in the 2001 regulation, the Republic of Austria had not failed to fulfil its obligations under Community law. The principle was respected while the delay in implementing it was admitted as legitimate.

The Court's judgment referred to a related issue, the prohibition of the employment of women in work of a high-pressure atmosphere and in diving work. The Commission considered that, as for the employment of women in the underground mining industry, a general prohibition of the employment of women in work in a high-pressure atmosphere and in diving work without individual assessment cannot be justified by women's alleged special needs of protection. The Court found that the absolute prohibition in the Austrian regulation of 1973 did not constitute a difference in treatment permitted under Article 2 (3) of Directive 76/207:

> "Legislation that precludes any individual assessment and prohibits women from entering the employment in question, when that employment is not forbidden to men whose vital capacity and red blood cell count are equal to or lower than the average values of those variables measured for women, is not authorized by virtue of Article 2 (3) of Directive 76/207 and constitutes discrimination on grounds of sex."

The Court then declared that, by maintaining in Articles 8 and 31 of the *Druckluft- und Taucherarbeiten Verordnung* (Regulation on work in a high-pressure atmosphere and diving work) of 25 July 1973 a general prohibition of the employment of women in work in a high-pressure atmosphere and in diving work, providing a limited number of exceptions in the former case, Austria had failed to fulfil its obligations under Articles 2 and 3 of Council Directive 76/207/EEC of 9 February 1976.

Maximum Weight Limits

ILO Standards

The Maximum Weight Convention No. 127 1967 was adopted on 28 June 1967 and entered into force on 10 March 1970. The Convention applies to regular manual transport of loads, and to all branches of economic activity in respect of which the Member State concerned maintains a system of labour inspection. A degree of protection is granted to women and young workers: their assignment to manual transport of loads other than light loads "shall be limited". When women and young workers are engaged in such transport, the maximum weight of such loads "shall be substantially less than that permitted for adult male workers".[12] The implementation of such policy is left to Member States. Twenty-five countries have ratified this Convention, which is to be revised.

The Maximum Weight Recommendation No. 128 1967 was also adopted to complement the Convention. Several articles elaborated on the principle that where adult women workers are engaged in the manual transport of loads, the maximum weight of such loads should be substantially less than that permitted for adult male workers. Article 16 provides that:

> "As far as possible, adult women workers should not be assigned to regular manual transport of loads."

And Article 17 provides that:

> "Where adult manual women workers are assigned to regular manual transport of loads, provision should be made –
>
> a. as appropriate, to reduce the time spent on actual lifting, carrying and putting down of loads by such workers;
>
> b. to prohibit the assignment of such workers to certain specified jobs, comprised in the manual transport of loads, which are especially arduous."

This instrument is also to be revised.[13]

---

12 Article 7.

13 New EU Members (Bulgaria, Hungary, Poland and Romania) who have ratified Convention 127 will have to denounce it. Older Members (France, Italy, Spain and Portugal) who have also ratified the Convention, will have to denounce it. See Commission of the EC, *Protective Legislation for Women in the Member States of the EC* (Brussels, 1987); see also ILO, *Meeting of Experts on Special Protective Measures for Women and Equality of Opportunity and Treatment* (Technical Background Paper, Geneva, 1989).

Conclusion

Social evolution and scientific and technical development outdate laws: international legislation and justice have been important, and at times, critical, actors in leading national governments or parliaments into adjusting to new social realities.

The evolution of concepts on the protection of women at work is shown by the initial position of the ILO on the need to protect women, the weaker sex, in working conditions, taking into account the traditional family responsibilities borne by women, and their reproductive role. Social evolution, the promotion of women's rights, the increasing number of women at work during the two World Wars, and progress in technology which made formerly hard work easier for all led to equality between women and men, and non discrimination between the sexes. For instance, ILO Conventions show the evolution from the prohibition of night work for women to the protection of all night workers without sex distinction.

The EU has not adopted any directives on the issues of protective measures for women as the general trend was to revise them. Already in 1958, the ILO Discrimination (Employment and Occupation) Convention No. 111 established the principle of non-discrimination on the ground of sex, and acknowledged that protective measures for women were tolerated until reviewed and revised where they had lost their purpose.

Both the ILO and the EU recognized at first the validity and the *raison d'être* of protective measures. Then both organizations realized, in the wake of the UN 1975 Decade for Women, that equality can be better achieved if certain unnecessary protective measures are abolished, resulting in the 1975 ILO Resolution and Plan of Action on the need to review all protective legislation applying to women in the light of up-to-date scientific knowledge and technical advances.

The EU followed in 1976 with Council Directive 76/207/EEC on the principle of equal treatment for men and women: there was to be no discrimination whatsoever on grounds of sex either directly or by reference to marital or family status. Similarly to Article 5 of Convention No. 111, Article 2(3) of Directive 76/207/EEC declared that "This Directive shall be without prejudice to provisions concerning the protection of women, particularly as regards pregnancy and maternity". Under Article 2(2), exceptions are then limited to occupational activities where the sex of the worker constitutes a "determining factor", and without prejudice to provisions concerning pregnancy and maternity.

Similarly to the 1975 ILO Resolution and Plan of Action, Article 9(2) of Directive 76/207/EEC requested Member States:

> "to periodically assess the occupational activities referred to in Article 2(2) in order to decide, in the light of social developments, whether there is justification for maintaining the exclusions concerned."

Extending protection to all the workers was promoted by the ILO as early as 1981 by Convention No. 155, which inspired the EU Directive 89/391/EEC in 1989 on the improvement in the safety and health of all workers without distinction of sex.

The 2002 Directive, which amended the 1976 Directive, and the case law of the ECJ then reinforced the fundamental principle of equality between women and men, in spite of problems of implementation at the national level. A right to accommodation has now replaced exclusion and outdated protection, although the 2002 Directive was to be "without prejudice to provisions concerning the protection of women, particularly as regards pregnancy and maternity".[14]

As a substitute for the abolition of protective measures for women at work, it is now admitted that equality between men and women can be achieved by protection for all workers regardless of sex, and, more generally, by implementing the ILO policy of "decent work".

As noted by the Director-General of ILO in his Report of June 1999:

> "The primary goal of the ILO today is to promote opportunities for women and men to obtain decent and productive work, in conditions of freedom, equity, security and human dignity. ... A gender perspective is therefore an imperative for the ILO, not merely for reasons of equity and fairness, but also because it is part of the very substance of the ILO's work today."[15]

A gender perspective is also an imperative for the EU and its Member States.

---

14 Article 7.

15 Report of the Director-General, "Decent Work", ILO, Geneva, International Labour Conference, 87th Session, June 1999, pp. 6 and 12.

Chapter 9

The Protection of Pregnancy and Maternity and Parental Leave

Background

Except in a few regions, women comprise at least one-third of the world's workforce. In more than 90 countries, over 50 per cent of women are economically active. More women than before are in the workforce throughout their child bearing years, as many families are dependent on income from both parents.[1] Yet, many women in the world are still subject to unequal treatment in employment due to their reproductive functions. They are subject to many forms of discrimination, ranging from pregnancy tests at the recruitment stage, to terminations during pregnancy or maternity leave, and loss of or insufficient wages during pregnancy and/or maternity leave. Even in countries having legislation providing for paid maternity leave, there is often a gap between law and practice. A 1998 ILO study found that just over 100 countries provide for maternity leave of 12 weeks or more, although in many cases, such leave is not remunerated. Only around 60 countries provide for maternity leave of 14 weeks or more, as set forth in ILO Convention No. 183.

The purpose of pregnancy and maternity protection is two-fold: first, to protect the health of the woman before and after birth, her child's health, and to protect the special relationship between a woman and her child over the period which follows pregnancy and childbirth,[2] and second, to provide a measure of job security – access to jobs for pregnant women, maintenance of salary and benefits during maternity leave, prevention of dismissal during maternity leave – generally to prevent discrimination of pregnant women and women on maternity leave.

---

1 ILO "Rules of the Game, A Brief Introduction to International Labour Standards" (2005), p. 6.

2 See the ECJ ruling in Case 184/83 *Hofmann* v. *Barmer Ersatzkasse* (1984) ECR 3047, paragraph 325.

ILO Standards

The ILO has adopted Conventions and Recommendations specifically concerning Maternity Protection, while other Conventions and/or Recommendations on other specific labour issues have included Articles giving pregnancy and maternity protection to women at work.

Article 5(1) of the Discrimination (Employment and Occupation) Convention No. 111 of 1958 established that:

> "Special measures of protection or assistance provided for in other Conventions or Recommendations adopted by the International Labour Conference shall not be deemed to be discrimination."

Special measures applicable to women only in view of their biological condition – pregnancy, giving birth, breastfeeding – therefore cannot be construed as breaching the principle of equal treatment of men and women.

At the global level, the ILO was a pioneer in this area with its Maternity Protection Convention No. 3 which was adopted by the first General Conference of the Organization on 28 November 1919. It sets the basic principles of protection which were later adapted or developed by the ILO and by the EU. The main principles were:

- A woman has the right to leave her work if she produces a medical certificate stating that her confinement will probably take place within six weeks;
- A woman is not permitted to work during the six weeks following her confinement;
- During her absence from work, she will be paid "benefits sufficient for the full and healthy maintenance of herself and her child, provided either out of public funds or by means of a system of insurance, the exact amount of which shall be determined by the competent national authority";
- As an additional benefit, she is entitled to free attendance by a doctor or certified midwife;
- If she is nursing her child, she is allowed half an hour twice a day during her working hours for this purpose;
- During her absence from work on maternity leave, or during illness arising out of pregnancy or confinement, it will be illegal for her employer to give her notice of dismissal, nor to give her notice of dismissal at such a time that the notice would expire during such absence, until her absence has exceeded a maximum period fixed by the national authority.

These provisions applied to women employed in industrial and commercial undertakings, – excluding agriculture, and also excluding family undertakings in which only members of the same family are employed.

This Maternity Protection Convention was revised on 28 June 1952 by Convention No. 103, which contained only a few clarifications or changes. The minimum maternity leave was for a period of 12 weeks, including a minimum period of compulsory leave of six weeks after confinement. Among the benefits granted were added freedom of choice of doctor and freedom of choice between a public and private hospital. Nursing periods were as prescribed by national laws, and they were to be counted as working hours and remunerated accordingly.

The new Convention applied to women employed in industrial and in non-industrial and agricultural occupations, including women wage earners working at home. Member States may provide for exceptions to the Convention for certain categories of non-industrial occupations, for occupations in agricultural undertakings, domestic work for wages in private households, women wage earners working at home, and undertakings engaged in the transport of passengers or goods by sea.

Recommendation No. 95 concerning Maternity Protection was also adopted on 28 June 1952. It provided for an extension of the period of maternity leave to 14 weeks, where necessary for the health of the woman. It gave details about the medical benefits to be granted, including other benefits in kind or in cash aimed at maintaining, restoring or improving the health of the woman protected, and her ability to work and to attend to her personal needs. It gave examples of legitimate reasons for dismissal during the protected period, such as serious fault, shutting down of the undertaking, or expiry of the contract of employment. Seniority rights of the woman should be preserved during her legal absence from work before and after confinement, as well as her right to reinstatement in her former work or in equivalent work paid at the same rate. Night work and overtime work should be prohibited for pregnant and nursing women. Work prejudicial to her health or that of her child – such as hard labour – should be prohibited during pregnancy and up to at least three months after confinement and longer if the women is nursing her child.

Following the adoption of several international instruments enhancing the rights of women by the UN and the ILO itself after 1952,[3] the General Conference of the ILO adopted on 15 June 2000 Maternity Protection Convention No. 183

3 Among them: The United Nations Convention on the Elimination of All Forms of Discrimination Against Women 1979, the United Nations Convention on the Rights of the Child 1989, the ILO's Declaration on Equality of Opportunity and Treatment of Women Workers 1975, the ILO's Declaration on Fundamental Principles and Rights at Work and its Follow-up 1998, the ILO Convention concerning Workers with Family Responsibilities 1981.

and Maternity Protection Recommendation No. 191, revising the Convention and Recommendation of 1952.

These showed several advances or changes in maternity protection provisions, although frequent references are made to national laws or rules as applicable standards, thus giving more reliance, and perhaps more leeway, on national authorities to apply or interpret the terms and requirements of the Convention. This increased flexibility was a stated goal of the ILO Employers group, the ILO Secretariat and some industrialized countries, who considered that it would facilitate ratification of the new Convention by a greater number of Member States.

The new Convention now covers all employed women. However, ratifying Members may, after consulting the representative organizations of the employers and workers concerned, exclude wholly or partly from the scope of the Convention limited categories of workers when its application to them would raise special problems of a substantive nature. This is a broad exception, that does not specify what these special problems might be.

The main advance is the increase of minimum maternity leave from 12 to 14 weeks in the Convention, and from 16 to 18 weeks in the Recommendation.

Cash benefits during maternity leave are to be no less than two-thirds of the woman's previous earnings in both the 1952 and the 2000 Conventions. The 2000 Recommendation is more generous: where practicable, and after consultation with the representative organizations of employers and workers, these benefits should be raised to the full amount of the woman's previous earnings. This Recommendation also gives more details on the range of medical benefits to be provided "to the extent possible".

Employment protection is strengthened, albeit by reference to national laws or regulations. It is now unlawful for an employer to terminate the employment of a woman during her maternity leave or during a period following her return to work to be prescribed by national laws or regulations, except on grounds unrelated to the pregnancy or birth of the child and its consequences or nursing. In a new, important clause, the burden of proving that the reasons for dismissal are unrelated to pregnancy or childbirth or its consequences or nursing "shall rest on the employer". Also important is the woman's right to return to the same position or an equivalent position paid at the same rate at the end of the maternity leave. The Recommendation specifies that the period of maternity leave should be considered as a period of service for the determination of her rights.

Equally important is a new Article 9 requiring States to adopt appropriate measures to ensure that maternity does not constitute a source of discrimination in employment, and, more specifically a prohibition from requiring a test for pregnancy when a woman is applying for employment, except for work prohibited or restricted for pregnant or nursing women, or where there is a recognized or significant risk to the health of the woman and child. The Recommendation offers measures to provide alternatives to work with a significant risk and gives examples of situations with risk.

Another measure, Article 10, makes it clear that nursing breaks or the reduction of working hours are counted as working time and remunerated accordingly.

As an innovation, the 2000 Recommendation entitles the employed father of the child to take leave for the unexpired portion of the postnatal maternity leave in case of the death of the mother before the expiry of postnatal leave. The employed mother or the employed father should be entitled to parental leave during a period following the expiry of maternity leave.

In the words of ILO Director-General Juan Somavia:

> "As is normal in a negotiation, the final text [of Convention 183] does not reflect everybody's aspirations. Some wanted a Convention limited to general principles, others wanted stronger and more extensive provisions than were finally agreed. But the net outcome on balance is an instrument which will help ensure that the interests, needs and rights of millions upon millions of mothers and children will be respected."

Mr Somavia added:

> "The challenge for us all is to see the cause of gender equality and the struggle for maternity protection as a basic need and a basic right. We have affirmed that all in society – employers, workers, governments, and society at large – share the responsibility for maternity protection. We look forward to working with you to make this a reality."[4]

ILO Standards on Other Labour Issues

A number of Conventions and Recommendations on other labour issues include articles giving maternity protection to women at work. Among them, Article 18 of the Maximum Weight Recommendation No. 128 1967 prescribes:

> "No woman should be assigned to manual transport of loads during a pregnancy which has been medically determined during the ten weeks following confinement if in the opinion of a qualified physician such work is likely to impair her health or that of the child."

4 Quotes from Mr Somavia from the International Labour Conference, 88th Session, Provisional Record 25 (Add.) "Reply by the Director-General to the discussion of his Report (addendum), 4. Maternity Protection" in *IBFAN News*, "Maternity Protection Coalition Report, 30 July 2000, Maternity Protection Convention and Recommendation 2000".

Article 11 of the Benzene Convention No. 136 1971, prohibits women medically certified as pregnant and nursing mothers to be employed in work processes involving exposure to benzene or products containing benzene.

According to Article 7 of the Night Work Convention 1990:

> "Measures shall be taken to ensure that an alternative to night work is available to women workers who would otherwise be called upon to perform such work ... before and after childbirth, for a period of at least sixteen weeks of which at least eight weeks shall be before the expected date of childbirth."

During these periods, which may be extended on health grounds, other prescriptions forbid the dismissal of women, except for justifiable reasons not connected with pregnancy or childbirth. Sufficient income and retention of status, seniority and access to promotion are also protected. Finally, these provisions cannot have the effect of reducing the protection and benefits connected with maternity leave.

Similar protection and prohibitions are found in Article 2 of the Protocol of 1990 to the Night Work (Women) Convention (Revised).[5]

EU Legislation

A series of Council Directives have defined EU policy concerning pregnancy and maternity protection. These have established general principles concerning equal treatment for men and women, and safety and health at work, more specific principles on the rights of pregnant women.

In Directive 76/207/EEC of 9 February 1976 on the implementation of the principle of equal treatment for men and women as regards access to employment, vocational training and promotion, and working conditions, Article 2(3) made clear that the Directive "shall be without prejudice to provisions concerning the protection of women, particularly as regards pregnancy and maternity".

Directive 89/391/EEC of 12 June 1989 on the introduction of measures to encourage improvements in the safety and health of workers at work prescribes that particularly sensitive risk groups must be protected against the dangers which specifically affect them.

Then, Directive 92/85/EEC on the introduction of measures to encourage improvements in the safety and health at work of pregnant workers and workers who have recently given birth or are breastfeeding,[6] adopted on 19 October 1992, has determined that this category of workers must be considered a sensitive risk

[5] Page 89.

[6] Tenth individual Directive within Article 16 (1) of Directive 89/391/EEC.

group in many respects and that measures must be taken with regard to their safety and health.[7]

This Directive, called in short the Pregnancy Directive, thus affirmed that the protection of this group was a legitimate exception to the principle of equal treatment of men and women at work, on the grounds of women's biological condition during and after pregnancy.

A summary of some of the provisions in the Pregnancy Directive follow – the proviso "in accordance with national legislation and/or practice" attached to these provisions is not repeated below in each clause:

- pregnant women are entitled to a continuous period of maternity leave of at least 14 weeks allocated before and/or after confinement – this must include compulsory maternity leave of at least two weeks allocated before and/or after confinement;
- pregnant women are entitled to time off, without loss of pay, in order to attend prenatal examinations, if these take place during working hours;
- the dismissal of workers during the beginning of their pregnancy to the end of maternity leave is prohibited, save in exceptional cases; in the latter case, the employer must cite duly substantiated grounds for her dismissal in writing;
- contractual employment rights, including the maintenance of payment to, and/or entitlement to an adequate allowance to those workers must be ensured;
- workers wronged by failure to comply with the obligations of the Directive should have access to a legal process, or recourse to other competent authorities;
- Annex I gives a non-exhaustive list of physical, biological and chemical agents, industrial processes and working conditions (including underground mining work) for which workers' activities may involve a specific risk of exposure; strictly technical adjustments may be made to this Annex as a result of technical progress, changes in international regulations or specifications and new findings in the area covered by the Directive;
- Annex II gives a non-exhaustive list of physical, biological, and chemical agents, and working conditions in which exposure is prohibited for pregnant women or breastfeeding women; This Annex may be amended

7 Preamble of Directive 92/85/EEC. Article 16 (1) of Directive 89/391/EEC states: "The Council, acting on a proposal from the Commission based on Article 118a of the Treaty, shall adopt individual Directives, inter alia, in the areas listed in the Annex".

only in accordance with the procedure laid down in Article 118a of the Treaty, i.e. adoption of Directives by the Council after consultation with the Economic and Social Committee.

Council Directive 2000/78/EC of 27 November 2000 establishing a general framework for equal treatment in employment and occupation, called in short the Framework Directive, makes no reference to Pregnancy and Maternity Protection, insofar as the 1992 Pregnancy Directive has determined the basic principles and modalities applicable to such cases.

Directive 2002/73/EC of 23 September 2002 on the implementation of the principle of equal treatment for men and women as regards access to employment, vocational training and promotion, and working condition amends Directive 76/207/EEC. Its Preamble refers explicitly to women's biological condition during and after pregnancy in relation to the principle of equal treatment:

"(12) The Court of Justice has consistently recognised the legitimacy, in terms of the principle of equal treatment, of protecting a woman's biological condition during and after pregnancy. It has moreover consistently ruled that any unfavourable treatment of women related to pregnancy or maternity constitutes direct discrimination."

Article 7 states that the Directive "shall be without prejudice to provisions concerning the protection of women, particularly as regards pregnancy and maternity".

The Charter of Fundamental Rights of the European Union adopted in December 2000 has affirmed a number of key principles, some of which are directly relevant to policies and practices in labour issues and equal treatment of men and women:

- Human dignity is inviolable, it must be respected and protected (Article 1);
- Discrimination based, *inter alia*, on sex is prohibited (Article 21);
- Equality between men and women must be ensured in all areas, including employment, work and pay. But this principle shall not prevent the maintenance or adoption of measures providing for specific advantages in favour of the under-represented sex (Article 23);
- Every worker has the right to fair and just working conditions (Article 31);
- Those whose rights and freedoms guaranteed by the law of the Union are violated have the right to an effective remedy and to a fair trial (Article 47).

Directive 2006/54/EC of the European Parliament and of the Council of 5 July 2006 on the implementation of the principle of equal opportunities and equal treatment of men and women in matters of employment and occupation has recast previous Directives, and brought together in a single text the main provisions in this field. It recalled that Article 141 (3) of the EC Treaty provides a specific legal basis for the adoption of Community measures to ensure the application of the principle of equal opportunities and equal treatment in matters of employment and occupation. The Directive also referred to the EU Charter and to developments in the case law of the ECJ.

As stated in its Preamble:

> "(23) It is clear from the case law of the Court of Justice that unfavourable treatment of a woman related to pregnancy or maternity constitutes direct discrimination on grounds of sex. Such treatment should therefore be expressly covered by this Directive.
>
> (24) The Court of Justice has consistently recognized the legitimacy, as regards the principle of equal treatment, of protecting a woman's biological condition during pregnancy and maternity and of introducing maternity protection measures as a means to achieve substantive equality. This Directive should therefore be without prejudice to Council Directive 92/85/EEC of 19 October 1992 on the introduction of measures to encourage improvements in the safety and health at work of pregnant workers and workers who have recently given birth or are breastfeeding. This Directive should further be without prejudice to Council Directive 96/34/EC of 3 June 1996 on the framework agreement on parental leave concluded by UNICE, CEEP and the ETUC.
>
> (25) For reasons of clarity, it is also appropriate to make express provision for the protection of the employment rights of women on maternity leave and in particular their right to return to the same or an equivalent post, to suffer no detriment in their terms and conditions as a result of taking such leave and to benefit from any improvement in working conditions to which they would have been entitled during their absence."

Recital (26) encourages Member States to consider examining the scope for their respective legal systems to grant working men an individual and non-transferable right to paternity leave. Recital (27) refers to paternity or adoption leave, to be considered by Member States.

Under Article 2(2) of the Directive, discrimination includes:

> "(c) any less favourable treatment of a woman related to pregnancy or maternity leave within the meaning of Directive 92/85/EEC."

Under Article 9:

"1. Provisions contrary to the principle of equal treatment shall include those based on sex, either directly or indirectly, for ...

(g) suspending the retention or acquisition of rights during periods of maternity leave or leave for family reasons which are granted by law or agreement and are paid by the employer."

Article 15 on return from maternity leave specifies that:

"A woman on maternity leave shall be entitled, after the end of her period of maternity leave, to return to her job or to an equivalent post on terms and conditions which are no less favourable to her and to benefit from any improvement in working conditions to which she would have been entitled during her absence."

According to Article 16, the Directive is without prejudice to the right of Member States to recognize distinct rights to paternity and/or adoption leave and decide on measures and conditions of their exercise.

Comparison of ILO and EU Law

EU law has clearly been inspired by the ILO standards on pregnancy and maternity protection which were initiated well before the creation of the European communities.

The basic elements of this protection were set in the first Maternity Convention No. 3 in 1919, when the ILO was founded: right to maternity leave during set periods before and after confinement, financial support during these periods, free medical and midwife assistance, nursing time allowance during work, prohibition of dismissal during maternity leave, or during illnesses arising out of pregnancy or confinement. While there was an evolution with regard to the extent of these benefits in the ILO Conventions from 1919 through the current No. 183 of 2000, it is interesting to note that the 14 weeks' period of maternity leave in that ILO Convention is the same in the EU Pregnancy Directive of 1992.

Under Article 5(1) of the Discrimination (Employment and Occupation) Convention No. 111 of 1958:

"Special measures of protection or assistance provided for in other Conventions or Recommendations adopted by the International Labour Conference shall not be deemed to be discrimination."

This same principle was adopted by Directive 76/207/EEC of 9 February 1976 on the implementation of the principle of equal treatment for men and women as regards access to employment, vocational training and promotion, and working conditions. More specifically, Article 2(3) made clear that the Directive "shall be without prejudice to provisions concerning the protection of women, particularly as regards pregnancy and maternity". This was repeated in the Pregnancy

Directive of 1992, which affirmed that the protection of pregnant workers and workers who have recently given birth or are breastfeeding are a "sensitive risk group" was a legitimate exception to the principle of equal treatment of men and women at work, on the grounds of women's biological condition during and after pregnancy.

EU Case Law

Numerous ECJ rulings and judgments have given interpretations of the spirit of these Directives, setting limits but also extending the protection given to pregnant women, and women on maternity leave.

Cases Related to Pregnancy

Access to Jobs

This is the first leading case with reference to the refusal of employment on account of pregnancy: *Dekker* v. *Stichting Vormingscentrum voor Jong Volwassenen (VJV-Centrum) Plus.*[8] In June 1981, Mrs Dekker applied for the post of instructor at the training centre for young adults run by the VJV. On 15 June, she informed the committee dealing with applications that she was three months' pregnant. Nevertheless, the committee put her name forward to VJV management board as the most suitable candidate for the job. By letter of 10 July 1981, however, the VJV informed Mrs Dekker that she would not be appointed. In the letter, the VJV explained that if she was employed, a social fund would not reimburse the social benefits that the VJV would have to pay her during her maternity leave. As a result, the VJV would be unable to employ a replacement during Mrs Dekker's absence and would thus be short-staffed.

Mrs Dekker appealed to the *Hoge Raad der Nederlanden* against the lower courts' decisions to dismiss her applications for an order requiring the VJV to pay her damages for her financial loss.

Taking the view that the appeal raised problems as to the interpretation of Council Directive 76/207, the *Hoge Raad* referred the following questions to the ECJ for a preliminary ruling:

> "1) Is an employer directly or indirectly in breach of the principle of equal treatment laid down in Articles 2 (1) and 3 (1) of the Directive ... if he refuses to enter into a contract of employment with a candidate, found by him to be suitable, because of the adverse consequences for him which are to be anticipated owing to the fact that the candidate was pregnant

[8] Case C-177/88 (1990) ECR I-3941.

when she applied for the post, in conjunction with rules concerning unfitness for work laid down by a public authority under which inability to work in connection with pregnancy and confinement is assimilated to inability to work on account of sickness?

2) Does it make any difference that there were no male candidates?

3) Is it compatible with Articles 2 and 3 that:

a) if a breach of the principle that the rejected candidate must be accorded equal treatment is established, fault on the part of the employer is also required before a claim based on that breach such as the present can be upheld;

b) if such a breach is established, the employer for his part can still plead justification, even if none of the cases provided in Article 2 (2) to (4) applies ..."

On the first question, the Court replied, in part, that "a refusal of employment on account of the financial consequences of absence due to pregnancy must be regarded as based, essentially, on the fact of pregnancy". This refusal therefore constitutes direct discrimination and the employer is in direct contravention of the principle of equal treatment embodied in Articles 2 (1) and 3 (1) of Directive 76/207.

On the second question, the Court ruled that the fact that no man applied for the job does not alter the answer to the first question.

On the third, the Court answered that "any infringement of the prohibition of discrimination suffices in itself to make the person guilty of it fully liable...".

Dismissal

In *Handels-og Kontorfunktionaerernes Forbund i Danmark v. Dansk Arbejsgiverforening,*[9] an employee was dismissed on account of absences due to an illness attributable to pregnancy or confinement.

Mrs Hertz, a part-time cashier and saleswoman, was employed by Aldi Marked on 15 July 1982. She gave birth to a child in June 1983 after a pregnancy marked by complications for most of which, with the consent of her employer, she was on sick leave. On the expiry of her maternity leave, she resumed work in late 1983. Between June 1984 and June 1985 she was again on sick leave for 100 working days. She and her employer agreed that her illness was a consequence of her pregnancy and confinement. By letter of 27 June 1985, Aldi Marked informed Mrs Hertz that it was terminating her contract of employment with the statutory four months' notice. Aldi Marked later stated that Mrs Hertz's periods

9 Case C-179/88 (1990) ECR I-3979.

of absence were the ground for her dismissal and that it was normal practice to dismiss workers who were often absent owing to illness.

The Danish Maritime and Commercial Court dismissed the action brought by Mrs Hertz against her dismissal. The *Hoejesteret*, to which an appeal was filed, referred the following questions to the ECJ for a preliminary ruling:

> "(1) Do the provisions of Article 5 (1), in conjunction with Article 2 (1), of Council Directive 76/207/EEC of 9 February 1976 on the implementation of the principle of equal treatment for men and women as regards access to employment, vocational training and promotion, and working conditions encompass dismissal as a consequence of absence due to illness which is attributable to pregnancy or confinement?
>
> (2) If the answer is affirmative, is protection against dismissal due to illness caused by pregnancy or confinement unlimited in time?"

Quoting the *Dekker* case, the Court first stated that the dismissal of a female worker on account of pregnancy constitutes direct discrimination on grounds of sex, as is a refusal to appoint a pregnant woman. On the other hand:

> "the dismissal of a female worker on account of repeated periods of sick leave which are not attributable to pregnancy or confinement does not constitute direct discrimination on grounds of sex, inasmuch as such periods of sick leave would lead to dismissal of a male worker in the same circumstances."

The Directive does not envisage the case of an illness attributable to pregnancy or confinement. It does, however, admit of national provisions guaranteeing women special rights on account of pregnancy and maternity, such as maternity leave. During such leave, a woman is protected against dismissal due to absence. In the case of an illness manifesting itself after the maternity leave, for the Court:

> "there is no reason to distinguish an illness attributable to pregnancy or confinement from any other illness. Such a pathological condition is therefore covered by the general rules applicable in the event of illness."

The Court then ruled that Article 5 (1) of the Directive, in conjunction with Article 2 (1), does not preclude dismissals which are the result of absences due to an illness attributable to pregnancy or confinement.

In the case of *Webb* v. *EMO Air Cargo (UK) Ltd.*,[10] an employee who was herself a replacement for a pregnant woman was dismissed when found pregnant.

---

10 Case C-32/93 (1994) ECR I-3567.

By order of 26 November 1992, the House of Lords referred this case to the ECJ under Article 177 of the Treaty on the interpretation of Directive 76/207/EEC. In the import operations department employing four employees – EMO had a total of 16 employees – Mrs Webb was recruited initially to replace a pregnant employee, Mrs Stewart, although she would continue to work for EMO when that employee would return to work. Mrs Webb did not know that she was pregnant when the employment contract was entered into. She started work on 1 July 1987. Two weeks later, she thought that she might be pregnant, which was confirmed a week later. On 30 July, she received a letter dismissing her.

Mrs Webb then brought proceedings before the Industrial Tribunal pleading direct discrimination on grounds of sex and, in the alternative, indirect discrimination. Quoting articles of the relevant national legislation (the Sex Discrimination Act) the Tribunal held that Mrs Webb had not been directly or indirectly discriminated against on grounds of sex. The Tribunal rejected her claims and dismissed her action on the grounds that the employers had shown that the reasonable needs of their business required that the person recruited to cover for Mrs Stewart during her maternity leave be available.

Appeals to the Employment Appeal Tribunal and then to the Court of Appeal were unsuccessful. She was granted leave by the Court of Appeal to appeal to the House of Lords, which stayed proceedings and submitted the following question for a preliminary ruling:

> "Is it discrimination on grounds of sex contrary to Directive 76/207 for an employer to dismiss a female employee ('the appellant')
>
> (a) whom he engaged for the specific purpose of replacing (after training) another female employee during the latter's forthcoming maternity leave,
>
> (b) when, very shortly after appointment, the employer discovers that the appellant herself will be absent on maternity leave during the maternity leave of the other employee, and the employer dismisses her because he needs the job holder to be at work during that period,
>
> (c) had the employer known of the pregnancy of the appellant at the date of appointment, she would not have been appointed, and
>
> (d) the employer would similarly have dismissed a male employee engaged for this purpose who required leave of absence at the relevance time for medical or other reasons?"

As was apparent from documents submitted to the Court, the question related to a contract of employment concluded for an indefinite period. As ruled by the

Court in the *Handels* case 1990,[11] the dismissal of a female worker on account of pregnancy constitutes direct discrimination on grounds of sex. The Court added other considerations as parts of the general context of Mrs Webb's case:

> "20. Furthermore, by reserving to Member States the right to retain or introduce provisions which are intended to protect women in connection with "pregnancy and maternity", Article 2 (3) of Directive 76/207 recognizes the legitimacy, in terms of the principle of equal treatment, first, of protecting a woman's biological condition during and after pregnancy and, second, of protecting the special relationship between a woman and her child over the period which follows pregnancy and childbirth ...
>
> 21. In view of the harmful effects which the risk of dismissal may have on the physical and mental state of women who are pregnant, have recently given birth or are breastfeeding, including the particular serious risk that pregnant women may be prompted voluntarily to terminate their pregnancy, the Community legislature subsequently provided, pursuant to Article 10 of Council Directive 92/85/EEC of 19 October 1992 on the introduction of measures to encourage improvements in the safety and health at work of pregnant workers and workers who have recently given birth or are breastfeeding,[12] for special protection to be given to women, by prohibiting dismissal during the period from the beginning of their pregnancy to the end of their maternity leave.
>
> 22. Furthermore, Article 10 of Directive 92/85 provides that there is to be no exception to, or derogation from, the prohibition on the dismissal of pregnant women during that period, save in exceptional cases not connected with their condition.
>
> 24. First, in response to the House of Lords' inquiry, there can be no question of comparing the situation of a woman who finds herself incapable, by reason of pregnancy discovered very shortly after the conclusion of the employment contract, of performing the task for which she was recruited with that of a man similarly incapable for medical or other reason.
>
> 25. As Mrs Webb rightly argues, pregnancy is not in any way comparable with a pathological condition, and even less so with unavailability for work on non-medical grounds, both of which are situations that may justify the dismissal of a woman without discriminating on grounds of sex. Moreover, in the Hertz judgment, cited above, the Court drew a

---

11 Case C-179/88 (1990) ECR I-3979.

12 OJ (1992) L 348/1.

> clear distinction between pregnancy and illness, even where the illness is attributable to pregnancy but manifests itself after the maternity leave. As the Court pointed out (in paragraph 16), there is no reason to distinguish such an illness from any other illness."

In conclusion, the Court ruled that:

> "Article 2(1) read with Article 5(1) of Council Directive 76/207/EEC of 9 February 1976 on the implementation of the principle of equal treatment for men and women as regards access to employment, vocational training and promotion, and working conditions precludes dismissal of an employee who is recruited for an unlimited term with a view, initially, to replacing another employee during the latter's maternity leave and who cannot do so because, shortly after her recruitment, she is herself found to be pregnant."

The same principle was applied by the Court in another preliminary ruling in *Mahlburg* v. *Land Mecklenburg.*[13] However, in contrast with the *Dekker* case, the unequal treatment in the *Mahlburg* case was not based directly on the woman's pregnancy, but on a statutory prohibition on employment attached to that condition, a prohibition imposed by national legislation as a protection for pregnant women. Based on the *Webb* case, the Court confirmed that:

> "the protection afforded by Community law to a woman during pregnancy and after childbirth cannot be dependent on whether her presence at work during maternity is essential to the proper functioning of the undertaking in which she is employed. Any contrary interpretation would render ineffective the provisions of the Directive."

The Court ruled that:

> "Articles 2 (1) and (3) of Directive 76/207/EEC ... precludes a refusal to appoint a pregnant woman to a post for an indefinite period on the ground that a statutory prohibition on employment attaching to the condition of pregnancy prevents her from being employed in that post from the outset and for the duration of the pregnancy."

A ruling similar to the first *Handels* case was given by the Court in the *Handels-og Konforfunctionaernes Forbund i Danmark*, acting on behalf of *Elisabeth Larsson* v. *Dansk Handel & Service*, acting on behalf of *Fotex Supermarked A/S.*[14]

In paragraph 23, the ruling stated:

[13] Case C-207/98 (2000) ECR-I 549.

[14] Case C-400/95 (1997) ECR I-2757.

> "Outside the periods of maternity leave laid down by the Member States to allow female workers to be absent during the period in which the problems inherent in pregnancy and confinement occur, however, and in the absence of any national or, as the case may be, Community provisions affording women specific protection, a woman is not protected under the Directive [76/207] against dismissal on grounds of periods of absence due to an illness originating in pregnancy. As has been pointed out above, as male and female workers are equally exposed to illness, the Directive does not concern illnesses attributable to pregnancy or confinement."

In *Habermann-Beltermann* v. *Arbeiterwohlfahrt, Bezirksverband Ndb./Opf.e.V.*,[15] an indefinite employment contract was terminated as the result of a prohibition on night-time work during pregnancy.

Mrs Habermann-Beltermann, a nurse qualified in the care of the elderly, applied for a post as a night attendant in a home for the aged. For family reasons, she was able to work at night only. An employment contract of indefinite duration was signed on 23 March 1992, which took effect on 1 April 1992. The contract stipulated that she was to be assigned night-time work only. She was absent from work because of illness from 29 April to 12 June 1992. A medical certificate dated 29 May 1952 stated that she was pregnant: her pregnancy was said to have begun on 11 March 1992.

By letter dated 4 June 1992, the enterprise terminated Mrs Habermann-Beltermann's employment, relying on a German law on the protection of mothers, whose paragraph 8 (1) states, in part:

> "It is prohibited to assign to women who are pregnant or breastfeeding overtime or night-time work between 8 p.m. and 6 a.m. or work on Sundays or public holidays ..."

Additionally, Paragraph 134 of the German Civil Code provides that "Any legal act contrary to a statutory prohibition shall be void except as otherwise provided by law".

The questions asked by the national court to the ECJ related to an employment contract for an indefinite period for the performance of night work, concluded between an employer and a pregnant employee, both of whom were unaware of the pregnancy.

For the Court, it was clear that the termination of an employment contract on account of the employee's pregnancy, whether by annulment or avoidance, concerns women alone and constitutes, therefore, direct discrimination on grounds of sex, as the Court has held in cases where a pregnant woman was

[15] Case C-421/92 (1994) ECR I-1657.

denied employment or dismissed, as in the *Dekker* and first *Handels* cases. However, unlike the *Dekker* case, the unequal treatment in this case was not based directly on a woman's pregnancy but was the result of a statutory prohibition on night work during pregnancy.

The answer to the questions submitted by the national court was that:

> "Article 2 (1), read in conjunction with Articles 3 (1) and 5 (1) of Directive 76/207/EEC, precludes an employment contract for an indefinite period for the performance of night-time work concluded between an employer and a pregnant employee, both of whom were unaware of the pregnancy, from being held to be void on account of the statutory prohibition on night-time work which applies, by virtue of national law, during pregnancy and breastfeeding, or from being avoided by the employer on account of a mistake on his part as to the essential personal characteristics of the woman at the time when the contract was concluded."

In the case of *Brown* v. *Rentokil Ltd.*[16] the Court referred to the *Dekker* case, the first *Handels* case 1990, and the *Habermann-Beltermann* and *Webb* cases, and re-affirmed that Articles 2 (1) and 5/1) of Directive 76/207 preclude the dismissal of a female worker at any time during her pregnancy for absences due to incapacity for work caused by illness resulting from that pregnancy. As to the worker's absence after maternity leave, this may be taken into account under the same conditions as a man's absence, of the same duration, through incapacity for work.

In *Tele Danmark A/S* v. *Handels-og Kontorfunktionaerernes Forbund i Danmark (HK)*[17] a worker on a fixed-term employment contract was dismissed, as she had not informed her employer, on recruitment, that she was pregnant.

In June 1995, Ms Brandt-Nielsen was recruited by Tele Danmark for six months from 1 July 1995. In August, she informed her employer that she was pregnant and expected to give birth in early November. On 23 August, she was dismissed on the ground that she had not informed Tele Danmark that she was pregnant when she was recruited. She worked for the whole month of September.

Under the applicable collective agreement, she would have been entitled to paid maternity leave starting eight weeks before the expected date of giving birth. In this case, it would have started on 11 September 1995.

On 4 March 1996 HK, acting on behalf of Ms Brandt-Nielsen, brought proceedings against Tele Danmark before a Danish District Court for compensation, on the ground that her dismissal was contrary to Paragraph 9 of the Equal Treatment Law. According to this Paragraph, an employer may not dismiss an employee on the ground that the latter has insisted on exercising her right of absence or has

---

16 Case C-394/96 (1998) ECR I-4185.

17 Case C-109/00 (2001) ECR I-6993.

been absent ... or otherwise on grounds of pregnancy, childbirth or adoption. Under Paragraph 16, if an employee is dismissed contrary to Paragraph 9, the dismissal shall be set aside if so requested, unless, in exceptional cases and after balancing the interests of the parties, it is found to be manifestly unreasonable to insist that the employment relationship be maintained or restored. If the dismissal is not set aside, compensation shall be paid.

The District Court, by judgment of 14 January 1997, dismissed the action on the ground that Ms Brandt-Nielsen, who had been recruited for a six-month period, had failed to say that she was pregnant at the recruitment interview, although she was expected to give birth during the fifth month of the contract of employment. By judgment of 15 April 1999, the Western Regional Court, hearing her appeal, ruled in her favour on the ground that it was not disputed that the dismissal was linked to her pregnancy.

Tele Danmark appealed against this decision to the *Hojesteret*, who stayed the proceedings and referred two questions to the ECJ for a preliminary ruling:

> "First, whether Article 5 (1) of Directive 76/207 and/or Article 10 of Directive 92/85, or other provisions in these Directives, or elsewhere in Community Law preclude a worker from being dismissed on the ground of pregnancy in the case where:
>
> (i) the woman in question was recruited as a temporary worker for a limited period; and
>
> (ii) when she entered into the contract of employment, the worker knew that she was pregnant but did not inform her employer of that fact; and
>
> (iii) her pregnancy meant that the worker was unable to work for a significant portion of her period of employment?
>
> Second, whether the fact that the employment occurs in a very large undertaking and that that undertaking frequently uses temporary workers have any bearing on the answer to Question 1?"

In its ruling, the ECJ submitted that a worker is not obliged to inform her employer of her pregnancy, since the employer is not entitled to take it into account on recruitment. Furthermore, as the Court has held on several occasions, the dismissal of a female worker on account of pregnancy constitutes direct discrimination on grounds of sex, contrary to Article 5 (1) of Directive 76/207. During the period from the start of pregnancy to the end of maternity leave, Article 10 of Directive 92/85 does not provide for any exception to, or derogation from, the prohibition of dismissing pregnant workers, save in exceptional cases not connected with their condition where the employer justifies the dismissal in writing. Moreover, the Court has held that a refusal to employ a woman on account of her pregnancy cannot be justified on grounds relating to the financial loss which an employer who appointed a pregnant woman would suffer for the duration of her maternity leave.[18]

Finally, Directives 76/207 and 92/85 do not make any distinction, as regards the scope of the principle of equal treatment for men and women, according to the duration of the employment relationship in question. Had the Community legislature wished to exclude fixed-term contracts, which represent a substantial proportion of employment relationships, from the scope of those directives, it would have done so expressly.

The answer to the first question was, consequently, that Article 5 (1) of Directive 76/207 and Article 10 of Directive 92/85 are to be interpreted as precluding a worker from being dismissed on the ground of pregnancy.

On the second question, the fact that the worker has been recruited by a very large undertaking which employs temporary workers frequently is of no relevance to the interpretation of these Articles.

In another case, a worker's fixed-term contract was not renewed because of her pregnancy: *Melgar* v. *Ayuntamiento de Los Barrios*.[19]

In its ruling, the Court confirmed the precedent ruling in stating that Directive 92/85 applies to both fixed-term and indefinite appointments. However, it gave a wider licence to Member States in applying exceptions to the prohibition of dismissal of pregnant workers, workers who have recently given birth or workers who are breastfeeding.

In June 1998, Mrs Melgar was engaged by the Municipality of Los Barrios (Spain) as an employee, working 20 hours a week, as home-help for retired persons without family. The contract, initially concluded for three months, was renewed twice, until 2 December 1998. A new fixed-term part-time contract was concluded on 3 December 1998, with a new task. The contract, which did not specify an expiry date, ended on 2 February 1999. Another similar contract started on 3 February 1999, again without an expiry date, ended on 2 May 1999. A fourth similar contract started on 3 May 1999.

On 12 May 1999, Mrs Melgar was notified by the Municipality that her contract would cease on 2 June 1999. Her employer had been informed about her pregnancy, and her child was born on 16 December 1999.

When offered a fifth contract on 7 June 1999, contract which would take effect on 3 June, Mrs Melgar refused to sign it and addressed a complaint to the Municipality in which she contended that her previous contract had not expired since she had been dismissed in a discriminatory way, in breach of her fundamental rights. For her, it was not a question of signing a new contract but simply to reinstate her in her employment, and she brought proceedings against the Municipality before the *Juzgado de lo Social Unico de Algesiras*.

---

[18] *Dekker*, para. 29.

[19] Case C-438/99 (2001) ECR I-6915.

The judge at that court stayed the proceedings and referred four questions to the ECJ, whose answers follow:

> "1. Article 10 of Directive 92/85 has direct effect and is to be interpreted to the effect that, in absence of transposition measures taken by a Member States within the period prescribed by the Directive, it confers on individuals rights on which they may rely before a national court.
>
> 2. In allowing derogations from the prohibition of dismissal of pregnant workers, workers who have recently given birth or workers who are breastfeeding in cases 'not connected with their condition which are permitted under national legislation and/or practice', Article 10 (1) of Directive 92/85 does not require the Member States to specify the particular grounds on which such workers may be dismissed.
>
> 3. Referring to the Tele Danmark judgment, the Court recalled that Directive 92/85 makes no distinction according to the duration of the employment relationship: it was therefore clear that the prohibition of dismissal laid down in Article 10 of Directive 92/85 applies to both fixed-term employment contracts and to those concluded for an indefinite period. It was also clear that non-renewal of a fixed-term employment contract, when it comes to the end of its stipulated term, cannot be regarded as a dismissal. However, when non-renewal is motivated by the worker's state of pregnancy, it constitutes direct discrimination on grounds of sex, contrary to Article 2 (1) and 3 (1) of Directive 76/207.
>
> 4. In providing that the dismissal of a pregnant worker, of a worker who has recently given birth or a worker who is breastfeeding may take place, in exceptional cases, 'and, where applicable, provided that the competent authority has given its consent', Article 10 (1) of Directive 92/85 is not to be interpreted as imposing on Member States any obligation to have a national authority, having found that there is an exceptional case justifying the dismissal of such as worker, give its consent prior to the employer's decision to dismiss the worker.

In the next case, the return to work of a pregnant woman before the end of parental leave was refused by her employer on the grounds of alleged fraud: *Busch v. Klinikum Neustadt GmbH & Co. Betriebs-KG.*[20]

Ms Busch worked as a nurse for the clinic starting in April 1998. After the birth of her first child in June 2000, she took parental leave which was to be for three years.[21]

---

20 Case C-320/01 (2003) ECR I-2041.

21 Under the German Federal Law on Parental Allowance and Parental Leave, workers

By letter of 30 January 2001, Ms Busch requested permission to terminate her parental leave early and return to full time work as a nurse, which was accepted by her employer. She returned to work on 9 April 2001. The next day, she informed her employer for the first time that she was seven months pregnant. Her maternity leave was to start on 23 May 2001, the required six weeks period prior to the expected date of birth. The clinic released her from her obligation to work with effect from 11 April 2001 and, by letter of 19 April 2001, rescinded its consent to her returning to work, on grounds of fraudulent misrepresentation and mistake as to an essential characteristic. The documents before the Court showed that Ms Busch wished to end her parental leave so that she would receive a maternity allowance, which is higher than the allowance paid during parental leave, and also the supplements to the maternity allowance. The case was referred to the ECJ by the national court with two questions, answered by the Court hereunder.

The ECJ found that when an employer takes an employee's pregnancy into consideration in the refusal to allow her to return to work before the end of her parental leave, that constitutes direct discrimination on grounds of sex. In this ruling, the Court referred to *Dekker* and *Mahlburg* concerning refusal to hire; *Webb* and *Tele Danmark* concerning dismissal; and, *Melgar* concerning refusal to renew a contract for a fixed-term. The Court added:

> "since the employer may not take the employee's pregnancy into consideration for the purpose of applying her working conditions, she is not obliged to inform the employer that she is pregnant."

Article 2 (1) of Directive 76/207 was interpreted by the Court as precluding an employer from contesting under national law the consent it gave to the reinstatement of an employee to return before the end of her parental leave on the grounds that it was in error as to her being pregnant.

Cases Related to Maternity Leave

In a number of cases, the Court has interpreted EU Directives 75/117 and 76/207 in relation to various benefits while on maternity leave: their purpose and limits, their duration, pay levels, pay rises, annual and sick leave, pension, and termination payments.

are entitled to parental leave until the date of the third birthday of a child born after 31 December 1991.

Benefits for Fathers

In *Hofmann* v. *Barmer Ersatzkasse*[22] a father's claim for maternity leave was rejected.

Mr Hofmann, the plaintiff, is the father of an illegitimate child, of which he has acknowledged paternity. He obtained unpaid leave from his employer for the period between the expiry of the statutory protective period of eight weeks which was available to the mother and the day on which the child reached the age of six months; during that time, he took care of the child while the mother continued her employment.

At the same time, Mr Hofmann submitted to the *Barmer Ersatzkasse*, the defendant in the case, a claim for payment of maternity leave provided by German law for the protection of working mothers. His request was refused and his appeal was also unsuccessful. An action brought before the Hamburg Social Court was dismissed by a judgment of 19 October 1982 on the grounds that the German law and the intention of the legislature indicated that only mothers could claim maternity leave. This court referred two questions to the ECJ.

The first one raised the question of the scope and limits of the principle of equal treatment. The plaintiff claims that the main object of the provisions of the German law is not to give social protection to the mother on biological and medical grounds but rather to protect the child.

The ECJ recalled that Directive 76/207 is designed to implement the principle of equal treatment for men and women as regards *inter alia* "working conditions". From its analysis, the Court found it apparent that the Directive is not designed to settle questions concerned with the organisation of the family, or to alter the division of responsibility between parents.

Furthermore, by reserving to Member States the right to retain or introduce provisions which are intended to protect women in connection with "pregnancy and maternity", the Directive recognizes the legitimacy, in terms of the principle of equal treatment, of protecting a woman's needs in two respects:

> "First, it is legitimate to ensure the protection of a woman's biological condition during pregnancy and thereafter until such time as her physiological and mental functions have returned to normal after childbirth; second, it is legitimate to protect the special relationship between a woman and her child which follows pregnancy and childbirth, by preventing that relationship from being disturbed by the multiple burdens which would result from the simultaneous pursuit of employment."

The Court also said that the Directive leaves Member States with a discretion as to the social measures which they adopt in order to guarantee, within the

[22] Case 184/83 (1984) ECR I-3047.

framework laid down by the Directive, the protection of women in connection with pregnancy and maternity and to offset the disadvantages which women, in comparison with men, suffer with regard to the retention of employment.

The Court concluded that:

> "Directive 76/207 must be interpreted as meaning that a Member State may, after the statutory protective period has expired, grant to mothers a period of maternity leave which the state encourages them to take by the payment of an allowance. The Directive does not impose on Member States a requirement that they shall, as an alternative, allow such leave to be granted to fathers, even where the parents so decide."

The *Hofmann* case would have had a different outcome after the adoption of the Parental Leave Directive 96/34 in December 1995.

Conditions of Work

The following cases raise the issue as to whether workers' conditions of work apply equally to women on maternity leave.

The first one, a collective case, refers to the amount of benefits received by women on maternity leave: *Gillespie and others* v. *Northern Health and Social Services Boards, Department of Health and Social Services, Eastern Health and Social Services Board and Southern Health and Southern Health and Social Services Board.*[23]

The case was initiated by 17 plaintiffs against their employers from various Northern Ireland Health Services concerning the amount of benefits they received during their maternity leave. Their entitlements under collective agreements were more favourable than those laid down by the general legislation, but included progressively lower rates after four and a further two weeks. In November 1988, negotiations with the health services resulted in pay increases which were not received by the plaintiffs.

They instituted proceedings before the Industrial Tribunal which dismissed their application, then to Court of Appeal in Northern Ireland. The Court stayed proceedings and referred questions to the ECJ for a preliminary ruling on the interpretation of Directives 75/117, 76/207, 89/391 and 92/85.

The Court found that the *Gillespie* case was concerned with women taking maternity leave provided by national legislation. They are in a special position which requires them to be afforded special protection, but which is not comparable either with that of a man or with that of a woman actually at work. As Directive 89/391 did not apply *ratione temporis* to the case, it was for the national legislation to set the amount of the maternity benefit.

The Court concluded that:

[23] Case C-342/93 (1996) ECR I-475.

> "the principle of equal pay laid down in Article 119 of the Treaty and set out in detail neither requires that women should continue to receive full pay during maternity leave, nor lays down specific criteria for determining the amount of benefit payable to them during that period, provided that the amount is not set so low as to jeopardize the purpose of maternity leave. However, to the extent that it is calculated on the basis of pay received by a woman before the commencement of maternity leave, the amount of benefit must include pay rises awarded between the beginning of the period covered by reference pay and the end of maternity leave, as from the date on which they take effect."

The *Gillespie* precedent was applied in 2004 in the *Alabaster* v. *Woolwich plc and Secretary of State for Social Security.*[24]

In answer to the questions referred to it by the Court of Appeal (England and Wales) (Civil Division) by order of 27 March 2002, the Court ruled, in part:

> "1. Article 119 of the EC Treaty [Articles 117 to 120 of the Treaty have been replaced by Articles 136 to 143 EC] must be interpreted as requiring that, in so far as the pay received by the worker during her maternity leave is determined at least in part on the basis of the pay she earned before her maternity leave began, any pay rise awarded between the beginning of the period covered by the reference pay and the end of the maternity leave must be included in the elements of pay taken into account in calculating the amount of such pay. This requirement is not limited to cases where the pay rise is back-dated to the period covered by the reference pay."

The Court included in this ruling an important statement on the "clear division" of functions between the national courts and the Court of Justice, by reference to Article 234 EC. In accordance with the Article, the Court may rule on the interpretation or validity of Community provisions only on the basis of the facts which the national court puts before it. Thus, within the framework of the procedure under this Article, it is not for the Court of Justice but for the national court to apply the Community rules which it has interpreted to national measures or situations.[25]

The next case also concerns the rights of pregnant women to salary and other benefits while on maternity leave, their rights to sick leave, annual leave and the accrual of pension rights: *Boyle and Others* v. *Equal Opportunities Commission.*[26]

---

24 Case C-147/02 (2004) ECR I-3101.

25 Para. 52.

26 Case C-411/96 (1998) ECR I-6401.

Questions of interpretation of Directives 75/117, 76/207, 89/391 and 92/85 were raised in proceedings between Mrs Boyle and others and their employer, the Equal Opportunities Commission (EOC) concerning the staff Maternity Scheme. The national court stated that the EOC was agreed to be an emanation of the State so the Directives at issue had a direct effect.

The six applicants in the main proceedings were all EOC employees of child-bearing age. They had completed at least one year's service with their employer. Three of them had taken maternity leave in the recent past. According to the EOC Staff Handbook, staff who are unfit to work because of illness are entitled to their full salary for a maximum of six months in any 12 month period. Thereafter they receive half pay up to a maximum of 12 months in any four year period. Another clause provides that any leave taken without pay reduces the annual leave entitlement by a proportion of the amount of the unpaid leave taken.

The dispute centered on the Maternity Scheme, several clauses of which were contested by the plaintiffs before the Industrial Tribunal, Manchester, as discriminating against female employees and thus contrary to Article 119 of the Treaty or Directives 75/117, 76/207 or 92/85. Having doubts as to the compatibility of these provisions with Community law, the Tribunal stayed proceedings and, on 15 October 1996, referred the questions to the ECJ for a preliminary ruling. Extracts from the Court's answer follow:

> "1. Article 119 of the EC Treaty, Article 1 of Council Directive 75/117 ... and Article 11 of Council Directive 92/85 ... do not preclude a clause in an employment contract which makes the payment, during the period of maternity leave referred to by Article 8 of Directive 92/85, of pay higher than the statutory payments in respect of maternity leave conditional on the worker's undertaking to return to work after the birth of the child for at least one month, failing which she is required to repay the difference between the amount of the pay she will have received during the period of maternity leave, on the one hand, and the amount of these payments, on the other.
>
> 2. Article 8 of Directive 92/85 and Article 5 (1) of Council Directive 76/207 ...do not preclude a clause in an employment contract from requiring an employee who has expressed her intention to commence her maternity leave during the six weeks preceding the expected week of childbirth, and is on sick leave with a pregnancy-related illness immediately before that date and gives birth during the period of sick leave, to bring forward the date on which her paid maternity leave commences either to the beginning of the sixth week preceding the expected week of childbirth, or to the beginning of the period of sick leave, whichever is the later.

> 3. A clause in an employment contract which prohibits a woman from taking sick leave during the minimum period of 14 weeks' maternity leave to which a female worker is entitled pursuant to Article 8 (1) of Directive 92/85, unless she elects to return to work and thus terminate her maternity leave, is not compatible with Directive 92/85. By contrast, a clause in an employment contract which prohibits a woman from taking sick leave during a period of supplementary maternity leave granted to her by the employer, unless she elects to return to work and thus terminate her maternity leave, is compatible with Directives 76/207 and 92/85.
>
> 4. Directives 92/85 and 76/207 do not preclude a clause in an employment contract from limiting the period during which annual leave accrues to the minimum period of 14 weeks' maternity leave to which female workers are entitled under Article 8 of Directive 92/85 and from providing that annual leave ceases to accrue during any period of supplementary maternity leave granted to them by their employer.
>
> 5. Directive 92/85 precludes a clause in an employment contract from limiting, in the context of an occupational scheme wholly financed by the employer, the accrual of pension rights during the period of maternity leave referred to by Article 8 of that directive to the period during which the woman receives the pay provided by that contract or national legislation."

In summary, the ruling gave satisfaction to the employer in most issues raised, except as in paragraphs 3 and 5 above.

The *Abdoulaye and Others* v. *Régie nationale des usines Renault SA*[27] case was initiated by a group of male workers alleging discrimination with regard to an allowance for pregnant women going on maternity leave.

The plaintiffs in the main proceedings are male workers at Renault. They claimed that Article 18 of the collective agreement on social benefits for Renault employees was incompatible with the prohibition of discrimination laid down in Article 119 of the Treaty, implemented by Article L.140-2 of the French *Code du Travail*. Article 18 of the agreement provides that "when taking maternity leave, a female employee shall be granted the sum of FRF 7,500". The plaintiffs pleaded that although the birth of a child concerns women alone from a strictly physiological point of view, it is, in at least equal measure, a social event which concerns the whole family, including the father, and to deny him the same allowance amounts to unlawful discrimination. The *Conseil de Prud'hommes* referred the question to the ECJ for a preliminary ruling.

27 Case C-218/98 (1999) ECR I-5723.

According to the case law of the Court, the principle of equal pay, like the general principle of non-discrimination of which it is a particular expression, presupposes that male and female workers whom it covers are in comparable situations.[28]

Renault mentioned several occupational disadvantages inherent in maternity leave, which arise for female workers as a result for being away from work: a woman on maternity leave may not be proposed for promotion; on her return, her period of service will be reduced by the length of her absence; a pregnant worker may not claim performance-related salary increases; a female worker cannot take part in training; since new technology is constantly changing the nature of jobs, the adaptation of a female worker returning from maternity leave becomes complicated.

The Court ruled:

> "The principle of equal pay laid down in Article 119 of the Treaty (Articles 117 to 120 of the Treaty have been replaced by Article 136 EC to 143 EC) does not preclude the making of a lump-sum payment exclusively to female workers who take maternity leave where that payment is designed to offset the occupational disadvantages which arise for those workers as a result of their being away from work."

The *Gomez v. Continental Industrias del Caucho SA.*[29] case concerns a claim to take annual leave at a time coinciding with maternity leave, the period of annual leave being established for all workers by collective agreement.

Ms Gomez was employed as a factory worker by Continental Industrias since 12 September 1994. She was on maternity leave from 5 May to 24 August 2001. She had been able to choose her holiday period in 2000 and, accordingly, she should not have been able to take her annual leave in September 2001 during the exceptional period reserved for six workers who had not been able to choose their holiday period during the previous year, September being otherwise excluded for leave in accordance with a collective agreement.

Ms Gomez nevertheless applied to take her annual leave from 25 August to 21 September 2001, or, alternatively, from 1 September to 27 September 2001, during a period following her maternity leave. Following her employer's refusal, she brought proceedings against Continental Industrias on 6 June 2001 before the Juzgados de lo Social de Madrid. This body referred questions on the interpretation of Directives 93/104 and 76/207 concerning the concurrent rights to annual leave and maternity leave to the ECJ for a preliminary ruling.

The Court stated that:

---

28 *Gillespie*, paras 16 -18.

29 Case C-342/01 (2004) ECR I-2605.

> "the entitlement of every worker to paid annual leave must be regarded as a particularly important principle of the Community social law from which there can be no derogation and whose implementation by the competent national authorities must be confined within the limits expressly laid down by Directive 93/104."[30]

It added, by reference to *Boyle*[31] that Article 5 (1) of Directive 76/207 is to be interpreted as meaning that a worker must be able to take her annual leave during a period other than the period of her maternity leave, even if the period of maternity leave coincides with the general period of annual leave fixed by a collective agreement for the entire workforce.

On a second question, the Court ruled that Article 11 (2) (a) of Directive 92/85 is to be interpreted as also applying to the entitlement of workers such as those of the case to a longer period of annual leave, provided by national law, than the minimum laid down by Directive 93/104.

Promotion

This case concerns the entitlement to a promotion of a woman based on periods of maternity leave: *Land Brandenburg* v. *Sass*.[32]

Mrs Sass, a German national, was employed starting on 1 July 1982 as a production manager at the *Hochschule für Film und Fernsehen "Konrad Wolff"* in Potsdam. Her employment relationship was governed by the Labour Code of the German Democratic Republic at the time of birth of her second child, entitling her to a 20 week maternity leave, which she took from 27 January to 16 June 1987.

Following the reunification of Germany (3 October 1990), the responsibility for Mrs Sass's employment relationship was transferred to *Land Brandenburg*, governed by the *Mutterschutzgesetz*, which prohibits the employment of women in the eight weeks following confinement, and a collective agreement. On her promotion to a higher grade in May 1998, Land Brandenburg counted the first 8 weeks of the maternity leave under the GDR entitlement towards the qualifying 15 years required for classification in a higher salary grade, but not the subsequent 12 weeks.

Mrs Sass brought an action before a national court of first instance claiming that the whole of her maternity leave, i.e. 20 weeks, should have been taken into account, claiming unlawful discrimination against women. The lower courts granted the claim, accepting that Mrs Sass was in a worse position than a male colleague because, having taken maternity leave which is exclusively available

---

30 Para. 43.

31 Para. 47.

32 Case C-284/02 (2004) ECR I-11143.

to women, she will not attain the higher salary grade until 12 weeks later than that male colleagues do. The *Bundesarbeitsgericht*, to which the case was then submitted, referred it to the ECJ for a preliminary ruling on the application of Directive 76/207.

The Court found that the 20 weeks of maternity leave provided by the GDR and the 8 weeks provided by the *Land Brandenburg* had the same objectives and the same purpose, to ensure the physical recovery of the mother following the birth and to allow her to care for her child herself. Therefore, the 20 weeks of leave must be considered to be statutory leave intended for the protection of women who have given birth and must also count towards a qualifying period for access to a higher salary grade. However, it was for the national court to ascertain whether these conditions are fulfilled.

Parental Leave

The following two cases refer to possible benefits granted to workers on parental leave, which may follow, on a voluntary basis, maternity leave. They show the fundamental difference between the employment relationships of the compulsory maternity leave and the voluntary parental leave.

The first one concerns the right to a Christmas bonus while on parental leave: *Lewen v. Lothar Denda.*[33]

In Germany, parental leave is governed by the law on the grant of the parental allowance and parental leave. It may be taken on a voluntary basis and regardless of sex. It begins, at the earliest, at the end of the period for the protection of mothers (maternity leave) and ends no later than the date on which the child reaches the age of three. During that period, the employment contract is suspended. The worker receives a parenting allowance, but no monthly remuneration.

Excerpts of the Court's rulings follow:

> "1. A Christmas bonus ... constitutes pay within the meaning of Article 119 of the Treaty ... even if it is paid voluntarily and even if it is paid mainly or exclusively as an incentive for future work or loyalty to the undertaking or both ...
>
> 2. Article 119 of the Treaty ... precludes an employer from excluding female workers on parenting leave entirely from the benefit of a bonus paid voluntarily as an exceptional allowance at Christmas without taking account of the work done in the year in the year in which the bonus is paid or of the periods for the protection of mothers (in which they prevented from working) where that bonus is awarded retroactively as pay for work performed in the course of that year. However, Article 119 does not preclude a refusal to pay such a bonus to a woman on parental

33 Case C-333/97 (1999) ECR I-07243.

> leave where the award of that allowance is subject to the sole condition that the worker be in active employment when it is awarded."

Moreover, although Article 119 does not preclude an employer, when granting that bonus, from taking periods of parenting leave into account, so that to reduce the benefit pro rata, it does preclude the employer from taking periods for the protection of mothers (in which they were prohibited from working) into account for the same purpose.

> "Neither Article 11 (2) of Directive 92/85 ... nor Clause 2 (6) of the Annex to Directive 96/34 ... covers the payment of the above bonus; consequently, neither provision precludes a refusal to pay the bonus or the taking into account of the aforementioned periods."

The second case relates to the possible accrual of a termination allowance during parental leave: *Österreichischer Gewerkschaftsbund, Gewerkschaft der Privatangestellten* v. *Wirtschafttkammer Österreich.*[34]

The claimant applied to the *Oberster Gerichtshof* for a declaration that the first parental leave of workers in an employment relationship must be taken into account in calculating the termination payment, as length of service, for up to eight months in the same way as military or civilian service. The fact that the relevant regulation does not take into account the periods of parental leave, in contrast to periods of military or civilian service, was claimed to constitute indirect discrimination. The *Gerichshof* referred the case to the ECJ for a preliminary ruling.

In answer to a first question, the Court's answer in paragraph 39 was that:

> "the benefit, for persons performing military service or, as an alternative, compulsory civilian service which may be extended voluntarily, consisting in the taking into account, for calculation of a termination payment they might subsequently be entitled to claim, of the duration of that service is to be regarded as part of their pay within the meaning of Article 141 EC."

The Court added that:

> "60. In the present case, parental leave is taken voluntarily by a worker in order to bring up a child. The voluntary nature of such leave is not lost because of difficulties in finding appropriate structures for looking after a very young child, however regrettable such a situation may be. Parental leave does not have the same purpose as maternity leave; it is regulated by different legislation, and may moreover be taken at periods other than those following maternity leave.

---

34 Case C-220/02 (2004) ECR I-5907.

61. The performance of national service, on the other hand, corresponds to a civic obligation laid down by law and is not governed by the individual interests of the worker.

65. Accordingly, the answer to Questions 2 and 3 must be that Article 141 EC and Directive 75/117 do not preclude the calculation of a termination payment from taking into account, as length of service, the duration of military service or the civilian equivalent performed mainly by men but not of parental leave taken most often by women."

Conclusion

As noted earlier in this Chapter, the ILO Conventions have not only inspired the EU legislation on pregnancy and maternity protection, but its Convention No. 3 of 1919, adopted at the first General Conference of the new organization, has defined the basic principles of the protection developed by the EU in its Directives.

However, the initial approach of the two organizations was different. The ILO was created, to a large extent, to protect workers, thus to protect women workers. The EU started immediately with the principle of equal treatment for men and women, and then developed the rights (rather than the protection) of pregnant women and women after confinement, as a legitimate exception to the principle of equal treatment of men and women at work, on the grounds of women's biological conditions during and after pregnancy.

The EU Directives set general principles and guidelines, but their application by Member States needed guidance or decisions by the ECJ. Its rulings were given in response to national courts or authorities requests for clarification of the intent or interpretation to be given to Article 119 of the Treaty, and of Council Directives 75/111, 75/117, 76/207, 92/85, 93/104.

In its many rulings, the ECJ has further confirmed, developed, defined or refined policies concerning pregnancy or maternity protection and generally strengthened this protection, even at the risk, in some cases, of favouring the employee at the expense of the employer (*Busch*).

Among these rulings:

- the Court confirmed the purposes and legitimacy of this protection, i.e. protecting a woman's biological condition during and after pregnancy, and – as an extension of this basic right – protecting the special relationship between a woman and her child over the period which follows pregnancy and childbirth (*Webb, Hofmann*); another motivation was to offset the disadvantages which women, by comparison with men, suffer with regard to the retention of employment (*Hofmann*) and, we might add, with regard to pay and other benefits.

- pregnancy is not in any way comparable with a pathological condition (*Webb*);
- a worker is not obliged to inform her employer of her pregnancy (*Tele-Danmark*);
- Directives 76/207 and 92/85 apply to both fixed-term and indefinite appointments (*Tele-Danmark and Handels 2001*);
- the dismissal of a female worker on account of pregnancy constitutes direct discrimination on grounds of sex, as is the refusal to appoint a pregnant woman (*Handels 1990*);
- manifesting itself after the maternity leave, there is no reason to distinguish an illness attributable to pregnancy or confinement from any other illness (*Handels 1990, 1997*).

In allowing derogations from the prohibition of dismissal of pregnant workers, workers who have recently given birth or workers who are breastfeeding in cases "not connected with their condition which are permitted under national legislation and/or practice" Article 10 (1) of Directive 92/85 does not require the Member States to specify the particular grounds on which such workers may be dismissed (*Melgar*).

On benefits, the Court has affirmed that there can be no derogation to every worker's entitlement to paid annual leave (*Gomez*). On parental leave, the Court excluded a period of parental leave from the calculation of a termination benefit, on the grounds that parental leave does not have the same purpose as maternity leave and, in a controversial decision, that men in military or civil service and women on parental leave are not in a comparable situation as the former respond to a civic obligation imposed in the public interest, while the latter is a matter between the worker and his/her family (*Österreichischer Gewerkschaftsbund*).

Chapter 10

WORKERS WITH FAMILY RESPONSIBILITIES AND CHILD CARE

Background

The ILO General Survey of the Committee of Experts 1978[1] emphasised that:

> "all measures promoting equal rights may prove meaningless for a vast proportion of women if – as a result of their family responsibilities – they must either give up their jobs entirely, or lose any chance of advancement because they can give only a smaller part of their attention and energy to their professional work."

The first seeds for measures of protection of workers with family responsibilities were already sown in the Employment (Women with Family Responsibilities) Recommendation No. 123 in 1965. Family responsibilities were a barrier to equality in employment and a major source of direct and indirect discrimination against women. On 25 June 1975 the ILO adopted a Resolution concerning a plan of action with a view to promoting equality of opportunity for women workers[2] The ILO Conference recognized that:

> "in order to make women's right to work outside the home without discrimination fully effective measures should be taken ... to encourage a more equitable sharing among family members of household tasks."

The equitable sharing of family responsibilities at home makes the sharing of work responsibilities more effective. In addition the importance of child care facilities has become a focus and was put on the agenda for action by the social partners.

---

1 Quoted in *Equality in Employment and Occupation*, Special Survey in respect of Convention No. 111, Report of the Committee of Experts, International Labour Conference 83rd session 1996, p. 19.

2 International Labour Conference, 1975 Part I, 8 (1) and (2).

ILO Standards

The adoption in 1981 of both the ILO Convention No. 156 on Workers with Family Responsibilities and Recommendation No. 165 marked a shift in traditional attitudes concerning the role of women, and a recognition that family responsibilities affect not only women workers but the family and society as a whole. Under this Convention all workers regardless of sex are to enjoy effective equality not only between men and women with family responsibilities, but between these and other workers. The twofold aim of the Convention is, first, to enable workers with family responsibilities to engage in employment without discrimination, and secondly, to reconcile work and family responsibilities, especially by providing child-care.

This Convention is ratified today by 156 countries including all 27 EU Member States.

Article 5 of the Convention provides that:

> "All measures compatible with national conditions and possibilities shall further be taken (a) to take account of the needs of workers with family responsibilities in community planning; and (b) to develop or promote community services, public or private, such as child-care and family services and facilities."

Child-care facilities are indispensable if both parents are working. The Recommendation spells out concrete measures to create employment and working conditions that meet the needs of workers with family responsibilities – such as reduced working hours, flexible working schedules, parental leave, child care and family services and facilities, tax relief, etc.

EU Legislation

Community law realised already in the 1970s that discrimination on the ground of marital or family status should be banned and the Equal Treatment Directive 1976 expressly provided in Article 2 (1) that:

> "For the purposes of the following provisions, the principle of equal treatment shall mean that there shall be no discrimination whatsoever on grounds of sex either directly or indirectly by reference in particular to marital or family status."

The 2002 amending Directive has reproduced the same provision without change. The fourth paragraph of Article 7 of the amending Directive provides in addition that:

> "The Directive shall also be without prejudice to the provisions of Council Directive 96/34/EC of 3 June 1996 on the Framework Agreement on

> Parental leave concluded by UNICE, CEEP and the ETUC[3] ... It is also without prejudice to the right of Member States to recognise distinct rights to paternity and/or adoption leave. Those Member States which recognise such rights shall take the necessary measures to protect working men and women against dismissal due to exercising those rights and ensure that, at the end of such leave, they shall be entitled to return to their jobs or to equivalent posts on terms and conditions which are no less favourable to them, and to benefit from any improvement in working conditions to which they would have been entitled during their absence."

These provisions on parental and paternity leave as well as adoption leave are the results of a long process to implement the policy of reconciling work and family responsibilities for both men and women on an equal basis.

EU Case Law

In the case of *Ulrich Hofmann* v. *Barmer Erstzkasse*, 1984,[4] the question arose for the first time as to whether a father who takes care of his less than six-month-old baby can claim for a 'maternity benefit' in circumstances where he had obtained from his employer unpaid leave of absence while the mother resumed employment as a teacher. The mother had maternity protection under German law, but not the father. The ECJ was requested to give a preliminary ruling on the question of whether Mr Hoffman could rely on the Equal Treatment Directive that protects against discrimination on the basis of sex in all conditions of work.

The Court ruled that the Directive:

> "... must be interpreted as meaning that a Member State may, after the protective period has expired, grant to mothers a period of maternity leave which the State encourages them to take by the payment of an allowance. The directive does not impose on Member States a requirement that they shall, as an alternative, allow such leave to be granted to fathers, even where the parents so decide."

The Parental Leave Directive of 1996 has corrected this inequality between mother and father. Mr Hoffman could claim today, on the basis of the 2002 Equal Treatment Directive and directly on the basis of the Parental Leave Directive of 1996, the same protection afforded to mothers.

Parental leave has been a long-standing item on the European Union's social policy agenda, and features in the 1989 Community Charter of the

---

3 OJ (1996) L 145/4.

4 Case 184/83 (1984) ECR 3047.

Fundamental Social Rights of Workers, which states that "measures should... be developed enabling men and women to reconcile their occupational and family obligations".

Clause 2 (1) of the Framework Agreement on Parental Leave reads as follows:

> "This agreement grants ... men and women workers an individual right to parental leave on the grounds of the birth or adoption of a child to enable them to take care of that child, for at least three months, until a given age up to 8 years to be defined by Member States and/or management and labour."

Even prior to the 1996 Directive, in 1992 the Council adopted a Recommendation on Child Care,[5] which dealt with promotion of childcare services whilst parents are working, studying or training. It further recommends special parental leave for parents who have responsibility for the care and upbringing of children and it promotes the sharing, between men and women, of occupational, family and upbringing responsibilities arising from the care of children.

After the adoption of the Directive further steps were taken to implement it. In 2003 Council Decision 2003/578/EC of 22 July 2003 on Guidelines for the Employment Policies of the Member States[6] expressed the following in Guideline No. 16:

> "Gender gaps in the labour market should be progressively eliminated, if the EU is to deliver full employment, increase quality at work and promote social inclusion and cohesion. This requires both a gender mainstreaming approach and specific policy actions to create the conditions for women and men to enter, re-enter, and remain in the labour market. The Barcelona European Council agreed that by 2010 Member States should provide childcare to at least 90% of children between three years old and the mandatory school age and at least 33% of the children under three years of age."

These are indeed ambitious targets. The 2005 Guidelines promote in Guideline No. 18:

> "... a lifecycle approach to work which achieves an increase in female participation and reduces gender gaps in employment, unemployment and pay. It aims at a better reconciliation of work and private life and the provision of accessible and affordable childcare facilities and care for other dependents."

---

5 Council Recommendation 92/24/EEC OJ (1992) L 123.

6 OJ (2003) L 197/13.

Childcare may prove to be a better policy area for closing the gender gap than affirmative action and quotas for women. This topic will be discussed in Chapter 14.

The Parental Leave Directive 1996 and the Guidelines on Child Care are the "European translation" of ILO Convention 156 on Workers with Family Responsibilities 1981.

The implementation of the 1996 Directive raised some difficulty in Luxembourg and the Commission brought an action against Luxembourg, *Commission* v. *Grand Duchy of Luxembourg* 2005,[7] because the implementing national legislation differed from the Directive. The Court declared that:

> "by providing that the right to maternity leave or adoption leave arising during parental leave replaces the latter which must then come to an end, without its being possible for the parent to defer the portion of the parental leave which he or she was unable to take and by limiting the grant of the right to parental leave to parents of children born after 31 December 1998, or in respect of whom adoption proceedings were initiated after that date, the Grand Duchy of Luxembourg has failed to fulfil its obligations under Council Directive 96/34/EC of 3 June 1996 on the Framework Agreement on Parental Leave concluded by UNICE, CEEP and the ETUC."

The Court made a distinction between the aims of maternity leave and parental leave and interpreted the Directive in a way that maternity leave does not replace parental leave but merely suspends it to continue at a later date.

The Directive applied to child care of children born before or after the entry into force of the Directive. Parental leave could arise in respect of a child below the age of eight years, whether he was born before or after 1998. Today, nine years later, this issue is irrelevant.

This precedent only proves that the Commission is very vigilant as regards the full and proper implementation of EU law.

The problem of equality of treatment between men and women arose in a case involving child-care, where nursery facilities were only open for mothers and exceptionally in cases of *force majeur* also for fathers. The Dutch Ministry of Agriculture made available subsidised nursery places for children of women officials. Men were entitled to this service in cases of emergency, determined by the employer. On 5 December 1995, Mr Lommers asked the Minister of Agriculture to reserve a nursery place for his child yet unborn. His request was rejected on 20 December 1995 on the ground that children of male officials could be given places in the nursery facilities in question only in cases of emergency. Mr Lommers brought an action against the Ministry on the ground

---

7 OJ (2005) C 143/11.

of sex discrimination: *Lommers* v. *Dutch Ministry of Agriculture* 2002.[8] The ECJ was asked to deliver a preliminary ruling as to whether Mr Lommers suffered discrimination in violation of the Equal Treatment Directive.

The Court ruled that:

> "Article 2 (1) and (4) of Council Directive 76/207/EEC of 9 February 1976 ... does not preclude a scheme set up by a Minister to tackle extensive under-representation of women within his Ministry under which, in a context characterised by a proven insufficiency of proper, affordable care facilities, a limited number of subsidised nursery places made available by the Ministry to its staff is reserved for female officials alone whilst male officials may have access to them only in cases of emergency, to be determined by the employer. That is so, however, only in so far, in particular, as the said exception in favour of male officials is construed as allowing those of them who take care of their children by themselves to have access to that nursery places scheme on the same conditions as female officials."

Following this ruling, all that Mr Lommers has to prove is that he is the parent who takes care of the children, in order to be entitled to access to the nursery. This is not a case of affirmative action for women constituting a discrimination of men as both women and men, when they are the sole care-takers of the children, are entitled to have access to the subsidised nursery provided by the Dutch Ministry of Agriculture.

Conclusion

The ILO Convention on Workers with Family Responsibilities, Convention No. 156 of 1981 opened up a new era of awareness that the contribution of women to the work force can be promoted by providing proper child care, so that women workers can reconcile their dual role in society, as mothers and as workers. The Convention employed a neutral term regardless of sex – "Workers with Family Responsibilities". The Convention anticipated the evolution of sharing of family responsibilities by men.

EU law developed in the spirit of the ILO Convention and departed from the ECJ ruling in the *Hofmann* Case of 1984. In 1996 it adopted the Parental Leave Directive that promoted the sharing of family responsibilities by men and women workers. The *Lommers* ruling of 2002 likewise respected the principle of equal treatment of men and women regarding entitlement to child care.

8 Case C-476/99 (2002) ECR I-2891.

The policy of the EU as reflected in the Guidelines for the Employment Policies of the Member States of 2003 and 2005 evidences the central importance of child care and the commitment to the aim of reconciliation of worker's responsibilities as regards work and the family.[9]

[9] Regulation (EC) No. 29/2004 of 8 January 2004 adopting the specifications of the 2005 ad hoc module on reconciliation between work and family life provided for by Council Regulation (EC) No. 577/98; OJ (2004) L 5/57.

Chapter 11

PART-TIME WORK AND INDIRECT DISCRIMINATION

Background

Part-time work is one form of atypical work. The European Parliament published a Working Paper on Atypical Work in the EU, Social Affairs Series 3 2000[1] which discusses the growing phenomenon of a flexible workforce. This group of workers is composed of over 80% of women. According to the European Parliament's Working Paper, atypical workers include part-timers (21 million people in the EU), those on fixed term contracts (14 million), home workers (10 million), or those engaged in a large number of other arrangements, such as seasonal work, casual work, tele-work, family work, or self-employment. The main common characteristic of all such groups is that their working arrangements differ from those of the 'typical employee' working full time on an indefinite contract.

Atypical work can provide considerable economic and social benefits to society. It opens up the labour market to people for whom full time employment is unfeasible or unattractive. It also provides more flexibility, mobility and dynamism to the labour market, which in turn may contribute to an innovative culture, improved economic performance and efficiency. However, since many labour and social protection laws and institutions are still based on the profile of the 'typical worker', the atypical workers are often discriminated.

The Working Paper states that:

> "atypical workers often find that regulations and criteria are – for no good reason – less favourable for them, or not tailored to their situations. As a consequence, atypical work often does not turn out to be an economic and social opportunity, but a position in which reduced working hours

1 European Parliament Directorate General for Research, Working Paper "Atypical Work in the EU", *Social Affairs Series 3-2000* <ec.europa.eu/employment_social/labour_law/docs/ep_paper_atypicalwork_en.pdf>.

> are combined with inferior working conditions and lower pay; a fate which – as was already stated – mostly concerns women."

The report concludes that atypical workers in the EU are less protected and have less rights to benefits. The nature of these differences in formal positions, such as unemployment benefit, paid sickness leave, and pensions and health insurance is mainly a matter of thresholds before an atypical worker is entitled to rights or benefits and exclusion from rights and benefits. Because women are over-represented in part-time work, temporary work, family work and, to a lesser extent, homework they are more affected by those inequalities of atypical work than men. A very high percentage of cases of sex discrimination are consequently related to part-time work. As most (80%) of the part-time workers are women, they are affected indirectly by the discrimination of part-time work. We shall focus on part-time work and not on other forms of atypical work because the legal instruments of both the ILO and the EU concentrate on this form of activity. The abundant case law of the ECJ is also dealing almost exclusively with part-time work, but for one recent case of *Wippel* v. *Peek and Cloppenburg GmbH & Co. AG* 2004[2] involving "work on demand" – a form of casual work. The Court excluded this type of work from the protection afforded by the Directive on Part-Time Work.

ILO Standards

The ILO adopted in 1994 the Convention on Part-Time Work No. 175. It entered into force on 28 February 1998. Only 11 countries have ratified it so far, including eight EU Member States: Cyprus, Finland, Italy, Luxembourg, Netherlands, Portugal, Slovenia and Sweden. The ILO also adopted in the same year the Recommendation No. 182 on Part-time Work.

Definitions

The Convention offers the following definition of a part-time worker:

> "Article 1
>
> For the purposes of this Convention:
>
> 1. the term part-time worker means an employed person whose normal hours of work are less than those of comparable full time workers;

[2] Case C-313/02 (2004) ECR I-9483.

2. the normal hours of work referred to in subparagraph (a) may be calculated weekly or on average over a given period of employment;
3. the term comparable full time worker refers to a full time worker who:
   1) is engaged in the same or a similar type of work or occupation; and
   2) has the same type of employment relationship;
   3) is employed in the same establishment or, when there is no comparable full time worker in that establishment, in the same enterprise or, when there is no comparable full time worker in that enterprise, in the same branch of activity, as the part-time worker concerned;
4. full time workers affected by partial unemployment, that is by a collective and temporary reduction in their normal hours of work for economic, technical or structural reasons, are not considered to be part-time workers.

Article 2

This Convention does not affect more favourable provisions applicable to part-time workers under other international labour Conventions."

Exclusions

Article 3 allows the exclusion from the application of the Convention of "particular categories of workers or of establishments when its application to them would raise particular problems of a substantial nature". This open door to exclusions was believed to facilitate a wider ratification of the Convention.[3] However, as we have mentioned above, the number of ratifications, thirteen years after the adoption of the Convention, is really low.

Article 3 provides as follows:

"This Convention applies to all part-time workers, it being understood that a Member may, after consulting the representative organizations of employers and workers concerned, exclude wholly or partly from its scope particular categories of workers or of establishments when its application to them would raise particular problems of a substantial nature.

3 See G. Politakis, "Deconstructing Flexibility in International Labour Conventions" in *Melanges en honneur de Nicolas Valticos, Les normes internationales du travail: Un patrimoine pour l'avenir* (B.I.T. Geneve, 2004(, at p. 473.

Each Member having ratified this Convention which avails itself of the possibility afforded in the preceding paragraph shall, in its reports on the application of the Convention under Article 22 of the Constitution of the International Labour Organization, indicate any particular category of workers or of establishments thus excluded and the reasons why this exclusion was or is still judged necessary."

An Equitable Basis

Article 4 prescribes that:

"Measures shall be taken to ensure that part-time workers receive the same protection as that accorded to comparable full time workers in respect of: 1. the right to organize, the right to bargain collectively and the right to act as workers' representatives; 2. occupational safety and health; 3. discrimination in employment and occupation."

Article 5 provides for the criteria of *pro rata* in the relation of part-time to full time work:

"Measures appropriate to national law and practice shall be taken to ensure that part-time workers do not, solely because they work part-time, receive a basic wage which, calculated proportionately on an hourly, performance-related, or piece-rate basis, is lower than the basic wage of comparable full time workers, calculated according to the same method."

Article 7 imposes equal conditions of work for part-time and full time workers as regards maternity protection, termination of employment, paid annual leave and paid public holidays, and sick leave, it being understood that pecuniary entitlements may be determined in proportion to hours of work or earnings.

Article 13 of the ILO Part-Time Work Recommendation, No. 182 provides expressly beyond the binding protection of the Convention No. 175 the following recommendations:

"In accordance with national law and practice, part-time workers should have access on an equitable basis, and as far as possible under equivalent conditions, to all forms of leave available to comparable full time workers, in particular paid educational leave, parental leave and leave in cases of illness of a child or another member of a worker's immediate family."

Article 14 recommends:

"Where appropriate, the same rules should apply to part-time workers as to comparable full time workers with respect to scheduling of annual leave and work on customary rest days and public holidays."

Article 15 recommends:

> "Where appropriate, measures should be taken to overcome specific constraints on the access of part-time workers to training, career opportunities and occupational mobility."

Thresholds

As we shall see, in practice problems arose as to the thresholds. When is a worker a part-time worker? Are ten hours work per week qualifying a worker to a *pro rata* status? Or can he or she be excluded from any of the benefits enumerated under Article 7?

In practice the main source of difference in treatment of part-time and full time workers is the threshold. All sorts of thresholds apply for the part-time worker before he or she is entitled to benefits or protection. This is the case for dismissal protection, paid holidays, the continuation of payment in case of sickness, maternity leave, unemployment benefit and the right to benefits in the event of illness.

In Denmark this threshold is 15 hours per week, in Germany 18 hours per week, in Spain and Ireland 12 hours per week, in France and the Netherlands there is no threshold.[4]

Article 8 of the ILO Convention answers some of these questions without suggesting the number of working hours required for the creation of a threshold. Part-time workers whose hours of work or earnings are below specified thresholds may be excluded, except in regard to employment injury benefits and non-statutory maternity protection measures.

Paragraph (1) provides:

> "Part-time workers whose hours of work or earnings are below specified thresholds may be excluded by a Member;
>
> (a) from the scope of any of the statutory social security schemes... except in regard to employment injury benefits.
>
> (b) from the scope of any of the measures taken in the fields covered by Article 7, except in regard to maternity protection measures other than those provided under statutory social security schemes."

The Convention does not suggest any specified thresholds. It is left to the discretion of the States and to the social partners.

Article 8 (2) provides that:

> "The thresholds referred to in paragraph 1 shall be sufficiently low as not to exclude an unduly large percentage of part-time workers."

---

4 See the European Parliament Working Paper on Atypical Work, 2000, p. 73 *et seq.*

Article 8 (3) further provides that:

> "A Member which avails itself of the possibility provided for in paragraph 1 above shall:
>
> (a) periodically review the thresholds in force,
>
> (b) in its reports on the application of the Convention under Article 22 of the Constitution of the ILO, indicate the thresholds in force, the reasons therefore and whether consideration is being given to the progressive extension of protection to the workers excluded."

Article 8 (4) provides for the tripartite mode of operation, namely:

> "The most representative organisations of employers and workers shall be consulted on the establishment, review and revision of the thresholds referred to in this Article."

The concern of the ILO to establish fair thresholds is also expressed in Article 8 of the Part-Time Work Recommendation No. 182 1994:

> (1) As appropriate, threshold requirements based on hours of work or earnings as specified under Article 8 of the Convention in the fields referred to in Article 7 should be progressively reduced.
>
> (2) The period required as a condition for protection in the fields referred to in Article 7 of the Convention should not be longer for part-time workers than for comparable full time workers.

The possibility of excluding certain categories of workers from the provisions of the Part-Time Work Convention according to Article 3, and the discretion left with regard to thresholds under Article 8, leave the door open to indirect discrimination of women workers who are denied the protection of part-time work.

It cannot be a coincidence that several provisions of Council Directive on Part-Time Work 97/81/EC of 15 December 1997[5] echo the provisions of the ILO Convention on Part-Time Work 1994. The definition of a part-time worker is identical in the two instruments, and other provisions, such as the scope of the protection of part-time workers, the *pro rata temporis* principle, and even the exclusion of certain categories of workers, seem likewise to be inspired by the Convention.

[5] OJ (1998) L 14/9.

EU Legislation

The EU Directive on Part-Time Work originated in a Framework Agreement on Part-Time Work concluded with the social partners UNICE, CEEP and the ETUC. Like the ILO tripartite system, the EU followed this method of elaboration of rules after consultation and co-decision of employers, employees and governments. The general cross-industry organisations, the Union of Industrial and Confederations of Europe (UNICE), The European Centre of Enterprises with Public Participation (CEEP) and the European Trade Union Confederation (ETUC) collaborated in the promulgation of the Framework Agreement which laid down the general principles and minimum requirements for part-time working, striving to eliminate discrimination against part-time workers and aiming at the development of the potential for part-time work on a basis which is acceptable for employers and workers alike.

The EU Commission had a much more ambitious initiative to propose to management and labour: a comprehensive project to protect all forms of atypical work against discrimination. However this project was not realised and the Framework Agreement on Part-Time Work entered into force at the dawn of the new millennium as a Council Directive recognizing the *pro rata temporis* principle of granting proportional remuneration and other conditions of work, such as leave, bonuses, amenities, privileges, etc., to part-time workers. Two European countries have already followed the *pro rata principle* before the adoption of the Part-Time Directive, France and the Netherlands.

The Framework Agreement attaches importance to measures which would facilitate access to part-time work for men and women in order to prepare for retirement, reconcile professional and family life, and extend education and training opportunities to improve their skills and career opportunities for the mutual benefit of employers and workers and in a manner which would assist the development of enterprises.

The purpose of this Framework Agreement is a contribution to the overall European strategy on employment.

Clause 1 defines the purpose as follows:

"(a) to provide for the removal of discrimination against part-time workers and to improve the quality of part-time work;

(b) to facilitate the development of part-time work on a voluntary basis and to contribute to the flexible organization of working time in a manner which takes into account the needs of employers and employees."

Clause 2 (1) traces the scope of application to part-time workers who have an employment contract or employment relationship as defined by the law, collective agreement or practice in force in each Member State.

Clause 2 (2) permits the exclusion of certain categories of part-time workers for objective reasons.

Clause 3 (1) defines the term 'part-time worker' to mean:

> "an employee whose normal hours of work, calculated on a weekly basis or on average over a period of employment of up to one year, are less than the normal hours of work of a comparable full time worker."

Clause 3 (2) defines the term 'comparable full time worker' to include:

> "a full time worker in the same establishment having the same type of employment ... Where there is no comparable full time worker in the same establishment, the comparison shall be made by reference to the applicable collective agreement or, where there is no applicable collective agreement, in accordance with national law, collective agreements or practice."

This wide provision is also to be found in a parallel Article 1 (c) (iii) of the ILO Convention.

Clause 4 enshrines the principle of non-discrimination and applies the *pro rata temporis* criteria in respect of employment conditions.

The Framework Agreement further provides that a worker's refusal to transfer from full time to part-time work or vice-versa should not in itself constitute a valid reason for termination of employment, without prejudice to termination in accordance with national law, collective agreements and practice, for other reasons such as may arise from the operational requirements of the establishment concerned.

The considerable number of cases that came up for decision by the ECJ, both before and after the adoption of the Directive in 1997, show that the issue of part-time work and indirect discrimination of women part-time workers has not been solved yet.

The definition of indirect discrimination is to be found in the Burden of Proof Directive 1997.[6]

Article 1 (2) lays down that

> "for purposes of the principle of equal treatment referred to in paragraph 1, indirect discrimination shall exist where an apparently neutral provision, criterion or practice disadvantages a substantially higher proportion of the members of one sex unless that provision, criterion or practice is appropriate and necessary and can be justified by objective factors unrelated to sex."

6 Directive 97/80; OJ (1998) L 14/6.

Discrimination affecting part-time workers in comparison to full time-workers is neutral and does not on the face of it consist necessarily of sex discrimination. However, if the practice disadvantages a substantially higher proportion of women it amounts to indirect sex discrimination.

The role of the social partners is emphasised in the Preamble of the Directive:

> "Whereas the social partners are best placed to find solutions that correspond to the needs of both, employers and workers ... they must be given a special role in the implementation and application of this Agreement."

Thus, in the spirit of the ILO, the social partners are not only the norm setting body, but also in charge of implementation and application of the Agreement side by side with the EU Commission and the Court of Justice.

The Directive, unlike the ILO Convention and the Recommendation, is silent on the question of thresholds, but deals expressly with the issue of exclusion "wholly or partly from the terms of the Agreement" of part-time workers who work on a casual basis. Clause 2 of the Agreement, defining the scope of the Agreement, permits such exclusions for objective reasons, after consultation with the social partners, and subjects them to a periodic review to establish if the objective reasons for making them remain valid. This Clause is in conformity with Article 3 (1) of the ILO Convention, which provides, as we have seen, that:

> "a Member may, after consulting the representative organisations of employers and workers concerned, exclude wholly or partly from its scope particular categories of workers or of establishments when its application to them would raise particular problems of a substantial nature."

EU Case Law

The Court of Justice had been requested to apply and interpret the EU law regarding part-time work way before the Part-Time Work Directive was adopted in 1997. The adoption of the Directive has moreover not stopped the flow of cases on various aspects of discrimination of part-time workers regarding pay, qualifications for access to jobs, conditions of work (such as bonuses, allowances, compensation, calculating length of service), and, finally, dismissals and redundancies. The fact that most of the requests for preliminary rulings came from Germany shows that their collective agreements, mainly in the public service, are indifferent to the problem of indirect discrimination.

Equal Pay

In the first case that came for a preliminary ruling, *Kingsgate* v. *Jenkins* 1981, discussed in Chapter 6, the issue of indirect sex discrimination of a part-time worker arose as regards pay. The ECJ adopted a pragmatic approach and did not rule on the general issue of protecting part-time workers on the basis of *a pro rata* approach. The employer was given a defence to discrimination through proving that the disparity of pay between part-time and full time workers was justified on objective grounds unrelated to sex.

Ten years later another case involving pay came up for a preliminary ruling, that of *Helga Nimz* v. *Hamburg* 1991.[7] It appeared from the documents before the Court that Mrs Nimz's employment was governed by the provisions of the Collective Wage Agreement for Federal Employees of 1987, which provided that, for the purposes of classification in a higher salary grade on completion of a probationary period, full account should be taken of the period of service of workers employed for at least three-quarters of normal working time, but that only one-half of such period of service should be taken into account in the case of workers whose working hours are between one-half and three-quarters of normal working time.

On the basis of that provision and in view of the fact that Mrs Nimz was employed for less than three-quarters of normal working time, her employer refused to classify her in the next higher salary grade on her completion of six years in the lower grade. In view of the fact that employees who work for at least three-quarters of normal working time are entitled automatically, on completion of six years' service, to be reclassified in the next higher salary grade, Mrs Nimz believed that she was the victim of unlawful indirect discrimination. She therefore brought a case before the Labour Court in Hamburg. That Court took the view that her application raised problems relating to the interpretation of Articles 117 and 119 of the EEC Treaty and of the Equal Pay Directive 75/117. It therefore decided to stay the proceedings and to refer certain questions to the ECJ for a preliminary ruling.

In its first question, the national court sought in substance to ascertain whether Article 119 of the Treaty precludes a collective agreement entered into within the national public service from providing that the period of service of workers employed for at least three-quarters of normal working time be taken fully into account for reclassification in a higher salary grade, but that only one-half of such period of service be taken into account in the case of employees whose working hours are between one-half and three-quarters of such normal working time, where the latter group of employees comprises an appreciably larger percentage of women than men.

---

[7] Case 184/89 (1991) ECR I-297.

A collective agreement such as that which allows employers to maintain a distinction as regards overall pay between two categories of workers, that is to say, those who work for a minimum number of hours per week or per month and those who perform the same type of work but do not work such a minimum number of hours, does constitute discrimination against women workers vis-à-vis male workers, if in fact a much lower percentage of men work on a part-time basis than women. Such an agreement must therefore in principle be regarded as contrary to Article 119 of the Treaty. The outcome would be different only if the difference in treatment between the two categories of workers could be shown to be based on objectively justified factors unrelated to any discrimination on grounds of sex.[8] In this regard, the City of Hamburg argued that full time employees or those who work for three-quarters of normal working time acquire more quickly than others the abilities and skills relating to their particular job. The German Government also relied on their more extensive experience.

The Court rejected this argument as being based on a "generalization" about certain categories of workers, which does not make it possible to identify objective criteria unrelated to any discrimination on grounds of sex[9] Although experience goes hand in hand with length of service, and experience enables the worker in principle to improve performance of the tasks allotted to him, the objectivity of such a criterion depends on all the circumstances in a particular case, and in particular on the relationship between the nature of the work performed and the experience gained from the performance of that work upon completion of a certain number of working hours. However, it is a matter for the national court, which alone is competent to evaluate the facts, to determine in the light of all the circumstances whether and to what extent a provision in a collective agreement such as that here at issue is based on objectively justified factors unrelated to any discrimination on grounds of sex.

The Court ruled that:

> "(1) Article 119 of the EEC Treaty must be interpreted as precluding a collective agreement, entered into within the national public service, from providing for the period of service of employees working at least three-quarters of normal working time to be fully taken into account for reclassification in a higher salary grade, where only one-half of such period of service is taken into account in the case of employees whose working hours are between one-half and three-quarters of those normal working hours and the latter group of employees comprises a considerably smaller percentage of men than women, unless the employer can prove

---

[8] See the ruling of 13 May 1986 in Case 170/84 *Bilka-Kaufhaus* v. *Karin Weber von Hartz* 1986 ECR 1607.

[9] See the ruling of 13 July 1989 in Case 171/88 *Rinner-Kuehn* v. *FWW Spezial-Gebaeudereinigung* 1989 ECR I-2743.

> that such a provision is justified by factors whose objectivity depends in particular on the relationship between the nature of the duties performed and the experience afforded by the performance of those duties after a certain number of working hours have been completed.
>
> (2) Where there is indirect discrimination in a provision of a collective agreement, the national court is required to set aside that provision, without requesting or awaiting its prior removal by collective bargaining or any other procedure, and to apply to members of the group disadvantaged by that discrimination the same arrangements as are applied to other employees, arrangements which, failing the correct application of Article 119 of the EEC Treaty in national law, remain the only valid system of reference."

Simply put, the Court found that the Collective Wage Agreement was discriminatory to part-time women workers and was to be declared null by the Hamburg Court. Presumably the national court would be right in applying *pro rata* criteria in lieu of doubling the qualifying period for part-time workers who are employed for between half-time and three quarters of the time of full time workers.

In the case of *The City of Berlin* v. *Monika Botel* 1992,[10] a question arose with regard to compensation for training courses attended by part-time employees. The ECJ dealt with such compensation as being part of pay.

The concept of "pay", within the meaning of Article 119 of the Treaty, comprises any consideration, whether in cash or in kind, whether immediate or future, provided that the worker receives it, albeit indirectly, in respect of his employment from his employer, and irrespective of whether the worker receives it under a contract of employment, by virtue of legislative provisions, or on a voluntary basis.

The ECJ ruled that:

> "Article 119 of the EEC Treaty and Council Directive 75/117/EEC of 10 February 1975, on the approximation of the laws of the Member States relating to the application of the principle of equal pay for men and women, preclude national legislation applicable to a much greater number of women than men from limiting to their individual working hours the compensation, in the form of paid leave or overtime pay, which staff council members employed on a part-time basis are to receive from their employer for attending training courses which impart the knowledge necessary for working on staff councils and are held during the full time working hours applicable in the undertaking but which exceed their own

[10] Case C-360/90 (1992) ECR I-3589.

> part-time working hours, when staff council members employed on a full time basis are compensated for attendance of the same courses on the basis of full time working hours. It remains open to the Member State to prove that such legislation is justified by objective factors unrelated to any discrimination based on sex."

In the following two cases the discrimination of the women part-time workers also consisted of the fact that they were not paid compensation for attendance at training courses providing members of staff committees with the knowledge necessary for performing their functions: *Freers and Speckmann* v. *Deutsche Bundespost* 1996[11] and *Kuratorium für Dialyse und Nierentransplantation e.V.* v. *Lewark* 1996.[12]

After the entry into force of the Part-Time Work Directive 1997, in *Elsner-Lakeberg* v. *Land Nordrhein-Westfalen 2004*,[13] the ECJ addressed the interpretation of Article 141 EC and Council Directive 75/117/EEC of 10 February 1975 on the approximation of the laws of the Member States relating to the application of the principle of equal pay for men and women.

The applicant, who had the status of a civil servant, worked part-time as a secondary school teacher for the defendant *Land*. Full time teachers at the applicant's school worked for 24.5 hours per week, whereas she worked 15 hours per week. In December 1999 the applicant was required to work 2.5 additional hours in that month. Her request for remuneration of those hours was refused on the basis that the relevant national legislation provided that excess hours worked by a teacher who is a civil servant would be remunerated only when the additional work exceeded three hours in a month. She therefore received no pay at all for the additional 2.5 hours worked. Having unsuccessfully pursued the administrative appeal procedure, the applicant brought proceedings before the Administrative Court. That Court considered that in accordance with the relevant national legislation the applicant was not entitled to remuneration for the additional hours worked. It asked however whether that legislation was compatible with Article 141 EC in conjunction with the Equal Pay Directive, since the effect was that part-time teachers who were civil servants and work no more than three additional teaching hours per month receive less total remuneration than that granted for the same number of hours worked to full time teachers who are civil servants. The German Administrative Court accordingly referred the following question to the ECJ:

Is it compatible with Article 141 EC in conjunction with Council Directive 75/117/EEC of 10 February 1975 on the approximation of the laws of the

11 Case C-278/93 (1996) ECR I-1165.

12 Case C-457/93 (1996) ECR I-243.

13 Case C-285/02 (2004) ECR C-285/02 (2004) ECR I-5861.

Member States relating to the application of the principle of equal pay for men and women, that men and women teachers, part-time as well as full time, who are officials in the Land North-Rhine Westphalia are not granted remuneration for excess hours worked if that additional work does not exceed three teaching [hours] in the calendar month?

AG Jacobs stated in his opinion that:

> "National legislation providing that both full time and part-time employees are not remunerated for additional hours worked where the result is that the overall pay of full time employees is higher than that of part-time employees for the same number of hours worked establishes different treatment for full time and part-time employees. If that different treatment affects considerably more women than men the legislation infringes Article 141 EC and Council Directive 75/117/EEC on the approximation of the laws of the Member States relating to the application of the principle of equal pay for men and women, unless there are objective factors unrelated to sex which justify such a difference in treatment."

The ECJ adopted AG Jacob's opinion and ruled accordingly.

Access to a Profession

In the case of *Birgitte Kording* v. *Senator fur Finanzen* 1997[14] the issue of indirect discrimination arose as regards the right to access to work as a tax adviser.

Pursuant to Paragraph 2 of the Law on Tax Consultancy, the right to practice as a tax adviser in Germany is restricted to persons or associations with the appropriate professional status. That status is conferred on persons who have passed the qualifying examination or have been exempted there from Paragraph 35 (1). Under Paragraph 38 (1) (4a) of the Tax Consultancy Law, exemptions are granted *inter alia* to:

> "former executive-class officers or employees of the revenue administration who have been employed for not less than 15 years in work connected with the taxes administered by the Federal or Land tax authorities, as case officers (*Sachbearbeiter*) or at least in an equivalent capacity."

At the material time, Paragraph 38 of the above mentioned Law gave no indication whether the requisite 15 years' experience could also be acquired by working on a part-time basis.

However, the operation of Paragraph 38 was modified by Paragraph 36 (3) of the 1994 Sixth Law amending the Law on Tax Consultancy, which states that the experience required for admission to the qualifying examination may

---

[14] Case C-100/95 (1997) ECR I-5289.

also be acquired through employment on a part-time basis. In the case of part-time employment involving working hours of no less than one-half of normal working hours, the total period required is extended on a *pro rata* basis, but may not exceed double the length of the period specified in subparagraphs (1) and (2). Where the number of hours worked on a part-time basis is any lower, those hours are not taken into account.

The new wording of Paragraph 38 (2) of the above Law, which was also amended by the 1994 Law, provides that Paragraph 36 (3) is also to apply for the purposes of gaining exemption from the qualifying examination. The duties carried out by Mrs Kording at the Bremen Principal Revenue Office were those of a case officer. By letter of 21 October 1992, she requested the Finance Senator to provide her with a written statement, binding on the administration, to the effect that as of 30 April 1993 she would be exempt, by virtue of the duties she had performed, from the qualifying examination.

On 11 February 1993 the Admissions Committee issued Mrs Kording with a written statement, binding on the administration, to the effect that the duties performed were such as to satisfy the relevant requirements but adding that Mrs Kording would not have acquired by 30 April 1993 the minimum length of professional experience – 15 years – required under the Law. According to that statement, in prescribing the length of practical experience required, the legislature had proceeded on the assumption that the work would be performed by way of a main occupation, that is to say, through full time employment. Consequently, in the case of an applicant employed part-time, the hours worked can be taken into account only on a *pro rata* basis.

On 9 March 1993 Mrs Kording brought proceedings before the Finance Court which, uncertain whether the German legislation is compatible with the Directive, accordingly referred the following question to the Court for a preliminary ruling:

> "Is there an infringement, in the form of indirect discrimination against women, of Article 3 (1) of Directive 76/207/EEC of 9 February 1976, or of other Community legislation, where, under domestic legislation (Paragraph 38 (1), No. 4 (a), second subparagraph, in conjunction with Paragraph 36 (3) of the Law on Tax Consultancy, the 15-year minimum period of employment as a case officer in the executive grade of the revenue administration, which is required for exemption from the tax consultants' examination, is proportionately extended in the case of part-time employment involving working hours of no less than one-half of the normal working hours, and where, of the 119 part-time executive-grade officers in the Bremen revenue administration, 110 are women (92.4%)?"

By its question the German Finance Court is essentially asking whether Article 3 (1) of the Directive precludes national legislation which provides that, in the case of part-time employment involving working hours of no less than one-half of normal working hours, the total length of professional experience required for exemption from the qualifying examination is to be extended on a *pro rata* basis.

It should be recalled that Article 3 (1) of the Directive prohibits any discrimination whatsoever on grounds of sex in the conditions, including selection criteria, for access to all jobs or posts, whatever the sector or branch of activity, and to all levels of the occupational hierarchy.

As the ECJ stated in *Finanzamt Köln-Altstadt* v. *Schumacker* 1995,[15] discrimination can arise only through the application of different rules to comparable situations or the application of the same rule to different situations.

As the German Finance Court has stated, the legislation applicable in the main proceedings does not involve any direct discrimination since, where the same work is performed on a part-time basis, the total length of service required of persons working as case officers in the revenue administration who wish to work as tax advisers without taking the examination is extended in exactly the same way for men as for women. It should therefore be determined whether a measure of that kind may amount to indirect discrimination.

The ECJ has consistently held that indirect discrimination arises where a national measure, albeit formulated in neutral terms, works to the disadvantage of far more women than men.[16] In that regard, it cannot be denied that measures such as those at issue in the main proceedings have an impact on part-time employees and place them at a disadvantage by comparison with those who work full time. To gain exemption from the qualifying examination, part-time employees must work several years longer than full time employees.

Moreover, the order for reference discloses that 92.4% of executive-grade employees working on a part-time basis in the Bremen revenue administration are women. In those circumstances, measures such as those at issue in the main proceedings give rise in practice to discrimination against women as compared with men and must in principle be regarded as contrary to the Directive. The position would be different only if the distinction between those two categories of employee were justified by factors unrelated to any discrimination on grounds of sex.[17]

---

15 Case C-279/93 (1995) ECR I-225 in para. 30.

16 See, to that effect, Case C-444/93 *Megner and Scheffel* v. *Innungskrankenkasse Rheinhessen-Pfalz* 1995 ECR I-4741, para. 24, and Case C-343/92 *De Weerd* 1994 ECR I-571, para. 33.

17 [17] See *inter alia* Case 170/84 *Bilka* v. *Weber von Hartz* (1986) ECR 1607, para. 29; Case 171/88 *Rinner-Kühn* (1989) ECR 2743, para. 12; and Case C-457/93 *Kuratorium für*

It is for the national court, which alone has jurisdiction to assess the facts and interpret the national legislation, to determine in the light of all the circumstances whether, and to what extent, a legislative provision which, although applying irrespective of gender, actually affects a greater number of women than men is justified by objective reasons unrelated to any discrimination on grounds of sex.[18] The defendant took the view that qualification as a tax adviser following exemption from the professional examination must be regarded as a possibility available by way of exception solely to persons who, through the performance of certain work over a specified length of time, are certain at least to have gained sufficient experience. The Senator thus maintained that the expertise necessary to enter that profession without taking the examination can only be acquired through employment, the length of which has been prescribed independently of individual cases and with the same implications for all applicants.

Mrs Kording, on the other hand, maintained that the variety of tasks and the quality of the work carried out by part-time employees are comparable to those of full time employees. The only difference lies in the volume of work handled.

In the *Nimz* case 1991 (paragraph 14), as we have seen above, the Court took the view that it is impossible to identify objective criteria unrelated to any discrimination on grounds of sex on the basis of an alleged special link between length of service and acquisition of a certain level of knowledge or experience, since such a claim amounts to no more than a generalization concerning certain categories of workers. Although experience goes hand in hand with length of service, and experience enables the worker in principle to improve performance of the tasks allotted to him, the objectivity of such a criterion depends on all the circumstances in each individual case, and in particular on the relationship between the nature of the work performed and the experience gained from the performance of that work upon completion of a certain number of working hours.

Furthermore, the German Finance Court had already found that the national law, as originally worded, made the exemption of revenue administration officials from the qualifying examination conditional on their having acquired, over the ten years preceding departure from the revenue service, five years experience in tax matters.

Mrs Kording stated in the proceedings before the national court, without being contradicted by the Finance Senator, that in 1972 the length of experience required had been extended from five to fifteen years in order to discourage the tendency among officials to enter private practice. Thus the legislative amendment was not based on considerations relating to qualifications.

Dialyse und Nierentransplantation v. *Lewark* (1996) ECR I-243, para. 31.

18 See Case 96/80 *Jenkins* v. *Kingsgate* 1981 ECR 911, para. 14; *Bilka*, para. 36; and *Rinner-Kühn*, para. 15.

In situations of this kind, where a part-time employee is treated less favourably than a full time employee, measures such as those applicable in the main proceedings give rise to indirect discrimination against women employees if substantially fewer men than women work part-time; the measures in question are therefore contrary to Article 3 (1) of the Directive. However, such inequality of treatment would be compatible with that provision if it were justified by objective factors unrelated to any discrimination on grounds of sex.

The answer to the question referred to the Court must therefore be that Article 3 (1) of the Directive precludes, in cases where far more women will be affected than men, national legislation which provides that, in the case of part-time employment involving working hours of no less than one-half of normal working hours, the total length of professional experience required for exemption from the qualifying examination for tax advisers is to be extended on a *pro rata* basis, save where such legislation is justified by objective factors unrelated to any discrimination on grounds of sex.

The *Kording* case is recorded here in such great detail because it should have served as a precedent in the case of *Katharina Rinke* v. *Aertztekammer Hamburg* 2003[19]. This case questions the legality not of national law, but rather of the EU requirement to complete a number of periods of full time training in order to qualify as a general medical practitioner, as laid down in Council Directive 93/16/EEC of 5 April 1993, (thereby facilitating the free movement of doctors and the mutual recognition of their diplomas, certificates and other evidence of formal qualifications), as it indirectly discriminates against women and violates Council Directive 76/207/EEC on the implementation of the principle of equal treatment for men and women. The question arises as to whether the prohibition of discrimination on grounds of sex constitutes a basic unwritten right under Community law that overrides any conflicting rule in secondary legislation.

Mrs Rinke has argued that the requirement affects a considerably higher percentage of women than men and that there is therefore indirect discrimination. She noted that experience shows that a higher percentage of women than men take advantage of the possibility of undertaking part-time training. The average age upon completion of basic medical training is approximately 28. For women this coincides with the age at which they have to give serious consideration as to whether or not to have children. Further training lasts three to five years. This is the period during which most women have their first child (or children). Since the necessary practical experience cannot be acquired on a part-time basis, this group is essentially denied access to this profession. That is because the part-time training which has been completed is not recognised and therefore they are unable to establish themselves in practice as general medical practitioners.

---

19 Case C-25/02 (2003) ECR I-8349.

Eurostat statistics show that part-time work is performed mainly by women. The statistics from 2001 onwards show that one third of working women work part-time compared to 6% of working men. They also show that in countries in which the percentage of part-time working women is low, this fact reflects an obstacle to access to the labour market.

The average age at which women in the EU have children is 28. Moreover, in all the Member States of the EU women spend considerably more time than men looking after children. Women aged between 20 and 49 spend an average of 45 hours or more a week looking after children whilst men spend well under 30 hours a week doing so (the EU average is 22 hours). Not only do women devote more time to childcare, it also has a bearing on whether or not they go out to work and whether they work full or part-time. The combination of childcare and work usually means that women work part-time whereas men at most work a few hours less in a full time job. Around 37% of women aged between 20 and 49 who look after children and work part-time work less than 30 hours a week. That is twice as many as women in the same age group who have no children or at least no childcare responsibilities.

In the *Rinke* case there is a requirement that postgraduate training be undertaken full time. Therefore, the effect of lowering barriers specific to women disappears. Consequently, this requirement affects women in relatively larger numbers than men.

The fact that this case concerns a training requirement makes the effects of the indirect discrimination on the disadvantaged group more serious than if it concerned a requirement to exercise a function or profession full time. The training requirement means that a barrier may arise to entry to the profession concerned. The disadvantaged group is affected not only as regards the pursuit of a chosen career but also as regards the opportunities to embark upon a particular career.

The principle of equal treatment for men and women in the labour market laid down and developed in Article 141 EC and the secondary law based thereon, including Directive 76/207, constitutes a specific case of the fundamental principle of the equality of men and women in the labour market. In its established case law the Court has regarded this principle as a fundamental right. Therefore, it follows that in drafting and developing its secondary law the Community legislature must at all times consider whether that secondary law is consistent with this fundamental legal principle.

The German Federal Administrative Court referred the following question to the ECJ:

> "Does the requirement laid down in Directives 86/457/EEC and 93/16/EEC, to the effect that certain components of the specific training in general medical practice-completion of which confers the right to use the title general medical practitioner-must be undertaken full time,

> constitute indirect discrimination on grounds of sex within the meaning of Directive 76/207/EEC."

The ECJ stated that:

> "It is clear from the statistical data referred to by the Advocate General (at points 36 and 37 of his Opinion) that the percentage of women working part-time is much higher than that of men working on a part-time basis. That fact, which can be explained in particular by the unequal division of domestic tasks between women and men, shows that a much higher percentage of women than men wishing to train in general medicine have difficulties in working full time during part of their training. Thus, such a requirement does in fact place women at a particular disadvantage as compared with men."

The Court did not ignore this reality and yet it produced an unexpected ruling validating the discriminatory provisions of Article 5 (1) of Council Directive 86/457/EEC of 15 September 1986 on specific training in general medical practice and Article 34 (1) of Council Directive 93/16/EEC of 5 April 1993 to facilitate the free movement of doctors and the mutual recognition of their diplomas, certificates and other evidence of formal qualifications, according to which part-time training in general medical practice must include a certain number of periods of full time training.

The Court refused to admit that the two Directives are incompatible with the Equal Treatment Directive and that indirect discrimination violates a fundamental human right that the Court is bound to respect as a higher norm. The objective reasons for the justification of discrimination in the *Rinke* case were too pale and disproportionate to the higher aim of equality of treatment.

The Court at the same time did not follow its own previous case law when dealing with part-time workers' indirect discrimination in similar (though not identical) cases, especially the *Kording* case, 1997, decided six years earlier. Not unlike the *Rinke* case, the *Kording* case deals with a qualification for access to a profession.

It is to be regretted that the ECJ did not follow the excellent opinion of Advocate General Geelhoed. Moreover, no reference whatsoever was made to the aims of the Directive on Part-Time Work 1997 that entered into force some three years before the ruling. The Directive applies to part-time work, but may also be interpreted to apply to practical work that is qualifying for access to a profession.

Unlike the *Rinke* case, the case of *Erika Steinicke* v. *Bundesanstalt für Arbeit* 2003[20] referred to the Framework Agreement on Part-Time Work. The ECJ ad-

[20] Case C-77/02 (2003) ECR I-9027.

dressed the interpretation of Article 141 EC and of Council Directives 75/117/EEC on the approximation of the laws of the Member States relating to the application of the principles of equal pay for men and women and 76/207/EEC on the implementation of the principle of equal treatment for men and women as regards access to employment, vocational training and promotion and working conditions as well as Directive 97/81/EC 1997 concerning the Framework Agreement on Part-Time Work concluded by UNICE, CEEP and the ETUC.

The Court ruled that:

> "Articles 2 (1) and 5 (1) of Council Directive 76/207/EEC of 9 February 1976 on the implementation of the principle of equal treatment for men and women as regards access to employment, vocational training and promotion, and working conditions must be interpreted as precluding a national provision, by virtue of which part-time work for older employees may be authorised for public servants only if they have worked full time for a total of at least three of the five years preceding such part-time work, when significantly more women than men work part-time and are consequently excluded by that provision from the scheme of part-time work for older employees, unless such provision is justified by objective factors unrelated to any discrimination on grounds of sex."

The consequence of this ruling is that older women who worked only part-time will nevertheless be authorised to continue to work in the public service as part-time workers. The German provision which excludes part-time workers who have not satisfied the requirement of working three years as full timers violates EU law.

This last case may also be classified as one that comes within the group of discriminatory exclusions from certain conditions of work to which we turn now.

Exclusion from Certain Grants or from Other Conditions of Work

It may be recalled that in the *Bilka* case 1986, discussed above in Chapter 6, the part-time employee was excluded from an occupational pension scheme based on a contractual agreement between the employer and the employees. The plaintiff claimed she was indirectly discriminated on the basis of sex. The Court ruled that Article 119 of the Treaty is infringed by an undertaking which excludes part-time employees from its occupational pension scheme, where that exclusion affects a far greater number of women than men, unless the undertaking shows that the exclusion is based on objective grounds.[21] The exclusion of part-time employees from a severance grant on termination was the topic of the preliminary ruling

[21] See also *Dietz* Case 1996 Case C-435/93 (1996) ECR I-5223.

in the case of *Maria Kowalska 1990*, already mentioned earlier, where the ECJ gave the following ruling:

> "(1) Article 119 of the EEC Treaty is to be interpreted as precluding the application of a clause in a collective wage agreement applying to the national public service under which employers may exclude part-time employees from the payment of a severance grant on termination of their employment when in fact a considerably lower percentage of men than of women work part-time, unless the employer shows that the exclusion is based on objectively justified factors unrelated to any discrimination on grounds of sex.
>
> (2) Where there is indirect discrimination in a clause in a collective wage agreement, the class of persons placed at a disadvantage by reason of that discrimination must be treated in the same way and made subject to the same scheme, proportionately to the number of hours worked, as other workers, such scheme remaining, for want of correct transposition of Article 119 of the EEC Treaty into national law, the only valid point of reference."

The Court applied in this case the *pro rata* principle with regard to a payment of a severance grant on termination of part-time work.

In the circumstances of the *Rinner-Kuehn* 1989[22] case the exclusion of a part-time employee from the receipt of wages during incapacity to work was considered a practice amounting to sex discrimination.

The German law on the continued payment of wages (*Lohnfortzahlungsgesetz*) of 27 July 1969 provides that an employer must continue to pay wages for a period of up to six weeks to any employee who, after the commencement of his employment and through no fault of his own, is incapable of working. However, employees whose contract of employment provides for a normal period of work of not more than 10 hours a week or 45 hours a month are excluded from the benefit of that provision.

On the basis of that provision and with reference to the fact that Mrs Rinner-Kuehn normally worked ten hours a week, her employer refused to pay her for a period of eight hours in which she was absent owing to illness.

Mrs Rinner-Kuehn appealed against that decision to the Labour Court in Oldenburg, seeking the continued payment of her wages during the absence caused by her illness. The national court considered that her application raised issues concerning the interpretation of Article 119 of the EEC Treaty and of Directive 75/117. It therefore stayed the proceedings and referred the following

[22] Case 171/88 (1989) ECR 2743.

question to the Court of Justice for a preliminary ruling. The Court followed the *Bilka* precedent and declared that:

> "Article 119 of the EEC Treaty must be interpreted as precluding national legislation which permits employers to exclude employees whose normal working hours do not exceed 10 hours a week or 45 hours a month from the continued payment of wages in the event of illness, if that measure affects a far greater number of women than men, unless the Member State shows that the legislation concerned is justified by objective factors unrelated to any discrimination on grounds of sex."

Another case of discriminatory exclusions of part-time workers is that of *Shirley Preston and Others* 2000.[23] The ECJ was consistent in its preliminary rulings in these cases.

Promotion

The issue of the calculation of length of service of a part-time worker for the purpose of promotion arose in the case of *Hellen Gerster* v. *Bavaria* 1997.[24]The provision of German law at issue in the main proceedings does not discriminate directly, since the method of calculating length of service in the case of part-time employees is not determined by gender. It is therefore necessary to consider whether such a provision may constitute indirect discrimination.

According to settled case law,[25] indirect discrimination arises where a national measure, although formulated in neutral terms, works to the disadvantage of far more women than men.

As we have seen, according to German law, part-time employees whose working hours exceed two-thirds of normal working hours are deemed to have worked full time for the purposes of calculating their length of service. Likewise, part-time employees whose working hours amount to at least one-half of normal working hours are regarded as working two-thirds of normal working hours. On the other hand, if the proportion of hours worked is any lower than one-half, those hours are totally disregarded for the purposes of calculating length of service. Accordingly, it is common ground that the provision of national law at issue in the main proceedings treats part-time employees less favourably than

---

23 Case C-78/98 (2000) ECR I-3201. See also *Deutsche Post AG* joint cases C-270/97 and C-271/97 (2000) ECR I-929) as well as *Deutsche Telekom AG* v. *Lilli Schroder* 2000 C-50/96 (2000) ECR I-799.

24 Case C-1/95 (1997) ECR I-5253.

25 See, to that effect, Case C-444/93 *Megner and Scheffel* v. *Innungskrankenkasse Rheinhessen-Pfalz 1995* ECR I-4741, para. 24; and Case C-343/92 *De Weerd (née Roks) and Others* 1994 ECR I-571, para. 33.

full time employees, since the former accrue length of service more slowly, they perforce gain promotion later.

Mrs Gerster maintains that, in the department where she completed her period of service, 87% of part-time employees are women. According to the national court's findings, this percentage reflects the situation across the board in the Bavarian civil service.

In a situation of that kind, it must be concluded that in practice provisions such as those at issue in the main proceedings result in discrimination against women employees as compared with men and must in principle be regarded as contrary to Directive 76/207. The position would be different only if the distinction between those two categories of employee were justified by factors unrelated to any discrimination on grounds of sex.[26] The Court has consistently held that it is for the national court, which alone has jurisdiction to assess the facts and interpret the national legislation, to determine in the light of all the circumstances whether, and to what extent, a legislative provision which, although applying irrespective of gender, actually affects a greater number of women than men, is justified by objective reasons unrelated to any discrimination on grounds of sex.[27]

According to the Bavarian State, the discrimination is objectively justified since the system is based on the administration's need to establish a general yardstick in terms of length of service against which the professional experience of employees can be assessed before they can be regarded as eligible for promotion to a higher grade. The Bavarian State maintains that civil servants who work part-time need to complete longer periods of service than those who work full time, if they are to acquire the professional skills and abilities necessary for duties at a higher level.

Mrs Gerster, on the other hand, argued that in her capacity as a part-time employee she had performed, in the course of the last 10 years of her professional life, duties attached to the grade to which she aspired to be promoted.

On that point, it should first be noted that, according to the Bavarian Administrative Court, the defendant stated that the amendment made to the German Law in 1995 was "intended to assist in making working life more compatible with family life". The protection of women – and men – both in family life and in the workplace is a principle broadly accepted in the legal systems of the Member

---

26 See *inter alia* Case 170/84 *Bilka* v. *Weber von Hartz* (1986) ECR 1607, para. 29; Case 171/88 *Rinner-Kühn* v. *FWW Spezial-Gebäudereinigung* (1989) ECR 2743, para. 12; and Case C-457/93 *Kuratorium für Dialyse und Nierentransplantation* v. *Lewark* (1996) ECR I-243, para. 31.

27 See *Jenkins* v. *Kingsgate* (1981) ECR 911, para. 14; Bilka, para. 36, and *Rinner-Kühn*, para. 15.

States as a natural corollary of the fact that men and women are equal, and is upheld by Community law.

It may be recalled that, in the *Nimz* case, the Court took the view that it is impossible to identify objective criteria unrelated to any discrimination on the basis of an alleged special link between length of service and acquisition of a certain level of knowledge or experience, since such a claim amounts to no more than a generalization concerning certain categories of worker. Although experience goes hand in hand with length of service, and experience enables the worker in principle to improve performance of the tasks allotted to him, the objectivity of such a criterion depends on all the circumstances in each individual case, and in particular on the relationship between the nature of the work performed and the experience gained from the performance of that work upon completion of a certain number of working hours. If the national court is satisfied that the competent authorities are in a position to establish that the measures chosen reflect a legitimate social policy aim, and are an appropriate means of achieving that aim and are necessary in order to do so, the mere fact that the legislative provision affects far more women than men cannot be regarded as an infringement of the Equal Treatment Directive 1976.

On the other hand, if the national court concludes that there is no special link between length of service and acquisition of a certain level of knowledge or experience, the requirement laid down in German law to the effect that part-time employees must complete a period of service more than one-third longer than that completed by a full time official in order to have approximately the same chance of promotion must be regarded as contrary to the provisions of the Directive.

Dismissal and Collective Redundancies

In the case of *Barbel Kachelmann* 2000,[28] Ms Kachelmann was employed by Bankhaus from 1 April 1991 as a qualified banker with certified German/English bilingual drafting skills. She was responsible for managing cases in the Recovery Department of the documentary transactions section of the Hamburg branch. She was employed on a part-time basis for 30 hours a week (76.92%); the number of working hours fixed by the collective agreement for full time work was 38 hours per week.

Owing to a reduction in the volume of its international activities, Bankhaus decided to merge its Recovery Department, which until then had been separate, with the rest of the documentary transactions section. That involved a partial reallocation of duties. Taking the view that it had excess staff, Bankhaus, by letter of 21 June 1996, gave Ms Kachelmann notice of dismissal on economic

28 Case C-322/98 (2000) ECR I-7505.

grounds with effect from 30 September 1996. Ms Kachelmann contested her dismissal before the Labour Court, Hamburg. She claims that, during the process leading to her being given notice of dismissal on economic grounds, Bankhaus did not make a selection on the basis of social criteria from amongst all workers performing the same duties. It did not compare Ms Kachelmann, who was working 30 hours a week, with full time workers working 38 hours a week, even though she had stated, before she was given notice of dismissal, that she would be willing to work on a full time basis.

By judgment of 18 February 1997 the Labour Court dismissed Ms Kachelmann's claim. It found that she could not be transferred to a full time post without amendment of her employment contract, so that her job and those of the full time workers were not comparable. Nor was Bankhaus under a duty to increase Ms Kachelmann's hours of work by amending her employment contract so that they could employ her on a full time basis for the sole purpose of avoiding her dismissal.

The applicant took the view that the practice was indirectly discriminatory and therefore it was contrary to the Directive to exclude part-time workers from the category of workers from whom the employer must make a selection on the basis of social criteria when making redundancies on economic grounds. She therefore appealed to the State Labour Court in Hamburg. Where national rules, although worded in neutral terms, work to the disadvantage of a much higher percentage of women than men, they discriminate indirectly against women, unless that difference in treatment is justified by objective factors unrelated to any discrimination on grounds of sex.[29] It is well known that the number of workers employed full time in Germany, and probably throughout the Community, is significantly higher in all sectors than the number of part-time workers. It follows that, where jobs are being cut, part-time workers are in general put at a greater disadvantage because they have less chance of finding another comparable job. Consequently, lack of comparability between full time and part-time workers in the selection process based on social criteria may give rise to a difference in treatment to the detriment of part-time workers and entail an indirect disadvantage for them.

Advocate General Saggio was of the opinion that German legislation was incompatible with the Equal Treatment Directive and caused indirect sex discrimination not justified on objective grounds.

The Court however did not follow AG Saggio's reasoning and ruled that:

> "Articles 2 (1) and 5 (1) of Council Directive 76/207/EEC of 9 February 1976 on the implementation of the principle of equal treatment for men and women as regards access to employment, vocational training and promotion, and working conditions must be interpreted as not

---

[29] See, in particular, Case C-226/98 *Jørgensen* (2000) ECR I-2447, para. 29.

> precluding an interpretation of a national rule, such as that contained in Article 1 (3) of the Kündigungsschutzgesetz in the version in force until 30 September 1996, which proceeds on the general basis that part-time workers are not to be compared with full time workers when an employer has to proceed to selection on the basis of social criteria when abolishing a part-time job on economic grounds."

The ruling of the Court is discriminatory to part-time workers and indirectly discriminatory to women workers, who are far more likely to be part-time workers than men. Each dismissal or redundancy case for economic reasons must be handled in conformity with the Council Directive 98/59/EC of 20 July 1998 on the approximation of the laws of the Member States relating to Collective Redundancies.[30] Although this Directive does not address the issue of part-time workers, it does require consultation with the workers' representatives in accordance with Article 2. It is inconceivable that there was an intention to exclude part-time workers working 30 out of 38 hours from selection on the basis of social criteria.

The selection process based on social criteria should take into account personal considerations both for full time and part-time workers and, even if the premise that there is lack of comparability between the two groups is correct, part-time workers merit a selection process even *inter se*. For example, a widow with three children who is working 30 hours per week (out of 38 hours) should be kept working in preference to a single woman who works the same number of hours and indeed should also be preferred to a single man working full time.

The ECJ should have followed the reasoning of AG Saggio. On what objective grounds can a redundancy without a selection process on the basis of social criteria be justified in the case of a part-time worker? The absence of a selection process may result in discrimination and great injustice to part-time workers and to women.

The following English joint cases are presented here in order to illustrate how the U.K. Employment Appeal Tribunal prevented such an injustice and protected part-time women workers against dismissal some fifteen years before the adoption of the EU Directive on Part-Time Work. In *Clarke* v. *Eley (IMI) Kynoc Ltd. and Eley (IMI) Kynock Ltd.* v. *Powell* 1982[31] the Employment Appeal Tribunal applied a selection process on the basis of social criteria to collective redundancies discriminatory to part-time women workers. The Appeal Tribunal ordered the respondents to re-instate the part-time workers without resorting to Community law or referring the case to the ECJ.

The facts of the joint cases were as follows:

---

30 OJ (1998) L 225/16.

31 1982 IRLR 482.

The respondent company manufactured ammunition. In 1981 they got into commercial difficulties and needed to declare some of their work force redundant. In October 1981 they made redundant all 60 of their part-time workers (who were all women including Mrs Clarke and Ms Powell) as well as 20 full time men and 26 full time women. For many years the practice (with the tacit agreement of the union) had been to make part-time workers redundant first and then apply the criteria of "last in, first out" (LIFO) to full time workers.

In January 1981 this practice was written into a redundancy agreement with the consent of the social partners, excluding the part-timers. Part-timers were those whose contractual hours of work a week were less than 30. If the LIFO test had been applied to the whole work force, the two applicants would have not been made redundant.

Mrs Clarke had worked for the company since 1967. She was employed to work 25 hours a week but frequently worked longer hours. She was the breadwinner of the family. Her children were grown up and she could have for some 6 years before her redundancy opted for a full time job. Ms Powell worked 17 hours a week though sometimes more. She had worked for the company since 1975. In 1978 she had had a child and since then her domestic commitments made it impossible for her to work full time.

The Employment Appeal Tribunal took the view that "although last in first out, may have a discriminatory effect, taking (i.e. dismissing) part-time workers first is grossly discriminatory". One may add, as part-time workers are predominantly women, they are victims of indirect discrimination.

The Tribunal based its decision on national law, but arrived at a ruling in conformity with the Equal Treatment Directive. It ordered the reinstatement of the redundant part-time workers and thus awarded them the most effective remedy in a time of recession and unemployment.

Work on Demand Is Not Part-Time Work

A new type of employment contract was discussed in the case of *Nicole Wippel* v. *Peek & Cloppenburg GmbH & Co. KG.*, 2004,[32] and the applicability of the Framework Agreement on Part-time Work was tested.

The reference to the ECJ for a preliminary ruling came in the context of a dispute between Ms Wippel, who was employed part-time on the basis of a framework contract of employment based on the principle of 'work on demand', and her employer, Peek & Cloppenburg GmbH & Co. KG (P&C), concerning the absence in her contract of employment of an agreement as to hours of work and organisation of working time.

---

32 See *supra*, note 2.

In June 2000, Ms Wippel brought proceedings before the Labour and Social Court, Vienna, claiming that P&C should pay to her the amount of EUR 11,929.23, together with costs and ancillary amounts. She maintained that P&C was liable to her for the difference between the amount due in respect of the maximum hours of work that could have been demanded of her and the actual number of hours which she worked. Ms Wippel asserted that the maximum monthly working time should have constituted the basis for calculating her remuneration for each of the months during which she worked for P&C.

Regarding the consent of the employees to the arrangement, she maintained that the only part played by workers was to reply 'yes' or 'no' to work offered to them. There was therefore no question of a 'consensus' and the contract of employment with P&C was *contra bonos mores*. If a worker employed under this scheme was not used for some time, the employer, P&C, would have virtually no liability for holiday pay, sick pay and termination payments. Ms Wippel also claimed that the absence in her contract of employment of an agreement as to working hours and the organisation of working time constituted discrimination on the ground of sex.

Clause 3 (1) of the Framework Agreement on Part-Time Work 1997, defines "part-time worker" as an employee:

> "whose normal hours of work, calculated on a weekly basis or on average over a period of employment of up to one year, are less than the normal hours of work of a comparable full time worker."

Clause 4 of the Framework Agreement on part-time work provides *inter alia*:

> "In respect of employment conditions, part-time workers shall not be treated in a less favourable manner than comparable full time workers solely because they work part-time unless different treatment is justified on objective grounds."

The Grand Chamber of the Court ruled that:

> "in circumstances where all the contracts of employment of the other employees of an undertaking make provision for the length of weekly working time and for the organisation of working time, they do not preclude a contract of part-time employment of workers of the same undertaking, such as that in the main proceedings, under which the length of weekly working time and the organisation of working time are not fixed but are dependent on quantitative needs in terms of work to be performed determined on a case-by-case basis, such workers being entitled to accept or refuse that work."

In essence the Court concluded that "work on demand" does not come under the Directive on Part-Time Work.

Conclusion

The provisions of the Part-Time Work Directive 1997 are similar to those of the ILO Part-Time Work Convention No. 175 of 1994. Both instruments aim at the protection of part-time workers against discrimination and thereby are indirectly protecting women workers against indirect discrimination.

The *pro rata temporis* principle is adopted to apply proportionate treatment between full time and part-time workers, not only as far as pay is considered, but also in all conditions of work, including access to a profession, on the one hand, and dismissal and redundancy, on the other hand.

The only justifiable disparity, according to both instruments, must be based on objective reasons that are not related to sex or to part-time work *per se*. These objective reasons should be pleaded and proved before the national judicial authorities by the employer to the satisfaction of the national courts.

Both the ILO and the EU aim to entitle part-time workers to *pro rata* bonuses, maternity allowances, separation allowances, sick leave, etc. allowing for low thresholds and not permitting the exclusion of part-time workers from certain benefits unless their working hours per week or month fall below 10 hours or less, according to national law or collective agreements. These two recent legal instruments will establish fairness and equality in a domain where women occupy 80% of the workforce. As part-time work is dominated by women, they stand to benefit from the standards of Convention No. 175 and from the Directive on Part-time Work.

Examining the contribution of the ECJ to the interpretation and application of EU Law, we find that a majority of the cases that came to the Court by way of requests for preliminary rulings originated in Germany, where legislation governing the public sector, and more particularly, collective wage agreements, included provisions allowing for indirect discrimination of women workers. Germany has not as yet ratified ILO Convention No. 175 on Part-Time Work 1994.

The ECJ in about 20 cases emphasized that EU law does not tolerate and indeed precludes national provisions that discriminate, albeit indirectly, women part-time workers, unless the employer can prove objective reasons unrelated to sex, to justify the disparity before the national court. Most indirect discrimination, where a neutral criteria affects to a greater extent women than men, occurs in the context of part-time work.

There is complete harmony between the ILO Part-Time Work Convention No. 175 of 1994 and the EU Directive of 1997. The Convention addresses the question of thresholds and the Directive only implicitly deals with thresholds when it provides for the possible exclusion of certain categories of part-time workers for objective reasons.

The interpretation and application of the EU provisions by the ECJ in its rich case law also conforms to the spirit of the ILO standards. The authors have found only two cases, the *Kachelmann* case 2000 and the *Rinke* case 2003 that are subject to criticism. The *Wippel* case that originated in Austria and involved an atypical contract of "work on demand" was not considered an ordinary part-time case falling under the Directive. Work on demand therefore does not enjoy the same protection as part-time work.

It is now established that part-time work enjoys a *pro-rata* relationship to full time work. However, maternity and injury are accorded full protection and remuneration and compensation are not based upon a *pro-rata* basis.

The burden of proof is on the employer to show that in case of disparity of pay or other conditions of work inequality is due to objective reasons entirely unrelated to sex discrimination.

The protection and promotion of part-time work goes hand in hand with the possibility of reconciling professional and family life in the spirit of ILO Convention No. 156 on Workers with Family Responsibilities.[33] The question remains whether part-time workers are granted a right not to be treated less favourably than comparable full time workers or is this right limited on the ground that disparity is justified on objective grounds other than their part-time status? The ECJ became aware of the need to keep the defence of objective justification within strict bounds as befits an exception.[34] The Court, however, decided in an empiric and pragmatic fashion on a case by case basis and left the question of the validity of objective reasons to the national courts that are nearer to the facts.

---

33 See also D. Meulders and B. Tytgat, "The Emergence of Atypical Employment in the European Community", in G. and J. Rodgers (eds), *Precarious Jobs in Labour Market Regulation: The Growth of Atypical Employment in Western Europe* (International Institute for Labour Studies. Brussels), at p. 181.

34 See also B. Hepple, "Equality and Discrimination", in *Liber Amicorum Lord Wedderburn*, (Clarendon Oxford Press, 1996), at p. 251 *et seq.*

Chapter 12

THE BURDEN OF PROOF AND INDIRECT DISCRIMINATION

Background

Although the question of burden of proof as such was not dealt with directly by the ILO, on the EU level the issue is quite relevant in the implementation of the law of equality and non-discrimination. Whilst the ILO has not elaborated any separate standard in the form of a Convention or a Recommendation on the shifting of the burden of proof in cases of sex discrimination, it nevertheless provided for the exception of objective reasons that the employer can resort to in order to justify a disparity in pay or treatment in all conditions of work and refute discrimination based on sex.

It is therefore appropriate to devote a chapter to the subject and examine the provisions of the EU Directive on the Burden of Proof 1997,[1] as well as the case law of the Court of Justice.

EU Legislation

The general principle with regard to the burden of proof in litigation is that it lies with the plaintiff:-*actori incumbit probatio.* However, this principle presents insurmountable problems in discrimination cases. The relevant documents are generally in the possession of the employer, while forms of indirect discrimination are by nature difficult to prove. To solve this problem the European Commission and the European Parliament considered that the burden of proof should be reversed. Under this proposal the plaintiff only has to establish "presumed discrimination". It would then be up to the employer (the defendant) to refute this presumption by proving that the principle of equal treatment has not been violated or that there were objective reasons, unrelated to sex, to justify it.

1 Directive 97/80, OJ (1998) L 14/6.

On 5 July 1995 the Commission submitted to the social partners a text based in particular on the case law of the ECJ. After consulting management and labour for the second time on 7 February 1996, the Commission clearly decided to present a new directive which aimed to adjust the burden of proof rather than reverse it completely.

Council Directive 97/80 on the Burden of Proof in Cases of Discrimination based on Sex was adopted on 15 December 1997. Recitals 18 and 19 of the Preamble explain the importance and aim of the Directive:

> "(18) Whereas the Court of Justice of the European Communities has therefore held that the rules on the burden of proof must be adapted when there is a *prima facie* case of discrimination and that, for the principle of equal treatment to be applied effectively, the burden of proof must shift back to the respondent when evidence of such discrimination is brought;
>
> (19) Whereas it is all the more difficult to prove discrimination when it is indirect; whereas it is therefore important to define indirect discrimination …"

The aim is to ensure that the measures taken by the Member States to implement the principle of equal treatment are made more effective, so all persons who consider themselves wronged because the principle of equal treatment has not been applied to them can claim their rights by judicial process after possible recourse to other competent bodies.

Definitions

Article 2 of the Directive provides certain definitions that were empirically elaborated by the ECJ in its case law but now are enshrined in a written legal text:

> "1. For the purposes of this Directive, the principle of equal treatment shall mean that there shall be no discrimination whatsoever based on sex, either directly or indirectly.
>
> 2. For purposes of the principle of equal treatment referred to in paragraph 1, indirect discrimination shall exist where an apparently neutral provision, criterion or practice disadvantages a substantially higher proportion of the members of one sex unless that provision, criterion or practice is appropriate and necessary and can be justified by objective factors unrelated to sex."

Article 3 defines the scope of the Directive to include:

> "(a) the situations covered by Article 119 of the Treaty now Article 141, and by Directives 75/117/EEC, 76/207/EEC and, insofar as

discrimination based on sex is concerned, 92/85/EEC and 96/34/EC.

(b) any civil or administrative procedure concerning the public or private sector which provides for means of redress under national law pursuant to the measures referred to in (a) with the exception of out-of-court procedures of a voluntary nature or provided for in national law."

Article 4 provides for the plaintiff to establish a presumption of discrimination and for the respondent (the employer) the burden of rebutting the presumption.

"1. Member States shall take such measures as are necessary, in accordance with their national judicial systems, to ensure that, when persons who consider themselves wronged because the principle of equal treatment has not been applied to them establish, before a court or other competent authority, facts from which it may be presumed that there has been direct or indirect discrimination, it shall be for the respondent to prove that there has been no breach of the principle of equal treatment.

2. This Directive shall not prevent Member States from introducing rules of evidence which are more favourable to plaintiff."

Workers only have to consider themselves wronged and supply evidence leading to a presumption of direct discrimination or less favourable treatment. A claim to apparent discrimination enables them to go to court and have the burden of proof reversed against the employer, who would have to prove that there has been no discrimination or that the discrimination is justified by objective reasons that have nothing to do with the person's sex. The Directive entered into force on 1 January 2001. The definition of indirect discrimination was gleaned from the decisions made over the years by the ECJ, often, in cases of discrimination in the context of part-time work, where a substantially higher proportion of women were affected, as discussed in Chapter 11.

EU Case Law

The issue of the burden of proof arose in the *Danfoss* case 1989.[2] A collective agreement between a staff union and an employers' association provided for the same basic minimum wage for all workers in the same pay category. The grading was based on a job classification. However, the collective agreement allowed the employing company to grant additional payments to individual employees of the

---

2 Case 109/88 (1989) ECR 3199.

same category for flexibility, vocational training and seniority. The pay system discriminated women in that their pay was lower by almost 7% than the pay of men within the same category.

The ECJ was requested to give a preliminary ruling on the question of the burden of proof as regards the claim of a violation of the principle of equal pay. The Court held that:

> "where an undertaking applies a system of pay which is totally lacking in transparency, it is for the employer to prove that his practice in the matter of wages is not discriminatory, if a female worker establishes, in relation to a relatively large number of employees, that the average pay for women is less than for men."[3]

The Court advocated the reversal of the burden of proof to ensure effectiveness in the implementation of the principle of equal pay and to render the system of pay more transparent.

In *Enderby* v. *Frenchay Health Authority* 1993,[4] discussed in Chapter 6 in relation to a claim for equal pay for work of equal value, the issue of the reversal of the burden of proof also arose. A speech therapist employed by the local National Health Authority brought an action for sex discrimination, in that speech therapists, who were almost all women, were paid less than the mostly male clinical psychologists and pharmacists, who performed work of equal value.

The Court ruled that the existence of a *prima facie* case of discrimination shifts the burden of proving objective justification to the employer:

> "Where significant statistics disclose an appreciable difference in pay between two jobs of equal value, one of which is carried out almost exclusively by women and the other predominantly by men, Article 119 of the Treaty requires the employer to show that that difference is based on objectively justified factors unrelated to any discrimination on grounds of sex."

In *Brunnhofer* v. *Bank der Oesterreichischen Postsparkasse AG* 2001[5] a claim for equal pay came before the Austrian Court. The latter requested a preliminary ruling from the ECJ, on the burden of proof and other matters. The Court clearly differentiated between the burden of proof placed on the plaintiff to show a *prima facie* case, and the burden of proof placed on the defendant to dispute the claim or to give an objective justification for the disparity:

---

3 At p. 3225.

4 Case C-127/92 (1993) ECR I-5525.

5 Case C-381/99 (2001) ECR I-4961.

> "As a general rule, it is for employees who consider themselves to be the victims of discrimination to prove that they are receiving lower pay than that paid by the employer to a colleague of the other sex and that they are in fact performing the same work or work of equal value, comparable to that performed by the chosen comparator; the employer may then not only dispute the fact that the conditions for the application of the principle of equal pay for men and women are met in the case but also put forward objective grounds, unrelated to any discrimination based on sex, to justify the difference in pay."

Once a plaintiff satisfies the court that there is *a prima facie* case of discrimination, the defendant has the burden of showing either that there was no violation of the principle of equal pay or that there were objective reasons to justify the disparity in pay.

Unlike the cases discussed so far concerning discrimination with regard to equal pay, *Vasiliki Nikoloudi* v. *Organismos Tilepikoinonion Ellados AE* 2005[6] concerns equal treatment in all conditions of work. The ruling of the ECJ referred to the Burden of Proof Directive for the first time after its adoption.

In this case part-time women employees working as cleaners were denied the possibility of appointment as established members of staff. They claimed that a much higher percentage of women than men was affected the provisions of the relevant collective agreements excluding them from staff status. The exclusion of the appointment of part-time temporary staff as established staff constitutes indirect discrimination.

The Court ruled that once the plaintiffs proved this situation to be the case:

> "such a situation is contrary to Article 3 of Directive 76/207 unless the difference of treatment between these workers and those working full time is justified by factors unrelated to any discrimination on grounds of sex. It is for the national court to determine whether that is the case."

The Court added that:

> "3. Where the total exclusion of part-time employment when calculating length of service affects a much higher percentage of female workers than male workers, it constitutes indirect discrimination on grounds of sex contrary to Directive 76/207, unless that exclusion is attributable to factors which are objectively justified and are unrelated to any discrimination on grounds of sex. It is for the national court to determine whether that is the case. The proportional counting of part-time employment when making that calculation is also contrary to Directive 76/207, unless the employer establishes that it is justified by factors whose objectivity

6 Case C-196/02 (2005) ECR I-1789.

depends in particular on the aim pursued by taking length of service into account and, should it be a question of recognition of experience acquired, on the relationship between the nature of the duties carried out and the experience which performance of those duties brings after a certain number of hours of work have been completed.

4. Where employees plead that the principle of equal treatment has been infringed to their detriment and establish facts from which it may be presumed that there has been direct or indirect discrimination. Community law, in particular Directive 97/80, is to be interpreted as meaning that it shall be for the respondent to prove that there has been no breach of that principle."

The burden of proof thus shifts to the employer once a presumption of direct or indirect discrimination is established by the employee in all claims of unequal pay or unequal treatment in conditions of work, coming within the scope of Article 3 of the Directive on the Burden of Proof 1997.

Conclusion

As we saw in Chapter 11 when dealing with indirect discrimination, the importance of the shifting of the burden of proof to the stronger party to the dispute recreates a balance and restores the equality of the parties before the law, which is a guarantee to a fair trial. Indirect discrimination is a natural consequence of discrimination of part-time workers, since many more women are involved than men. By the very definition of indirect discrimination, women are the victims, as they are more affected by the disparity between part-time workers and full time workers, part-time workers consisting mainly of women.

The shifting of the burden of proof permits the employer to justify the discrimination for objective reasons unconnected with sex. This allows for extra-legal considerations and the rule of market forces, recognised also by the ILO. The ECJ often leaves the decision as to the validity of the objective reasons to be decided by the national judge, who is admittedly nearer to the facts.

Both the Directive on the Burden of Proof and the Directive on Part-time Work have undergone a legislative history which is closer to the practice of the ILO. These Directives originated in Framework Agreements between the social partners, very much like the elaboration of ILO standards through the tripartite method of consultation and collaboration.

If the ECJ succeeds in giving the upper hand to considerations of equality, then the two exceptions of objective reasons and of the inherent requirement of a job, as laid down both by the ILO Conventions and the EU Directives, should be given strict interpretations, as befits exceptions.

As we have seen, Article 4 (2) of the Directive on the Burden of Proof highlights the shifting of the burden of proof as a minimum norm and Member States are free to protect plaintiffs further by the adoption of rules of evidence in their favour: "The Directive shall not prevent Member States from introducing rules of evidence which are more favourable to the plaintiff."

Chapter 13

The Dignity of the Worker: Sexual Harassment

Background

The issue of sexual harassment at work became a public concern originally in North America, which led to administrative regulations and judicial recognition that sexual harassment is part of sex discrimination and thus condemned under relevant anti-discrimination acts or regulations.

This process then reached Europe, when a report submitted to the Commission of the EC in 1987 gave evidence of the reality and scope of the problem and made a number of recommendations to the EU and its Member States.[1]

The report linked the risk of sexual harassment to the victim's vulnerability on the basis of a survey conducted in Belgium: although any woman can be subjected to sexual harassment, the researchers found that unmarried, divorced or separated women, young women, and women working in traditionally male jobs were at special risk. Both the Belgian survey and research carried out in the Netherlands made clear that sexual harassment is linked with work status, as it is disproportionately perpetrated by male supervisors or managers upon female subordinates – it is a reflection of power. A survey in Spain found that 84 per cent of the women questioned had experienced some form of what they regarded as sexual harassment. In another Dutch study, 58 per cent of the women said that they had been sexually harassed. The Rubenstein report concluded from these and other surveys in Europe that "for millions of women in the EEC today, sexual harassment is an unpleasant and unavoidable part of their working lives". As its consequences, he wrote that:

> "Sexual harassment pollutes the working environment and can have a devastating effect upon the health and safety of those affected by

---

1 Michael Rubenstein, "The Dignity of Women at Work: A Report on the Problem of Sexual Harassment in the Member States of the European Communities", Part II: Appendix, October 1987 (Commission of the European Communities, Doc. V/412/1/87-EN).

> it. It imposes costs upon employers impeding economic efficiency and reducing profitability. It distorts the operation of the labour market by depriving women of opportunities that are available to men without sexual conditions."

This chapter will first consider the position of ILO and then measures taken by the EU.

The Position of the ILO

The ILO has not envisaged initiating a Convention on sexual harassment, but has relied on Convention No. 111 which prohibits discrimination in employment and occupation on (among others) the ground of sex to deal with this issue, and thus to rely on governments to enforce requirements contained in the Convention on this particular problem.

In a General Observation concerning Convention No. 111 published in 2003[2] the Committee of Experts on the Application of Conventions and Recommendations has noted and drawn attention to the various manifestations of sex discrimination covered by the Convention. It has noted the efforts made by numerous governments to address sexual harassment in the working environment. It noted that sexual harassment undermines equality at work by calling into question the integrity and dignity and the well-being of workers, and also damages an enterprise by weakening the bases upon which work relationships are built and impairing productivity.

The Committee earlier expressed its view that sexual harassment is a form of sex discrimination and should be addressed within the requirements of the Convention – i.e. without the need for a new Convention.

The Committee urged governments to take appropriate measures to prohibit sexual harassment in employment and occupation. Over the years, the Committee has reviewed various national legislative and policy approaches, judicial decisions and collective agreements on this subject, revealing similar approaches, definitions and procedures. It has provided guidance to the ratifying States of the Convention.

These definitions contain the following key elements:

> "(1) (*quid pro quo*): any physical, verbal or non-verbal conduct of a sexual nature and other conduct based on sex affecting the dignity of women and men, which is unwelcome, unreasonable, and offensive to the recipient; and a person's rejection of, or submission to, such

2 CEACR: General Observation concerning Convention No. 111, Doc. No. 52003111.

conduct is used explicitly or implicitly as a basis for a decision which affects that person's job; or

(2) (hostile work environment): conduct that creates an intimidating, hostile or humiliating working environment for the recipient."

Considering that some national initiatives fall short of the full protection against sexual harassment, the Committee decided that it would be helpful to provide guidance to ratifying States. The Committee has requested governments to provide information in their next report on the following points:

- whether sexual harassment has been prohibited in employment and occupation, and if so, how, e.g. through laws, policies, or codes;
- the definition of sexual harassment. Specifically, does it include *quid pro quo*, as well as hostile working environment?
- the scope of who is protected, i.e. job or training applicants ranging to full time applicants;
- the scope of protection, i.e. vocational education, vocational training, access to employment, conditions of employment and performing work in any occupation;
- the scope of liability, i.e. employers, supervisors and co-workers and, where possible, clients or other persons met in connection with performance of work duties;
- administrative mechanisms to address sexual harassment, including procedural protection for victims and accused harassers;
- enforcement mechanisms and procedures, including information on labour inspection activities;
- court decisions;
- educational and awareness-raising measures;
- cooperation with employers' and workers' organizations in addressing sexual harassment through policies and collective agreements.

At the time of writing, ILO had not published any comprehensive report on governments' reports.

The Position of the EU

A number of recommendations were first issued by the Council, the Commission and the European Parliament, starting in 1984, culminating with the adoption in

1991 of a Code of Conduct. This was followed by legislation: Directive 2002/73/ EC of the European Parliament and of the Council of September 2002 and the 2006 Directive.

Recommendations and the Code of Conduct

In accordance with the Council recommendation of 13 December 1984 on the promotion of positive action for women,[3] a number of Member States have carried out a variety of positive action measures and actions having a bearing on respect for the dignity of women at the workplace.

In its resolution of 11 June 1986 on violence against women,[4] the European Parliament called upon national governments, equal opportunity committees and trade unions to carry out concerted information campaigns to create a proper awareness of the individual rights of all members of the labour force.

More specifically, the 1987 report emphasized that existing remedies available under the sex discrimination laws of Member States were not appropriate to prevent sexual harassment. For its author:

> "The inadequacies of existing legal remedies are so patent, the discrepancies between the provisions in Member States so vast, that only a legal instrument with binding force will provide the necessary impetus for voluntary action to be taken. There is no reason to believe that moral suasion, in the form of a Recommendation or a Code of Practice, in itself will have the impact necessary to rectify the injustices currently suffered."

The report made a strong appeal for a Directive, a legal framework which would reduce the need for litigation by encouraging the prevention of sexual harassment, rather than stimulating law suits by concentrating on sanctions after the damage had been inflicted. However, such a preventative approach would not succeed without national legislation to stimulate change:

> "An effective law will focus attention on the problem. It will make solving the problem a priority for employers and it will alert the victims of sexual harassment to their rights."[5]

Following this report, the Advisory Committee on Equal Opportunities for Women and Men, in its opinion of 20 June 1988, unanimously recommended that there should be a code of conduct on sexual harassment in the workplace covering harassment of both sexes. In a resolution of 29 May 1990 on the protection of

3 OJ (1984) L 331/34.

4 OJ (1986) C 176/79; (4) COM (89) 568 final, 29.11.1989.

5 Rubenstein report, paras 1.14, 12.6.

the dignity of women and men at work[6] the Council affirmed that conduct based on sex affecting the dignity of women and men at work, including conduct of superiors and colleagues, constitutes an intolerable violation of the dignity of workers or trainees, and called on the Member States and the institutions and organs of the European Communities to develop positive measures designed to create a climate at work in which women and men respect one another's human integrity.

On 27 November 1991, the Commission adopted a recommendation on the protection of the dignity of women and men at work, which includes a definition of sexual harassment, also reproduced in its code of conduct.[7] Article 1 provides that:

> "Member States take action to promote awareness that conduct of a sexual nature, or other conduct based on sex affecting the dignity of women and men at work, including conduct of superiors and colleagues, is unacceptable if:
>
> (a) such conduct is unwanted, unreasonable and offensive to the recipient;
>
> (b) a person's rejection of, or submission to, such conduct on the part of employers or workers (including superiors or colleagues) is used explicitly or implicitly as a basis for a decision which affects that person's access to vocational training, access to employment, continued employment, promotion, salary or any other employment decisions;
>
> and/or
>
> (c) such conduct creates an intimidating, hostile or humiliating work environment for the recipient; ... and that such conduct may, in certain circumstances, be contrary to the principle of equal treatment with the meaning of Articles 3, 4 and 5 of Directive 76/207/EEC, Article 2."

It recommended that Member States take action in the public sector to implement the Commission's code of practice on the protection of the dignity of women and men at work, annexed to the Recommendation. The action of Member States would then create a climate at work in which women and men respect one another's human integrity, as an example to the private sector. Employers

---

6 OJ (1990) C 157/3.

7 Commission Recommendation of 27 November 1991 on the protection of the dignity of women and men at work (92/131/EEC), Article 1; and Annex, "A code of practice on measures to combat sexual harassment".

and employee representatives should be encouraged to develop measures to implement the Code (Articles 2, 3 and 4).

The code of conduct contains recommendations to employers: as measures of prevention, they should issue a policy statement which expressly states that all employees have a right to be treated with dignity, that sexual harassment at work will not be permitted or condoned and that employees have a right to complain about it should it occur. Other recommended measures include training of managers and supervisors, clear complaints procedures, encouragement of informal resolution of problems, offers of advice and assistance, independent and objective investigations, and disciplinary rules to be applied to inappropriate behaviour at work. The code also includes recommendations to trade unions and recalls the role of employees in preventing or discouraging sexual harassment.

The code, although not binding, was an important step taken by the EU as guidance to Member States and to employers.

In July 1996 and March 1997 consultations of the Commission with the social partners confirmed the importance of protecting the dignity of the individual worker, but the social partners did not agree on the need to negotiate a collective agreement on the issue of sexual harassment.

EU Legislation

Under Article 2 of the Treaty of Amsterdam, which entered into force on 1 May 1999, equal treatment between men and women became an explicit objective of the Community. Article 3 imposes on the Community the obligation to aim at eliminating inequalities, and to promote equality between men and women in all its activities. These developments were an explicit embodiment of the Court's statement that the elimination of discrimination based on sex forms part of fundamental rights.[8] Article 13 and 141 (3) of the Treaty gave a specific legal base as regards aspects covered by Directive 76/207/EEC. As noted in previous Chapters, this Directive is the foundation of EU law and policy in the area of gender equality in employment.

The Charter of Fundamental Rights of the EU

The Charter, adopted in December 2000, has affirmed or confirmed a number of key principles, some of which are relevant to harassment and sexual harassment:

- Human dignity is inviolable, it must be respected and protected (Article 1);

---

[8] Ruling of 15 June 1978 in Case 149/77 *Defrenne III*, (1977) ECR 1365, para. 27.

- Discrimination based, *inter alia*, on sex is prohibited (Article 21);
- Those whose rights and freedoms guaranteed by the law of the Union are violated have the right to an effective remedy and to a fair trial (Article 47).

The Charter may become legally binding on all Member States in 2009.

The 2002 Amendment and Sexual Harassment

Directive 2002/73/EC of the European Parliament and of the Council of 23 September 2002 amends Directive 76/207/EEC on the implementation of the principle of equal treatment for men and women as regards access to employment, vocational training and promotion, and working conditions. Both the European Parliament and the Commission were instrumental in initiating this Directive, which was preceded and followed by a number of other steps.

On 7 June 2000, the Commission wrote that a very important and sensitive issue like sexual harassment could not be ignored any more and must be addressed at Community level. It submitted a proposal for a Directive of the European Parliament and the Council, which was finally adopted in 2002.[9]

The Directive affirms that:

> "harassment related to the sex of a person and sexual harassment are contrary to the principle of equal treatment between women and men; it is therefore appropriate to define such concepts and to prohibit such forms of discrimination. To this end it must be emphasized that these forms of discrimination occur not only in the workplace, but also in the context of access to employment and vocational training, during employment and occupation."

The definitions of harassment and sexual harassment are in new Article 2(2):

> "harassment: where an unwanted conduct related to the sex of a person occurs with the purpose or effect of violating the dignity of a person, and or creating an intimidating, hostile, degrading, humiliating or offensive environment.
>
> sexual harassment: where any form of unwanted verbal, non-verbal or physical conduct of a sexual nature occurs, with the purpose or effect of violating the dignity of a person, in particular when creating an intimidating, hostile, degrading, humiliating or offensive environment."

---

9 Proposal for a Directive of the European Parliament and of the Council amending Council Directive 76/207/EEC on the implementation of the principle of equal treatment for men and women as regards access to employment, vocational training and promotion, and working conditions, COM (2000) 334 final, 2000/0142 (COD), 7 June 2000.

The definition of sexual harassment reflects that adopted by the Commission in its Code of Practice of 1991.

Article 3 confirms that harassment and sexual harassment within the meaning of the Directive "shall be deemed to be discrimination on the grounds of sex and therefore prohibited".

Member States are encouraged, in accordance with national law, through collective agreements or the practice of employers and those responsible for access to vocational training, to take measures to prevent all forms of discrimination on grounds of sex, in particular harassment and sexual harassment at the workplace. Member States should ensure that judicial and/or administrative procedures (and if appropriate, conciliation procedures) for the enforcement of obligations under the Directive are available to all persons who consider themselves wronged by failure to apply the principle of equal treatment to them.

Member States should introduce in their legal systems such measures as are necessary to protect persons from any adverse treatment or adverse consequence as a reaction to a complaint or to legal proceedings aimed at enforcing compliance with the principle of equal treatment.

Member States should ensure that associations, organizations or other legal entities which have a legitimate interest in ensuring that the provisions of the Directive are complied with, may engage, on behalf or in support of the complainant, with his or her approval, in any judicial and/or administrative procedure provided for the enforcement of obligations under this Directive.

The Directive lays down minimum requirements, thus giving Member States the option of introducing or maintaining more favourable provisions. Member States should provide for effective, proportionate and dissuasive penalties in cases of breaches of the obligations under the Directive. The Directive forbids Member States from restricting compensation or reparation for losses or damage sustained by a prior upper limit, except in:

> "cases where the employer can prove that the only damage suffered by an applicant as a result of discrimination within the meaning of [the] Directive is the refusal to take his/her job application into consideration."

Directive 2006/54/EC (recast)

Directive 2006/54/EC of the European Parliament and of the Council of 5 July 2006 on the implementation of the principle of equal opportunities and equal treatment of men and women in matters of employment and occupation has recast previous Directives, and brought together in a single text the main provisions in this field. On the issue of harassment and sexual harassment, Recital (6) of its Preamble has re-affirmed that:

> "Harassment and sexual harassment are contrary to the principle of equal treatment between men and women and constitute discrimina-

tion on grounds of sex for the purpose of this Directive. These forms of discrimination occur not only in the workplace, but also in the context of access to employment, vocational training and promotion. They should therefore be prohibited and should be subject to effective, proportionate and dissuasive penalties."

Employers and those responsible for vocational training are encouraged to take measures to combat such discrimination as well as preventive measures. The definitions of harassment and sexual harassment contained in Directive 2002/73/EC are repeated in Article 2 of the Directive.

This Directive will enter into force in 2008.

EU Case Law

At the time of writing, there was not yet any case law of the ECJ concerning the implementation and/or interpretation of Directive 2002//73. The Directive entered into force only in 2005. However a number of positive developments in the area of fighting against sexual harassment in several countries were reported by the Commission in May 2005.[10]

Judgments by criminal courts, district courts or labour courts in cases of sexual harassment have taken place in Slovenia, Lithuania, Ireland and Sweden. Also in Slovenia, the Office for Equal Opportunities has proposed a regulation on the protection of human dignity at work in state bodies, judicial organs and local community bodies. A Portuguese expert has organized, in November 2004, a seminar on harassment at the work place at the Faculty of Law of Lisbon University. In Malta, the Commission for the Equality of Men and Women was working on a Sexual Harassment Code of Practice. The Norwegian Gender Equality Ombud has started a project on the respect of the regulation on sexual harassment in high schools. In Spain, the "Comprehensive Act on Gender Violence" of 28 December 2004 includes civil, criminal, social and educational measures aimed at fighting gender violence through a global and unified strategy. Specialized judicial instances – Courts of Violence against Women – will be created within the criminal jurisdiction, and a National Observatory on Gender-based Violence will be established.

10 "General report on developments in EU Gender Equality Law, June 2004-May 2005" by the Commission's Network of legal experts in the fields of employment, social affairs and equality between men and women, pp. 19-21.

Conclusion

The ILO, while concerned about sexual harassment at work, has found no need for a new Convention on this specific issue, and continues to rely on Convention No. 111 to deal with related problems. The Organization has however felt that guidance will be necessary for ratifying States and will publish a comprehensive report on government's laws, policies, codes and practices.

The EU started at the same point, by relying first on Equal Treatment Directive 76/207/EEC, then went on to adopt a Code of Practice before finally adopting the new Directive 2002/73/EEC.

The problems facing potential targets of sexual harassment and victims are now recognized as a serious threat to men's and women's dignity and integrity, and a threat to enterprises' good management, and governments are urged to take appropriate legislative and judicial action to prevent or to sanction such behaviour.

Action starts at the national level. National legislation should provide a legally binding framework for the creation or development of effective policies and procedures to identify and fight against this serious violation of both individual human rights and equal treatment at work.

Employers and trade unions have to be convinced that this is a real, widespread and serious problem, often hidden from sight. Victims fear retribution by superiors or even from management, shame from colleagues or their families or friends, and moral damage from the attacks on their dignity and modesty. They have to be convinced that they will be protected if they complain.

At the international level, the role of the ILO and the EU is, as in other labour issues, to set minimum standards, offer guidance and procedures, and prod governments into action. Monitoring of governments' action in the ILO system is done by requiring both periodic reports on the implementation of a Convention and a review by an intergovernmental committee. The EU also requires governments to report on their implementation of Directives, but additional judicial control is provided by the ECJ whose decisions are to be applied by governments.

Changing social mores is a slow process, particularly in such a sensitive area as sexual behaviour. Continuous efforts are needed by social partners, governments, NGOs and international organizations to ensure that the requirements of Convention No. 111, Directives 2002/73/EC and 2006/54/EC are properly transposed and implemented at the national level.

Chapter 14

POSITIVE OR AFFIRMATIVE ACTION

Background

The question of equality between persons that are not equal for all purposes is thorny, especially in our times when the principle of non-discrimination has been extended to include not only the classic grounds of sex and race, but also disability, age and sex orientation.

Aristotle was already of the opinion that "equality between non-equals is as bad and discriminatory as inequality between equals". The ECJ adopted this approach when it stated that:

> "It is well settled that discrimination involves the application of different rules to comparable situations or the application of the same rule to different situations".[1]

Eminent jurists expressed the view that equality between non-equals may amount to "mockery to the poor". The poor require positive action to redress the gap between them and the rich. So do persons who have been victims of past discrimination on grounds of race and sex.

Positive action empowers the victim of discrimination. There is consensus today that in order to achieve equality in practice and not merely in theory, the law should privilege the underprivileged, at least on a transitional basis, until the gap is narrowed or breached between these groups.

Philosophically we are not dealing with equal rights, we are dealing with a human right to a difference. Such a conception will help us in the implementation of real equality, equal opportunity and the empowerment of the underprivileged, the disabled, ethnic groups and women.

The consensus for empowerment is broken over the methods to be adopted. The option of quotas that was imposed in some legal systems was not generally accepted. First, in the case of women workers, they preferred to be promoted on

---

1 *Brown* Case C-394/96 (1998) ECR I-4185 at para. 30. See also the *Gillespie* Case C-342/93 (1996) ECR I-475.

the basis of merit and not on the basis of quotas. Secondly, quotas for women often result in reverse discrimination of men.

ILO Standards

Neither the ILO standards nor EU law have advocated affirmative action and quotas. As we shall see, ILO Convention No. 111 merely provided that:

> "Any Member may, after consultation with representative employers' and workers' organisations, where such exist, determine that other special measures designed to meet the particular requirements of persons who, for reasons such as sex, age, disablement, family responsibilities or social or cultural status, are generally recognised to require special protection or assistance, shall not be deemed to be discrimination."[2]

These measures cannot be interpreted to cover affirmative action. However, in both the General Survey prepared in 1988 and in its Special Survey on Convention No. 111 undertaken in 1996[3] the Committee of Experts observed that the adoption of affirmative action measures is often extremely useful in the first stages of eliminating discrimination, as the mere banning of discrimination is not sufficient to eliminate it in practice. Most importantly, the surveys stressed the need for governments to take a comprehensive approach, involving both legislative and practical measures, to address all sources of discrimination and to encourage understanding and acceptance of the principle of equality.

EU Legislation

Not unlike the ILO instruments, the 1976 EU Directive on Equal Treatment for Men and Women as regards access to employment, vocational training, promotion and working conditions did not address the issue of affirmative or positive action as we understand it today. However, Article 2 paragraph (4) echoing the ILO provision, stipulates that:

---

2 Article 5 (2).

3 See *Equality in Employment and Occupation*, General Survey by the Committee of Experts on the Application of Conventions and Recommendations, International Labour Conference, 75th Session 1988; see also "Special Survey on Equality in Employment and Occupation in respect of Convention No. 111", Report of the Committee of Experts on the Application of Conventions and recommendations, International Labour Conference, 83rd Session 1996.

> "The Directive shall be without prejudice to measures to promote equal opportunity for men and women, in particular by removing existing inequalities that affect women's opportunities."

Article 2 did not directly support policies of affirmative action or quota systems as the wording was considered vague.

In 1984 a Recommendation was adopted that was more precise, but Recommendations have no binding force. According to the third recital in the Preamble to Council Recommendation 84/635/EEC of 13 December 1984 on the promotion of positive action for women,[4] existing legal provisions on equal treatment, which are designed to afford rights to individuals, are inadequate for the elimination of all existing inequalities unless parallel action is taken by governments, both sides of industry and other bodies concerned to counteract the prejudicial effects on women in employment which arise from social attitudes, behaviour and structures. Referring expressly to Article 2 (4) of the 1976 Directive, the Council recommended that the Member States:

> "adopt a positive action policy designed to eliminate existing inequalities affecting women in working life and to promote a better balance between the sexes in employment, comprising appropriate general and specific measures, within the framework of national policies and practices, while fully respecting the spheres of competence of the two sides of industry, in order:
>
> (a) to eliminate or counteract the prejudicial effects on women in employment or seeking employment which arise from existing attitudes, behaviour and structures based on the idea of a traditional division of roles in society between men and women;
>
> (b) to encourage the participation of women in various occupations in those sectors of working life where they are at present under-represented, particularly in the sectors of the future, and at higher levels of responsibility in order to achieve better use of all human resources."

As we shall see when discussing the case law of the ECJ, the Court interpreted these provisions narrowly.

The written law of the EU changed with the adoption of the Treaty of Amsterdam in 1997 and the amendment of the original Article 119 of the Treaty of Rome.

Article 141 paragraph 4 now reads as follows:

4 OJ (1984) L 331/34.

> "with a view of ensuring full equality in practice between men and women in working life, the principle of equal treatment shall not prevent any Member State from maintaining or adopting measures providing for specific advantages in order to make it easier for the under-represented sex to pursue a vocational activity or to prevent or compensate for disadvantages in professional careers."

This new provision in a primary source of law paved the way for the adoption of the amending directive of the 1976 Directive on Equal Treatment, namely Directive 2002/73/EC of the European Parliament and of the Council of 23 September 2002 amending Council Directive 76/207/EEC on the implementation of the principle of equal treatment for men and women as regards access to employment, vocational training and promotion, and working conditions.

The Directive emphasises in its Preamble in Recital (4) that:

> "Equality between women and men is a fundamental principle, under Article 2 and Article 3 (2) of the EC Treaty and the case law of the Court of Justice. These provisions proclaim equality between women and men as a 'task' and an 'aim' of the Community and impose a positive obligation to promote it in all its activities."

This is the first time the term positive obligation or action appears in a legal text. However, affirmative action is not a term used in the context of EU law.

The Directive further states in its Preamble in Recital (14) that:

> "Member States may, under Article 141 (4) of the Treaty, maintain or adopt measures providing for specific advantages, in order to make it easier for the under-represented sex to pursue a vocational activity or to prevent or compensate for disadvantages in professional careers. Given the current situation, and bearing in mind the Declaration No. 28 to the Amsterdam Treaty, Members States should in the first instance aim at improving the situation of women in working life."

Article 8 of the Directive provides that:

> "Member States may maintain or adopt measures within the meaning of Article 141 (4) of the Treaty with a view to ensuring full equality in practice between men and women."

Member States were to implement the Directive in their internal laws by 5 October 2005. The Directive has by now become the law of the EU on the matter of equal treatment of men and women at the work place, including positive action for women.

As explained in previous Chapters, the consolidating Directive of 2006 recasts and codifies the *acquis communautaire* in this field in one instrument.

Finally, Article 23 of the EU Charter of Fundamental Rights, that received legal backing in December 2007, provides that:

> "Equality between men and women must be ensured in all areas, including employment, work and pay.
>
> The principle of equality shall not prevent the maintenance or adoption of measures providing for specific advantages in favour of the under-represented sex."

EU Case Law

As we have seen, the Community adopted a policy of positive action, but did not go as far as introducing preference to women in domains where past discrimination prevented them from assuming an equal role, or where women were under-represented. It was only in the mid-1990s with the controversy over the *Kalanke* v. *the City of Bremen* case in 1995[5] that the issue came fully to the fore.

Mr Kalanke, the plaintiff in the main proceedings, held a diploma in horticulture and landscape gardening, and had worked since 1973 as a horticultural employee in the Parks Department and acted as permanent assistant to the Section Manager. Ms Glissmann, also holder of a diploma in landscape gardening since 1983 had also been employed as a horticultural employee in the Parks Department since 1975.

They both competed for a post with the Bremen landscape gardening Authority having the same qualifications. The Authority chose Ms Glissman because of the policy of affirmative action in favour of women adopted by the City of Bremen. The German Federal Administrative Court pointed out that the case did not involve a system of strict quotas reserving a certain proportion of posts for women, regardless of their qualifications, but rather a system of quotas dependent on candidates' abilities. Women enjoy no priority unless the candidates of both sexes are equally qualified. The German Federal Administrative Court, considering, however, that doubts remain in that regard has stayed the proceedings and sought a preliminary ruling from the ECJ on the following question:

> "Must Article 2 (4) of Council Directive 76/207/EEC of 9 February 1976 on the implementation of the principle of equal treatment for men and women as regards access to employment, vocational training and promotion, and working conditions, be interpreted as also covering statutory provisions under which, when a position in a higher pay bracket is being assigned, women with the same qualifications as men applying for the same position are to be given priority if women are under-represented,

5 Case C-450/93 (1995) ECR I-3051.

> there being deemed to be under-representation if women do not make up at least half of the staff in the individual pay brackets in the relevant personnel group within a department, which also applies to the function levels provided for in the organization chart?"

In its order for reference, the national court pointed out that a quota system such as that in issue might help to overcome in the future the disadvantages which women currently face and which perpetuate past inequalities, inasmuch as it accustoms people to seeing women also filling more senior posts. The traditional assignment of certain tasks to women and the concentration of women at the lower end of the scale are contrary to the equal rights criteria applicable today. In that connection, the national court cited figures illustrating the low proportion of women in the higher career brackets among city employees in Bremen, particularly if sectors such as education, where the presence of women in higher posts is now established, are excluded.

The ECJ came, however, to the conclusion that the policy of the City of Bremen went beyond the provisions Article 2 (1) and (4) if the automatic priority of women results in discrimination of men. The Court ruled that:

> "The answer to the national court's questions must therefore be that Article 2 (1) and (4) of the Directive precludes national rules such as those in the present case which, where candidates of different sexes short listed for promotion are equally qualified, automatically give priority to women in sectors where they are under-represented, under-representation being deemed to exist when women do not make up at least half of the staff in the individual pay brackets in the relevant personnel group or in the function levels provided for in the organization chart."

The Court thus protected Mr Kalanke's right to equal opportunity. The European Commission had to consider the appropriate measures to respect the Court's decision, while preserving the policy of positive action for women. It issued a Communication[6] in which it explained that the ruling prohibits rigid quotas for women' s employment, but does not stand in the way of promoting measures which are not discriminatory.

In *Helmut Marschall* v. *Land Nord-Rhein-Westfalen* 1997[7] the rationale of the *Kalanke* case was accepted. The ECJ clarified its position that quotas are compatible with the European Equal treatment Directive if they do not give absolute and unconditional priority to women in a way which discriminates against men.

In this case Mr Marschall, a teacher, sought to be nominated to a higher teaching post. The post was, however, filled by a women of equal qualifications

---

6 COM (96) 88 final.

7 Case C-409/95 (1977) ECR I-6363.

due to the positive action programme in the public service practised by the Land of Nord-Rhein-Westfalen. Mr Marschall claimed discrimination.

Called to give a preliminary ruling in this case, the ECJ distinguished the facts of the *Kalanke* case from the present ones. Whereas the quota system of the City of Bremen to promote women was rigid and absolute, resulting in reverse discrimination to men, the quota system of the Land Nord-Rhein-Westfalen was not absolute and required an objective consideration and assessment of the male candidates. Thus the priority given to the woman teacher was considered compatible with the Equal Treatment Directive 1976. The principle that may be gleaned from this case is therefore, that quotas are not prohibited, unless they give absolute and unconditional priority to women in a way which discriminates men. The Court observed that even where candidates are equally qualified, male candidates tend to be promoted in preference to female candidates particularly because of prejudices and stereotypes concerning the role and capacities of women in working life, so that the mere fact that a male candidate and a female candidate are equally qualified does not mean that they have the same chances.[8]

The ECJ's ruling is as follows:

> "A national rule which, in a case where there are fewer women than men at the level of the relevant post in a sector of the public service and both female and male candidates for the post are equally qualified in terms of their suitability, competence and professional performance, requires that priority be given to the promotion of female candidates unless reasons specific to an individual male candidate tilt the balance in his favour is not precluded by Article 2 (1) and (4) of Council Directive 76/207/EEC of 9 February 1976, on the implementation of the principle of equal treatment for men and women as regards access to employment, vocational training and promotion, and working conditions, provided that:
>
> – in each individual case the rule provides for male candidates who are equally as qualified as the female candidates a guarantee that the candidatures will be the subject of an objective assessment which will take account of all criteria specific to the candidates and will override the priority accorded to female candidates where one or more of those criteria tilts the balance in favour of the male candidate, and
>
> – such criteria are not such as to discriminate against the female candidates."

The Court thus approved the provision of the Law on the Advancement of Women of the Land Nord-Rhein-Westphalia which contains a safety clause in favour of

8 Marschall, paras 29 and 30.

men. It ruled that a provision of this kind, which requires that when men and women candidates are equally qualified, priority be given to the promotion of women is compatible with Article 2 (4) of the Equal Treatment Directive.

> "It could help to redress the balance with respect to the disadvantages suffered by women candidates arising from existing prejudices and stereotypes concerning the role and capacities of women in working life. Thus a provision which accords priority to women when male and female candidates are equally qualified does not breach European Community law."[9]

The difference between the *Kalanke* case and the present case lies in the existence of a safety clause in favour of men which guarantees that the candidature of men will be the subject of an objective assessment that will take account of all criteria specific to all candidates.

Badeck v. *Land Hessen* 2000[10] gave the ECJ the opportunity to examine the validity of another model of German affirmative action legislation. Forty-six parliamentarians contested the legality of the affirmative action law of Hessen and its compatibility with the Equal Treatment Directive. The *Staatsgerichtshof* forwarded several questions to the ECJ.

The ECJ examined carefully the provisions of the Law of the Land of Hessen, which was adopted as a transitory measure for thirteen years only, and its considerations and reasoning may be summarised as follows:

> "The provision which required opening half of the posts in all departments in the public service for women whose qualifications are equal to those of men, unless there are prevailing legal reasons not to do so, is not precluded by the Directive. This provision is not absolute and rigid and it was to be in force only during two years until the quota was fulfilled. Therefore Article 2 (1) and (4) of the Directive does not preclude a national rule which, in sectors of the public service where women are under-represented, gives priority, where male and female candidates have equal qualifications, to female candidates where that proves necessary for ensuring compliance with the objectives of the women's advancement plan, if no reasons of greater legal weight are opposed, provided that that rule guarantees that candidatures are the subject of an objective assessment which takes account of the specific personal situations of all candidates."

---

9 See Maria Boehmer, "Affirmative Action in Germany – Laws, Effects and Perspective" in *The Status of Women at the Dawn of the Twenty-first Century* (UNESCO, 2001), p. 64.

10 Case C-158/97 (2000) ECR, p. 1875.

In the second part of its question, the *Staatsgerichtshof* asks whether Article 2 (1) and (4) of the Directive precludes a national rule which prescribes that the binding targets of the women's advancement plan for temporary posts in the academic service and for academic assistants must provide for a minimum percentage of women which is at least equal to the percentage of women among graduates, holders of higher degrees and students in each discipline. The answer is that Article 2 (1) and (4) of the Directive does not preclude such a rule. In the third part of its question, the *Staatsgerichtshof* asks whether Article 2 (1) and (4) of the Directive precludes a national rule for the public service which allocates at least half the training places to women in trained occupations in which women are under-represented and for which the State does not have a monopoly of training.

Since the quota applies only to training places for which the State does not have a monopoly, and therefore concerns training for which places are also available in the private sector, no male candidate is definitively excluded from training. Taking an overall view of training (public and private sectors), the provision at issue therefore merely improves the chances of female candidates in the public sector.

The measures are thus intended to eliminate the causes of women's reduced opportunities of access to employment and careers, and moreover are measures regarding vocational orientation and training. Such measures are therefore among the measures authorised by Article 2 (4) of the Directive, which are intended to improve the ability of women to compete on the labour market and to pursue a career on an equal footing with men. Therefore Article 2 (1) and (4) of the Directive does not preclude such a rule. In the fourth part of its question, the Staatsgerichtshof asks whether Article 2 (1) and (4) of the Directive precludes a national rule which guarantees, where male and female candidates have equal qualifications, that women who are qualified are called to interview, in sectors in which they are under-represented.

The fifth part of the *Staatsgerichtshof*'s question asks whether Article 2 (1) and (4) of the Directive precludes a national rule under which, when appointments are made to employees' representative bodies and administrative and supervisory bodies, at least half the members must be women.

The ECJ ruled as follows:

> "Article 2 (1) and (4) of Council Directive 76/207/EEC of 9 February 1976 on the implementation of the principle of equal treatment for men and women as regards access to employment, vocational training and promotion, and working conditions does not preclude a national rule which
>
> – in sectors of the public service where women are under-represented, gives priority, where male and female candidates have equal qualifications, to female candidates where that proves necessary for ensuring

compliance with the objectives of the women's advancement plan, if no reasons of greater legal weight are opposed, provided that that rule guarantees that candidatures are the subject of an objective assessment which takes account of the specific personal situations of all candidates,

- prescribes that the binding targets of the women's advancement plan for temporary posts in the academic service and for academic assistants must provide for a minimum percentage of women which is at least equal to the percentage of women among graduates, holders of higher degrees and students in each discipline,
- in so far as its objective is to eliminate under-representation of women, in trained occupations in which women are under-represented and for which the State does not have a monopoly of training, allocates at least half the training places to women, unless despite appropriate measures for drawing the attention of women to the training places available there are not enough applications from women,
- where male and female candidates have equal qualifications, guarantees that qualified women who satisfy all the conditions required or laid down are called to interview, in sectors in which they are under-represented,
- relating to the composition of employees' representative bodies and administrative and supervisory bodies, recommends that the legislative provisions adopted for its implementation take into account the objective that at least half the members of those bodies must be women."

The Court rendered a comprehensive ruling based on the 1976 Equal Treatment Directive and found that there was no need to rule on the interpretation of Article 141 (4) EC.

In future cases it is Article 141 (4) EC that represents the up-to-date law together with Article 8 of the 2002 Amending Equal Treatment Directive that entered into force in 2005, and not Article 2 of the 1976 Directive.

The *Badeck* case can serve as a leading precedent for future affirmative action with flexible quotas that are compatible with Community Law. These flexible quotas were recognised by the Court when applied to jobs in the public service, academic posts, in vocational training, regarding pre-recruitment interviews and in the composition of representative and administrative bodies.

The cases discussed so far had their origin in Germany where some of the *Lander* adopted policies of affirmative action for women. *Abrahamsson* v. *Fogelquist*

2000[11] originated in Sweden when the Rector of the Goeteborg University appointed a women to the post of Professor although her qualifications were not as high as those of a male candidate (and also of another female candidate). This appointment was with the purpose of augmenting the number of women Professors. The Rector was of the opinion that the difference in the level of the personal qualifications would have no influence on the quality of teaching and that this appointment advances the cause of affirmative action for women.

The "discriminated" candidates brought action in the Swedish Court basing their claim on the fact that the appointment violated the principles of equality under Swedish Law, the Equal Treatment Directive 1976 and Article 141 of the Treaty of Amsterdam.

The Swedish Court referred the case to the ECJ for a preliminary ruling, seeking to ascertain whether Article 2 (1) and (4) of the Directive preclude national legislation, such as the Swedish legislation at issue in the main proceedings, which provides for positive discrimination in recruitment in favour of candidates of the under-represented sex in the sector of higher education.

In its ruling in the case of *Badeck and Others* 2000[12] the Court held that a measure which is intended to give priority in promotion to women in sectors of the public service where they are under-represented must be regarded as compatible with Community law where it does not automatically and unconditionally give priority to women when women and men are equally qualified, and where the candidatures are the subject of an objective assessment which takes account of the specific personal situations of all candidates.

In contrast to the national legislation on positive action examined by the Court in its *Kalanke, Marschall* and *Badeck* rulings, the Swedish legislation at issue allows giving preference to a candidate of the under-represented sex who, although sufficiently qualified, does not possess qualifications equal to those of other candidates of the opposite sex.

As a rule, a procedure for the selection of candidates for a post involves assessment of their qualifications by reference to the requirements of the vacant post or of the duties to be performed.

The clear aim of positive action is to achieve substantive, rather than formal, equality by reducing *de facto* inequalities which may arise in society and, thus, in accordance with Article 141 (4) EC, to prevent or compensate for disadvantages in the professional career of persons belonging to the under-represented sex.

It is essential in that connection that the application of criteria such as those mentioned above must be transparent and amenable to review in order to obviate any arbitrary assessment of the qualifications of candidates.

---

11 Case C-407/98 (2000) ECR I-5539.

12 Case C-158/97 (2000) ECR I-1875, para. 23.

As regards the selection procedure at issue, it does not appear from the relevant Swedish legislation that assessment of the qualifications of candidates by reference to the requirements of the vacant post is based on unambiguous criteria that prevent or compensate for disadvantages in the professional career of members of the under-represented sex.

On the contrary, under that legislation, a candidate for a public post belonging to the under-represented sex and possessing sufficient qualifications for that post must be chosen in preference to a candidate of the opposite sex who would otherwise have been appointed, where that measure is necessary for a candidate belonging to the under-represented sex to be appointed. It follows that the legislation at issue automatically grants preference to candidates belonging to the under-represented sex, provided that they are sufficiently qualified, subject only to the proviso that the difference between the merits of the candidates of each sex is not so great as to result in a breach of the requirement of objectivity in making appointments.

The scope and effect of that condition cannot be precisely determined, with the result that the selection of a candidate from among those who are sufficiently qualified is ultimately based on the mere fact of belonging to the under-represented sex, and that this is so even if the merits of the candidate so selected are inferior to those of a candidate of the opposite sex. Moreover, candidatures are not subjected to an objective assessment taking account of the specific personal situations of all the candidates. It follows that such a method of selection is not such as to be permitted by Article 2 (4) of the Directive.

Thus, even though Article 141 (4) EC allows the Member States to maintain or adopt measures providing for special advantages intended to prevent or compensate for disadvantages in professional careers in order to ensure full equality between men and women in professional life, it cannot be inferred that the Article allows a selection method of the kind at issue in this case which appears, on any view, to be disproportionate to the aim pursued.

Restricting the scope of a positive discrimination measure of the kind in point here is not capable of changing its absolute and disproportionate nature.

The ECJ ruled as follows:

> "1. Article 2 (1) and (4) of Council Directive 76/207/EEC of 9 February 1976 on the implementation of the principle of equal treatment for men and women as regards access to employment, vocational training and promotion, and working conditions and Article 141 (4) EC preclude national legislation under which a candidate for a public post who belongs to the under-represented sex and possesses sufficient qualifications for that post must be chosen in preference to a candidate of the opposite sex who would otherwise have been appointed, where this is necessary to secure the appointment of a candidate of the under-represented sex and the difference between the respective merits of the candidates is not

so great as to give rise to a breach of the requirement of objectivity in making appointments.

2. Article 2 (1) and (4) of Directive 76/207 and Article 141 (4) EC also preclude national legislation of that kind where it applies only to procedures for filling a predetermined number of posts or to posts created as part of a specific programme of a particular higher educational institution allowing the application of positive discrimination measures.

3. Article 2 (1) and (4) of Directive 76/207 does not preclude a rule of national case law under which a candidate belonging to the under-represented sex may be granted preference over a competitor of the opposite sex, provided that the candidates possess equivalent or substantially equivalent merits, where the candidatures are subjected to an objective assessment which takes account of the specific personal situations of all the candidates.

4. The question whether national rules providing for positive discrimination in the making of appointments in higher education are lawful cannot depend on the level of the post to be filled."

The ECJ followed its own previous precedents and insisted that, where positive action is absolute and rigid, as in the Swedish Law, not leaving any scope for an objective assessment, which takes account of the specific personal situations of the other candidates, it violates the cardinal rules of equality under Community law.

The *Schnorbus* v. *Land Hessen* ruling,[13] also delivered by the ECJ in 2000, involved a case of *prima facie* indirect discrimination of women. The facts were as follows: In October 1997 Ms Schnorbus passed the First State Examination in law. Under federal and Land Hessian legislation, in order to obtain a post in the judicial service or in the higher civil service, a person must have undergone practical legal training and then have passed the Second State Examination. To that end, she applied to the Hessian Ministry of Justice and European Affairs, (hereinafter the Ministry) for admission to the training starting in January 1998.

By letter of 16 December 1997, the Ministry rejected her application, informing her that, since too many applications had been received, it had been necessary for it to make a selection. By letter of 11 February 1998, the Ministry informed her that, for the same reasons, she could not be admitted to the next period of training, starting in March 1998, for which she had maintained her application.

She then lodged an objection, on 13 February 1998, to the refusal of admission to practical legal training, arguing, in particular, that the selection procedure

---

13 Case C-79/99 (2000) ECR I-10997.

discriminated against women because of the preference accorded to applicants who had completed compulsory military or civilian service, which can be done only by men. That objection was dismissed on 2 April 1998, on the ground that the rule in question, which was designed to counterbalance the disadvantage suffered by applicants who were obliged to complete military or civilian service, was based on an objective distinguishing factor. At the same time, she brought an application for interim relief before the Administrative Court in Frankfurt am Main, seeking appointment as a trainee with effect from the beginning of March 1998. That court upheld her application by order of 23 February 1998, but that order was set aside on 27 February 1998 by the Higher Administrative Court of Hessen. On 9 April 1998, she brought an action before the Administrative Court in Frankfurt am Main, seeking a declaration that the refusal of the Ministry to admit her was unlawful and an order requiring Land Hessen to employ her as a trainee for the period of training commencing in May 1998. Having learned, by letter of 28 April 1998, that it had finally been possible to allocate her a place following the selection made for that period of training, she withdrew her action in respect of that period of training but maintained her claims that the previous decisions should be declared unlawful in so far as they constituted, in her opinion, discrimination against her as a woman. The German Court referred the matter to the ECJ for a preliminary ruling.

The ECJ ruled as follows:

> "1. National provisions governing the date of admission to the practical legal training which is a necessary prerequisite of access to employment in the civil service fall within the scope of Council Directive 76/207/EEC of 9 February 1976 on the implementation of the principle of equal treatment for men and women as regards access to employment, vocational training and promotion, and working conditions.
>
> 2. National provisions such as those at issue in the main proceedings do not constitute discrimination directly based on sex.
>
> 3. National provisions such as those at issue in the main proceedings constitute indirect discrimination based on sex.
>
> 4. Directive 76/207 does not preclude national provisions such as those at issue in the main proceedings, in so far as such provisions are justified by objective reasons and prompted solely by a desire to counterbalance to some extent the delay resulting from the completion of compulsory military or civilian service. The priority granted those who performed military or civilian service did not violate the norm of equality. The situation of candidates who have performed military service is different from that of candidates – men and women alike – who have not performed such service. Different situations call for different treatment. The difference is not based on sex and is justified on objective reasons."

The promotion of equal opportunities for women can be done in many ways. Perhaps one of the most efficient ways is to provide child care facilities where women can place their children whilst they are at work. The following case deals with the issue of child care facilities. The Court was requested to give a preliminary ruling in the case of *Lommers* v. *The Dutch Minister of Agriculture* 2002[14] which dealt with the question of positive action in favour of women regarding subsidised child care. Here the question was not one of quotas to access the public service as in the majority of the previous cases. In the present case the issue was more of affirmative action in relation to conditions of work. Mr Lommers brought an action for sex discrimination against the Dutch Minister of Agriculture in that the Ministry supplied child care facilities for women employees. Men working at the Ministry could avail themselves of these facilities only in emergency cases.

The ECJ ruled that:

> "Article 2 (1) and (4) of Council Directive 76/207/EEC of 9 February 1976 on the implementation of the principle of equal treatment for men and women as regards access to employment, vocational training and promotion, and working conditions does not preclude a scheme set up by a Minister to tackle extensive under-representation of women within his Ministry under which, in a context characterised by a proven insufficiency of proper, affordable care facilities, a limited number of subsidised nursery places made available by the Ministry to its staff is reserved for female officials alone whilst male officials may have access to them only in cases of emergency, to be determined by the employer. That is so, however, only in so far, in particular, as the said exception in favour of male officials is construed as allowing those of them who take care of their children by themselves to have access to that nursery places scheme on the same conditions as female officials."

The issue of child care is of primary importance for workers with family responsibilities, as we have seen in Chapter 10 when dealing with ILO Convention No. 156 1981. The initiative of the Dutch Minister in providing subsidised facilities for mothers with small children is in the spirit both of the ILO and the EU Directive. Lommers felt discriminated in that the facility is open to fathers exceptionally only in cases of emergency. However, the ECJ ruling interpreted these cases to include the situation where the fathers are the primary care givers of the children. In this way all Mr Lommers has to do is to apply for child care services as a father who takes care of the child by himself and his position will be equal to that of a mother and he will merit to have access to the child care facility.

One may add that subsidised child care facilities may be more pragmatically efficient than quotas when we attempt to reconcile family responsibilities with

---

14 Case C-476/99 (2002) ECR I-2891.

breaching the gap between the participation of women and men in the world of work.

Conclusion

The principles that one may glean from the rulings of the ECJ regarding positive action in the public service in the last decade may be summarised briefly as follows:

1. Affirmative or positive action for women that is rigid and absolute and results in reverse discrimination to men is prohibited by Community law. (*Kalanke* case).
2. Flexible positive action (i.e. quotas) that takes into consideration the objective circumstances of the other candidates is permitted by Community law. (*Marschall* and *Badeck* cases.)
3. A system of quotas is permissible regarding vocational training, but is prohibited regarding access to jobs. (*Badeck* case).
4. A system to facilitate interviews for women in the pre-recruitment phase is permissible. (*Badeck* case).
5. Quotas that facilitate the equal representation of women on administrative bodies are lawful. (*Badeck* case).
6. Positive action in academic posts is permissible when the qualifications of the candidates are identical and consideration of the objective circumstances of all candidates is taken into account. (*Abrahamsson* case).
7. The granting of subsidised child-care to mothers as a measure of positive action is permissible when fathers are also given the same facilities in cases where they are the care-takers of the children. (*Lommers* case).

The rulings of the Court have clarified the issue of positive action under EU Law. As we have seen, the measures of empowerment of women are within the competence of the Member States. Article 137 of the Treaty of Amsterdam provides that the Community will support and complement the actions of the Member States in the field of equality and equal opportunity. Here we are reminded of the principle of subsidiarity. The major task is in the hands of the Member States, while the Community and the Court of Justice are assisting and supervising the actions of the Member States. As we have seen, half of the cases were referred from Germany, where some of the Länder have adopted positive action legislation and programmes. There was also one case from Sweden and one from the Netherlands. Positive action in favour of women is regulated by the Member States but must be compatible with EU law.

There is no definition of 'positive action'. Nevertheless, positive action generally can be viewed to cover many different measures and strategies which are undertaken in order to compensate for past injustices suffered by women by redressing current inequalities amongst men and women, primarily in employment. The Commission of the European Community has stated that:

> "the concept of positive action embraces all measures which aim to counter the effects of past discrimination, to eliminate existing discrimination and to promote equality of opportunity between women and men, particularly in relation to types or levels of jobs where members of one sex are significantly under-represented."

EU policy regarding equality between women and men takes a comprehensive approach which includes legislation, mainstreaming and positive action. The key objective is to eliminate inequalities and promote gender equality throughout the European Community in accordance with Articles 2 and 3 of the EC Treaty that advocate gender mainstreaming, as well as Article 141 which enshrines the principle of equality between women and men in matters of employment and occupation, and Article 13 that combats sex discrimination within and outside the work place.

PART IV
NEW CHALLENGES AND THE DECENT WORK AGENDA

Chapter 15

CHALLENGES, ACHIEVEMENTS AND TRENDS

In labour law as in other legal domains, changes and progress are a continuing development, and law reflects cultural and social changes as well as scientific and technological developments. As the German jurist Rudolf von Jhering already said at the end of the Nineteenth Century: "Law is in a perpetual process of becoming".[1] This book has shown, we hope, the considerable evolution of labour law at the global and regional levels in the domain of equality between men and women at work.

Both the ILO and the EU have defined rules of fair conditions of work, social justice and equality, the ILO being the pioneer and standard-setter in this field: ILO standards have a global scope, while the EU legislates within the realm of EU Member States. The ILO has been a source of inspiration for EU developments in the labour area and more particularly in the equal treatment of men and women at work.

ILO standards are aimed at universality and have to take into account wide differences in traditions, cultures, social norms, economic development and ambitions, and in particular the specific concerns of the two main groups, the industrialized and the developing countries, although there are sub-groups in each. ILO Conventions have had to find compromises acceptable to all groups or supervised derogations in order to allow for gradual progress and to encourage more ratifications. The ILO Conventions are enforceable at the national level after ratification by Member States, and are then subject to reporting and international monitoring.

The EU has been able to go deeper and faster insofar as its Member States have, generally, a common tradition of values and practices in the labour area, although equal treatment of men and women is more of a recent development.

EU Directives are binding for all EU Member States, and are enforceable through an infrastructure of control by the European Commission and the ECJ.

1 Free translation of *Der Kampf um's Recht* (Vienna 1874), reproduced and prefaced by Felix Ermacora (Propylaen Verlag, Berlin, 1992), p. 69.

The ECJ has gone into details of implementation and interpretation of Directives, which, at times, have opened new tracks.

The EU has adopted, since the 1990s, a requirement of compulsory consultation with social partners on the discussion and formulation of social directives, i.e. employers' and workers' representatives, thus following the ILO's pattern of its tripartite composition – governments, employers' and workers' representation – in formulating and adopting ILO Conventions. Like the ILO, the EU has to take into account the different interests of governments, often allied with employers' groups, and of trade unions groups with their own history of past struggles and concern for the workers' security of employment and welfare, followed only in later years by the recognition that women and men at work must be granted equal treatment.

The Charter of Fundamental Rights of the European Union adopted in December 2000 was given legal force at Strasburg in December 2007.[2] The Charter confirmed a number of key principles, some of which are directly relevant to policies and practices in labour issues and equal treatment of men and women:

- Human dignity is inviolable, it must be respected and protected (Article 1);
- Discrimination based, *inter alia*, on sex is prohibited (Article 21);
- Equality between men and women must be ensured in all areas, including employment, work and pay. But this principle shall not prevent the maintenance or adoption of measures providing for specific advantages in favour of the under-represented sex (Article 23);
- Every worker has the right to fair and just working conditions (Article 31);
- Those whose rights and freedoms guaranteed by the law of the Union are violated have the right to an effective remedy and to a fair trial (Article 47).

Equality of men and women at work has become mainstreamed and elevated to a fundamental right.

Directive 2006/54/EC of the European Parliament and of the Council of 5 July 2006 on the implementation of the principle of equal opportunities and equal treatment of men and women in matters of employment and occupation has recast previous Directives, and brought together in a single text the main provisions in this field. It recalled that Article 141 (3) of the Treaty provides a

2 The Presidency Council at Strasburg, Proclamation of the Institutions of the EU on 12 December 2007.

specific legal basis for the adoption of Community measures to ensure the application of the principle of equal opportunities and equal treatment in matters of employment and occupation. The Directive also referred to the EU Charter and to developments in the case-law of the ECJ.

In accordance with Article 137 of the Treaty of Amsterdam, the Community will support and complement the actions of the Member States in the field of equality and opportunity. Under the principle of subsidiarity, the measures of empowerment of women are within the competence of the Member States, while the role of the Community and the ECJ is to assist and supervise the action of Member States. The Community has thus shared powers with the Member States in the domain of social law, including equality at work. This field is, however, not anymore predominantly covered by national laws, as the activity on the Community level has deepened and become more intensive in the last decade.

From the perspective of enforcement of equality, most national courts in the Member States have resorted to the procedure of preliminary rulings of the ECJ, starting with Belgian courts in 1971 in the three *Defrenne* Cases. The rulings provide a harmonised judicial basis for the implementation and interpretation of Directives at the national level, creating a consistent and uniform legal regime at EU level.

The ILO/EU Parallels

A few important developments and achievements of EU legislation and their connection with ILO standards are summarized hereunder.

In the equal pay area, EU Equal Pay law, i.e. Article 119 (now 141) of the EU Treaty and the Equal Pay Directive 1975, are the European translation of ILO Convention No. 100. The extension of Equal Pay for Equal Work to cover Work of Equal Value via the 1975 Directive brought EU law in line with the ILO standard. The definition of pay under EU law is inspired by the ILO definition of 'Remuneration' in Convention No. 100. The exception to the principle of Equal Pay elaborated by the ECJ's case law, where the employer can prove objective reasons unrelated to sex, is expressly provided for by ILO Convention No. 100 in Article 3 (3).

Although there are no references to the ILO standards in EU Directives and the ECJ is silent as to the impact of ILO Convention No. 100, the influence of the universal norms is great and the provisions of the Convention are followed and given effective application in the Member States via the ECJ's case law and its control powers.

In effect, the ILO standards on equal pay concerning their scope, the definition of "pay" and derogations, have all been taken over by the EU law.

The same influence of ILO Conventions is found in the equal treatment area. The *corpus juris* on EU equality at work is to be found in the Directive on Equal

Treatment 1976 that was inspired by ILO Convention No. 111 concerning Discrimination in Employment and Occupation 1958.

EU practice and ECJ decisions have consistently enlarged the scope of application of the Equal Treatment Directive 1976, covering a wide spectrum of employment issues from access to jobs to termination of employment. In this domain, the striking evolution towards unisex jobs deserves to be underlined. All jobs and occupations that were segregated and legitimately closed to women some fifty years ago are now open to women (albeit no access to army combat jobs).

In the EU, all stages of employment – access, promotion, vocational training and conditions of work – come under the rule of equal treatment. As a difference, the ILO Convention and not the EU law refers to education, while EU law expressly includes dismissal as a part of employment policy, which is only covered implicitly by the ILO.

The audacious decision of the ECJ in the *Marshall* 1986 case endowed women with a right to work, beyond the age of retirement, in spite of the fact that the ages of retirement are still different for men and women. Women can now work until the legal age of retirement for men.

The ILO Conventions have also inspired the EU legislation on pregnancy and maternity protection: Convention No. 3 of 1919, adopted at the first General Conference of the new organization, defined the basic principles of such protection, which were then used and developed by the EU in its Directives and the many rulings of the ECJ.

Extending protection to all workers without distinction of sex was promoted by the ILO as early as 1981 by the Occupational Safety and Health Convention No. 155. The EU followed in 1989 with Council Directive 89/391/EEC on the introduction of measures to encourage improvements in the safety and health of workers at work. The Directive refers to "workers" without distinction as to sex.

In the domain of protective measures for women workers, a similar interaction between ILO and the EU took place. Already in 1958, the ILO Discrimination (Employment and Occupation) Convention No. 111 established the principle of non-discrimination on the ground of sex, yet acknowledged that the various protective measures for women required observance. Such measures were not incompatible with equality, and were not deemed to be discrimination. ILO protective measures have gradually given place to health and safety measures for the whole workforce regardless of sex.

The EU followed in 1976 with Council Directive 76/207/EEC which adopted the principle of equal treatment in all conditions of work. The 2002 amending Directive has confirmed this principle.

The 1976 Directive permitted protective measures on a temporary basis until reviewed and revised because they had become purposeless. Exceptions are now limited only to occupational activities where the sex of the worker constitutes a "determining factor", and without prejudice to provisions concerning pregnancy and maternity. These exceptions follow the ILO derogations.

The ILO Employment (Women with Family Responsibilities) Recommendation No. 123 of 1965 emphasized that all measures promoting equal rights may prove meaningless for a vast proportion of women if – as a result of their family responsibilities – they must either give up their jobs entirely, or lose any chance of advancement. On 25 June 1975 the ILO adopted a Resolution concerning a plan of action with a view to promoting equality of opportunity for women workers. The Conference recognized that:

> "in order to make women's right to work outside the home without discrimination fully effective measures should be taken ... to encourage a more equitable sharing among family members of household tasks."

The adoption in 1981 of the ILO Convention on Workers with Family Responsibilities No. 156 and Recommendation No. 165 marked a shift in traditional attitudes concerning the role of women, and a recognition that family responsibilities affect not only women workers but the family and society as a whole.

EU law developed in the spirit of the ILO Convention No. 156 and departed from the ECJ ruling in the *Hofmann* Case 1984. It adopted in 1996 the Parental Leave Directive (96/34/EC) that promoted the sharing of family responsibilities by men and women workers. Its Preamble encouraged Member States to take measures to reconcile work and family life, and encouraged men to assume an equal share of family responsibilities and to take parental leave (Recitals 6 and 8).

The *Lommers* ruling of 2002 laid down the principle of the equitable sharing of subsidized child care facilities by mothers and fathers. Where the father is the child-caretaker he is as entitled as a mother to a subsidised nursery.

The policy of the EU as reflected in the Guidelines of 2003 and 2005 for the Employment Policies of the Member States evidences the central importance of child care and the commitment to the aim of reconciliation of workers' responsibilities as regards work and the family.

A further important step towards equality is marked by the provisions of the Part-Time Work Directive 1997 that follow those of ILO Convention No. 175 1994. Both instruments aim to protect part-time workers against discrimination and thereby protect women workers against indirect discrimination.

Both the ILO and the EU aim to entitle part-time workers to *pro rata* bonuses, maternity allowances, separation allowances, sick leave, etc., prohibiting the exclusion of part-time workers from certain benefits unless their working hours per week fall below 10 hours or less, according to national law or collective agreements.

While the ILO has not elaborated any separate standard in the form of a Convention or a Recommendation on the question of burden of proof in cases of sex discrimination, it nevertheless provided for the exception of objective reasons that the employer can resort to in order to justify a disparity in pay or treatment in all conditions of work and refute discrimination based on sex. The issue is relevant for the EU in the implementation of the policies on equality and non-discrimination. It resulted in the adoption of the EU Directive on the Burden of Proof 1997.

This Directive and the Directive on Part-time Work have undergone a legislative history close to the practice of ILO. These Directives originated in Framework Agreements between the social partners, much like the elaboration of ILO Standards through the tripartite method of consultation and collaboration.

The ILO, while concerned about sexual harassment at work, has found no need for a new Convention on this specific issue, and continues to rely on Convention 111 to deal with related problems. The EU first relied on the Equal Treatment Directive 76/207/EEC, then went on to adopt a Code of Practice on the Protection of the Dignity of the Worker 1991 before finally adopting a new Directive 2002/73/EC amending Directive 76/207/EEC and recognizing sexual harassment as a form of sex discrimination.[3]

Neither the ILO standards nor EU law initially advocated affirmative action and quotas as means to ensure the implementation of the principle of equality between men and women. However, in 1996 the ILO Committee of Experts observed that the adoption of affirmative action measures is often extremely useful in the first stages of eliminating discrimination. Not unlike the ILO instruments, the 1976 Directive on Equal Treatment for Men and Women did not address the issue of affirmative or positive action, except in paragraph 4 of its Article 2:

> "The Directive shall be without prejudice to measures to promote equal opportunity for men and women, in particular by removing existing inequalities that affect women's opportunities."

Referring to this Article, in 1984 the Council recommended that Member States adopt a positive action policy designed to eliminate existing inequalities affecting women in working life and to promote a better balance between the sexes in employment. The ECJ then advocated flexible positive action in the public service, rather than rigid or absolute quotas. The Court also decided that the granting of subsidized child-care to mothers as a measure of positive action is permissible when fathers are also given the same facilities in cases when they are the principal care takers of their children.

In 2007, the ILO acknowledged that affirmative action measures that are integrated in human resources policies can help employers create more

[3] As strongly recommended by the Rubenstein report of 1987.

inclusive workplaces, and has improved the representation of groups affected by discrimination.[4]

Altogether, the impact of ILO standards on EU law and practice is more than evident although there is no acknowledgment in EU legislation or case law. The EU has followed the ILO guiding models. Only more recently has there been collaboration and interaction between the ILO and the EU. Will this recent joint effort between global and regional forces bring about cross-fertilisation and open up new avenues to eliminate discrimination? This query brings us to assess the achievements so far and trace the roadmap for future action.

The Slow Road to Equality between Women and Men in the EU

In 2006, several important events had a bearing on gender equality in the EU: the adoption by the European Commission of the Roadmap for equality between women and men[5] for the period 2006-2010, and the adoption by the European Council of the Pact for Gender Equality.[6] In addition, a Regulation creating a European Institute for Gender Equality, a new regulation of the Structural Funds,[7] and the Community strategic guidelines on cohesion[8] for the period 2007-2013 were also adopted in 2006. The latter foresee both specific measures and the integration of the gender perspective in all actions. Their implementation will be primarily the task of the Member States.

A 2007 report on equality between men and women in the EU by the Commission to the Council, the European Parliament, the European Economic and Social Committee and the Committee of the Regions shows some progress and many roadblocks.[9]

Over the last few years, progress has been achieved towards the Lisbon target of reaching an employment rate for women of 60 percent by 2010. Women were still more likely to be unemployed than men as the unemployment rate was 9.9 percent among women in 2005 whereas it was 7.9 percent among men. In

---

4 *Equality at Work: Tackling the Challenges: Global Report under the follow-up to the ILO Declaration on Fundamental Principles and Rights at Work* (ILO, Geneva, 2007), p. xi.

5 Doc. COM (2006) 92 final.

6 Conclusions of the Presidency, 7775/1//06/Rev. 1.

7 Regulation (EC) No. 1922/2006, and Regulations (EC) 1081/2006 and 1083/2006; OJ (2006) L 403/9, 20 December 2006 – L 210/12, 5 July 2006; – L 210/25, 11 July 2006.

8 Council Decision 2006/702/EC.

9 Report from the Commission to the Council, the European Parliament, the European Economic and Social Committee and the Committee of the Regions on equality between women and men 2007, Doc. COM (2007) 49 final, 7 February 2007, and Annex.

2006, the share of women employees working part-time was 32 percent in the EU while the corresponding figure for men was 7.7 percent. Only 29 percent of scientists and engineers in the EU are women. The average number of female members of national parliaments was 24 percent in 2006, an increase of 1 percentage point since 2004.

Although women now represent the majority of new higher education graduates (59 percent), their fields of study remain strongly stereotyped: technical studies attract only one female graduate in ten, compared with four male graduates in ten.

The report notes the persistence of gender gaps in the European labour market. Women earn an average of 15 percent less than men for each hour worked, one point below its level in 1999.

What are the remedies?

The combined efforts of the ILO and the EU promise to have significant results.

The ILO Prescriptions

In its 2007 report,[10] the ILO has adopted gender equality as a universal strategic goal, making it a mainstream objective of its Decent Work Country Programmes. The elimination of discrimination is at the heart of "decent work" for all women and men, which:

> "is founded on the notion of equal opportunities for all those who work or seek work and a living, whether as labourers, employers or self-employed, in the formal or the informal economy."[11]

One approach recommended by the report is to complement conventional anti-discrimination policy measures, such as coherent and comprehensive laws, effective enforcement market policies by adding measures on job search, recruitment and placement, training, hiring subsidies, job-creation programmes, and support services.

Businesses should be persuaded to modify their human resources management policies and practices with a view to achieving greater diversity in their work-forces through a number of non-regulatory measures.

For the ILO, one method of establishing pay equality is through job evaluation methods that are free from gender bias: a well-known albeit complex human resources technique.

---

10 *Equality at Work: Tackling the Challenges*: see note 4.

11 *Time for Equality at Work, Global Report under the follow-up to the ILO Declaration on Fundamental Principles and Rights at work* (ILO, Geneva, 2003), p. 1.

Workplace family policies are required for both men and women to help overcome the problems of workers with family responsibilities in better balancing work-family issues in a world of longer working hours and work patterns that disadvantage women and affect their careers. Childcare arrangements, especially for children under three years old, should become a priority. New policies have encouraged fathers to take parental leave.

Part-time work should be more equally distributed between women and men. However, in many countries, opportunities for women are concentrated in low-status jobs. One exception is the Netherlands, which through greater labour market regulation has introduced part-time work throughout all segregated sectors and occupations to achieve a more even distribution of part-time work between women and men.[12]

The critical role of the social partners is highlighted by the ILO in key areas such as collective bargaining to bring about concrete change in the working lives of those subject to discrimination. In the field of collective bargaining trade unions, especially in the industrialized countries, are putting work-family reconciliation high on their agenda, partly as a way of increasing membership. However, issues such as family care provisions are still absent from collective agreements in other countries, including new EU Member States. The social partners can also contribute to the elimination of discrimination and the promotion of equality at work by removing discriminatory practices within their own structures, and in the types of services that they supply to their members.

The EU Prescriptions

As contained in a 2007 Report, the EU prescriptions follow the ILO prescriptions as to principles and policies, but they are more precise as they address a quasi-homogeneous group of countries, and are enforceable through the binding directives and the Court's decisions.[13] As in the ILO, the social partners and national authorities are called upon to define and implement innovative effective policies.

The Spring European Council of 2006 stressed that policies on gender equality are essential instruments for economic growth, prosperity and competitiveness. In order to fully exploit the potential of European workforce productivity, it is essential to promote women's long-term participation in the labour market and to eliminate the disparities between men and women across the board. Equality policies will need the active support of Community cohesion policy and effective implementation of legislation on equal treatment.

12 *Equality at Work: Tackling the Challenges*, note 3, p. xii.

13 EU Doc. COM (2007) 49 final, section 3 "Challenges and Policy Orientations".

According to the 2007 report, the priorities set out in the Roadmap for gender equality will require action in the following areas.

1. Eliminating gender gaps in the labour market. Access to high quality paid employment is the guarantor of the economic independence of both women and men. Nevertheless, some very major disparities persist between the sexes, in particular regarding arrangements for working time (part-time work, temporary contracts) and sectors and professions. It is essential to analyse and tackle the factors underlying these disparities. Among these:

- The causes of labour market segregation, which essentially originates in stereotype choices of education, training and careers, should be actively combated;
- Efforts aimed at eliminating obstacles to women's access to decision-making and managerial positions need to be intensified;
- Efforts to reduce the gender pay gap should be continued. Particular attention should be given to the low level of wages in professions which tend to be dominated by women and to the reasons which lead to reduced earnings in professions and sectors in which women become more prominent;
- The development, implementation and monitoring of "flexicurity" should take account of their different impacts on women and men and should avoid stressing the "flexibility" aspect for women and the "security" aspect for men.

2. Encouraging a better balance of private and family responsibilities between women and men. Numerous constraints restrict the free choice of individuals to reconcile their professions and their private lives, for example, the lack of childcare services, financial factors, career setbacks, the risk of losing one's skills, the difficulties of returning to employment and the pressure to conform to stereotypes.

- Parental leave should be targeted at both men and women, it should be financially attractive, it should be taken over several periods, its duration should not be a barrier to returning to work;
- Parental leave should make it possible for fathers to be involved in domestic and family responsibilities from the day their children are born.

3. Ensuring that policies on gender equality have the full support of EU cohesion and rural development policies.

4. Ensuring effective implementation of the legislative framework on the equal treatment of men and women with the active support of Member States and the social partners.

When summing up the priorities of the ILO and the EU, one may conclude that they converge. They both single out the same aims and means:

1. Desegregation of jobs,
2. Balancing home and work responsibilities,
3. Banning discrimination of part-time workers.
4. The EU now prohibits different retirement ages for men and women as being contrary to the principle of equal treatment.

Both the ILO and the EU subscribe to the ILO-initiated "Decent Work Agenda" (2000-2005) in which gender equality occupies pride of place. The ILO, the locomotive, and the EU, the trailer, have the same road map to advance equality.

Trends

The new Millennium brought awareness to discrimination beyond gender discrimination in the EU, and EU law added other grounds based on race, ethnic origin, religion or belief, disability, age or sexual orientation. The 2000 Race Directive implements the principle of equal treatment irrespective of racial or ethnic origin and the 2000 General Framework Directive affords protection against discrimination on the basis of age, invalidity and sexual orientation. These three new grounds go beyond the protection of ILO Convention No. 111.[14] EU law now recognizes that there are underprivileged sensitive groups who are less equal than others at the workplace, and that they need specific protection and positive (affirmative) action.

The widening of combat against discrimination and the inclusion of new underprivileged groups of society should not dilute the closing of the gender gap. There is real apprehension that positive action for women may be jeopardised, especially if these different new groups compete to be represented against under-represented women entitled to positive action. Equality for women thus acquires a new challenge.

Furthermore, the steady progress against discrimination, inequalities in income, job opportunities, job retention and career prospects continues to be an up-hill effort, compounded by the globalization of the market system and global

---

14 Council Directive 2000/43/EC concerning Equal Treatment irrespective of Race and Ethnic Origin OJ (2000) L 180/22 and Council Directive 2000/78/EC establishing a General Framework for Equal Treatment in Employment and Occupation; OJ (2000) L 303/16.

competition. As noted by Hepple,[15] "The ECJ has also recently taken a robust approach to attempts to use 'market forces' to justify indirect discrimination".

This road to equality of women and men was paved by the ILO and followed by the EU. The substantive law of the European Community was inspired by ILO standards. In more recent years the EU adhered also to the ILO's model of the tripartite system of representation – governments, employers, workers – in defining or revising labour law policies and in their implementation and monitoring.

The new Millennium witnessed the novel initiatives of the ILO Decent Work Agenda. Decent work sums up the aspirations of people in their working lives. It involves opportunities for work that is productive, freely chosen and delivers a fair income. There should be equality of opportunity and treatment for all women and men, security in the workplace, social protection for the worker and his/her family, prospects for personal development and social integration, as well as freedom for people to express their concerns, organise and participate in the decisions that affect their lives. It includes also the core labour standards such as the prohibition of child labour and of forced labour, prohibition of discrimination in employment and freedom of association and collective bargaining. The World Commission on the Social Dimension of Globalisation proposed that decent work for all should become a global goal for all international, regional, national and local public and private actors.[16]

In the words of the Director General of the ILO, Juan Somavia:

> "The primary goal of the ILO today is to promote opportunities for women and men to obtain decent and productive work, in conditions of freedom, equity, security and human dignity."

As early as May 2001 there was an exchange of letters between the Commission of the EC and the ILO[17] which proclaimed their shared commitment to social and economic progress, to improving living and working conditions, and to promoting employment. Since the first agreement between the ILO and the Communities in 1958, the two organizations have progressively developed their cooperation to further these aims. This new exchange of letters serves, first, to identify the areas in which new challenges have emerged for both the organizations, and second, to establish on that basis the priority areas in which cooperation between the ILO and the Commission would be most beneficial. These letters illustrate

15 Bob Hepple, "Equality and Discrimination", in *European Community Labour Law Principles and Perspectives on European Labour Law: Liber amicorum Lord Wedderburn* (Clarendon Press Oxford, 1996), pp, 237-259.

16 Report of the World Commission on the Social Dimension of Globalisation, February 2004, § 280, 492-493, 502-510 and Annexe I.

17 OJ (2001) C 165/12.

the convergence of the aims and priorities of the two organisations in relation to the Decent Work Agenda.

In the letters, the ILO identifies four strategic objectives as crucial to its mandate in the context of globalization: fundamental principles and rights at work, the promotion of employment for women and men, the enhancement of social protection and the promotion of social dialogue. Together, these constitute the essence of "Decent Work". The process of European integration, for its part, has acquired a strong and dynamic social dimension. In this context, the promotion of equality is now at the heart of the EU's agenda for employment, social policy and industrial relations. It is the driving force for a thriving economy, more and better jobs and an inclusive society. Moreover, the process of enlargement of the European Union will require the new Member States to adhere to the framework of the European social model.

The letters recall that in 1995 the World Summit for Social Development defined a social floor for the global economy in terms of the ILO Conventions covering four basic principles: freedom of association and collective bargaining, freedom from forced labour, freedom from discrimination, and the abolition of child labour. In this context, the ILO has reinforced its role as the focal point for international efforts to promote opportunities for women and men to obtain decent and productive work through the adoption of the Declaration on Fundamental Principles and Rights at Work. In the European Union, a reference to fundamental social rights is now included in the Treaty itself, as is the possibility of concrete action by the Community against discrimination and social exclusion. Furthermore, the European Union has proclaimed a Charter of Fundamental Rights.

The European Union has also developed an extensive employment strategy which seeks to maximize the employment potential of the European economy while respecting the principle of gender equality. It should further be noted that the ILO and the European Community now have common goals with respect to the promotion of social protection.

In a Communication of 18 May 2004 on "The social dimension of globalisation: the EU's policy contribution on extending the benefits to all", the European Commission supports the promotion of decent work for all as a global goal. In December 2004, the European Council highlighted the importance of the social dimension of globalisation. In March 2005, the Council adopted conclusions on the same issue.

In conclusion, this book has recounted the pioneering role of the ILO and the impressive progress achieved by the EU in the area of equality of men and women at work. It has also shown the influence of ILO Conventions on EU law and the case law of the ECJ. The Community Court faithfully translated into practice the standards of the ILO as they were adopted by EU legislation.

Finally this study has demonstrated the need for continued international initiatives, at both the global and regional levels, in standard-setting and monitoring, such as the recent Decent Work Agenda.

We hope that our account of the EU's model might help other countries and regions on their own road to equality, and might assist the new Member States of the Union to approximate their social laws with EU laws.

Annexes

SELECT ILO CONVENTIONS – EXCERPTS

The Equal Remuneration Convention, No. 100, 1951

...

Article 1

For the purpose of this Convention –

(a) the term *remuneration* includes the ordinary, basic or minimum wage or salary and any additional emoluments whatsoever payable directly or indirectly, whether in cash or in kind, by the employer to the worker and arising out of the worker's employment;

(b) the term *equal remuneration for men and women workers for work of equal value* refers to rates of remuneration established without discrimination based on sex.

Article 2

1. Each Member shall, by means appropriate to the methods in operation for determining rates of remuneration, promote and, in so far as is consistent with such methods, ensure the application to all workers of the principle of equal remuneration for men and women workers for work of equal value.

2. This principle may be applied by means of –

(a) national laws or regulations;

(b) legally established or recognised machinery for wage determination;

(c) collective agreements between employers and workers; or

(d) a combination of these various means.

Article 3

1. Where such action will assist in giving effect to the provisions of this Convention measures shall be taken to promote objective appraisal of jobs on the basis of the work to be performed.

2. The methods to be followed in this appraisal may be decided upon by the authorities responsible for the determination of rates of remuneration, or, where such rates are determined by collective agreements, by the partíes thereto.

3. Differential rates between workers which correspond, without regard to sex, to differences, as determined by such objective appraisal, in the work to be performed shall not be considered as being contrary to the principle of equal remuneration for men and women workers for work of equal value.

Article 4

Each Member shall co-operate as appropriate with the employers' and workers' organisations concerned for the purpose of giving effect to the provisions of this Convention.

Article 5

The formal ratifications of this Convention shall be communicated to the Director-General of the International Labour Office for registration.

Article 6

1. This Convention shall be binding only upon those Members of the International Labour Organisation whose ratifications have been registered with the Director-General.

2. It shall come into force twelve months after the date on which the ratifications of two Members have been registered with the Director-General.

3. Thereafter, this Convention shall come into force for any Member twelve months after the date on which its ratification has been registered.

Article 7

1. Declarations communicated to the Director-General of the International Labour Office in accordance with paragraph 2 of Article 35 of the Constitution of the International Labour Organisation shall indicate –

a) the territories in respect of which the Member concerned undertakes that the provisions of the Convention shall be applied without modification;

b) the territories in respect of which it undertakes that the provisions of the Convention shall be applied subject to modifications, together with details of the said modifications;

c) the territories in respect of which the Convention is inapplicable and in such cases the grounds on which it is inapplicable;

d) the territories in respect of which it reserves its decision pending further consideration of the position.

2. The undertakings referred to in subparagraphs (a) and (b) of paragraph 1 of this Article shall be deemed to be an integral part of the ratification and shall have the force of ratification.

3. Any Member may at any time by a subsequent declaration cancel in whole or in part any reservation made in its original declaration in virtue of subparagraph (b), (c) or (d) of paragraph 1 of this Article.

4. Any Member may, at any time at which the Convention is subject to denunciation in accordance with the provisions of Article 9, communicate to the Director-General a declaration modifying in any other respect the terms of any former declaration and stating the present position in respect of such territories as it may specify.

Article 8

1. Declarations communicated to the Director-General of the International Labour Office in accordance with paragraph 4 or 5 of Article 35 of the Constitution of the International Labour Organisation shall indicate whether the provisions of the Convention will be applied in the territory concerned without modification or subject to modifications; when the declaration indicates that the provisions of the Convention will be applied subject to modifications, it shall give details of the said modifications.

2. The Member, Members or international authority concerned may at any time by a subsequent declaration renounce in whole or in part the right to have recourse to any modification indicated in any former declaration.

3. The Member, Members or international authority concerned may, at any time at which this Convention is subject to denunciation in accordance with the provisions of Article 9, communicate to the Director-General a declaration modifying in any other respect the terms of any former declaration and stating the present position in respect of the application of the Convention.

Article 9

1. A Member which has ratified this Convention may denounce it after the expiration of ten years from the date on which the Convention first comes into force, by an act communicated to the Director-General of the International Labour Office for registration. Such denunciation shall not take effect until one year after the date on which it is registered.

2. Each Member which has ratified this Convention and which does not, within the year following the expiration of the period of ten years mentioned in the preceding paragraph, exercise the right of denunciation provided for in this Article, will be bound for another period of ten years and, thereafter, may

denounce this Convention at the expiration of each period of ten years under the terms provided for in this Article.

Article 10

1. The Director-General of the International Labour Office shall notify all Members of the International Labour Organisation of the registration of all ratifications, declarations and denunciations communicated to him by the Members of the Organisation.

2. When notifying the Members of the Organisation of the registration of the second ratification communicated to him, the Director-General shall draw the attention of the Members of the Organisation to the date upon which the Convention will come into force.

Article 11

The Director-General of the International Labour Office shall communicate to the Secretary-General of the United Nations for registration in accordance with Article 102 of the Charter of the United Nations full particulars of all ratifications, declarations and acts of denunciation registered by him in accordance with the provisions of the preceding articles.

Article 12

At such times as may consider necessary the Governing Body of the International Labour Office shall present to the General Conference a report on the working of this Convention and shall examine the desirability of placing on the agenda of the Conference the question of its revision in whole or in part.

Article 13

1. Should the Conference adopt a new Convention revising this Convention in whole or in part, then, unless the new Convention otherwise provides –

a) the ratification by a Member of the new revising Convention shall ipso jure involve the immediate denunciation of this Convention, notwithstanding the provisions of Article 9 above, if and when the new revising Convention shall have come into force;

b) as from the date when the new revising Convention comes into force this Convention shall cease to be open to ratification by the Members.

2. This Convention shall in any case remain in force in its actual form and content for those Members which have ratified it but have not ratified the revising Convention.

The Discrimination (Employment and Occupation) Convention, No. 111, 1958

Article 1

1. For the purpose of this Convention the term *discrimination* includes –

(a) any distinction, exclusion or preference made on the basis of race, colour, sex, religion, political opinion, national extraction or social origin, which has the effect of nullifying or impairing equality of opportunity or treatment in employment or occupation;

(b) such other distinction, exclusion or preference which has the effect of nullifying or impairing equality of opportunity or treatment in employment or occupation as may be determined by the Member concerned after consultation with representative employers' and workers' organisations, where such exist, and with other appropriate bodies.

2. Any distinction, exclusion or preference in respect of a particular job based on the inherent requirements thereof shall not be deemed to be discrimination.

3. For the purpose of this Convention the terms *employment* and *occupation* include access to vocational training, access to employment and to particular occupations, and terms and conditions of employment.

Article 2

Each Member for which this Convention is in force undertakes to declare and pursue a national policy designed to promote, by methods appropriate to national conditions and practice, equality of opportunity and treatment in respect of employment and occupation, with a view to eliminating any discrimination in respect thereof.

Article 3

Each Member for which this Convention is in force undertakes, by methods appropriate to national conditions and practice –

(a) to seek the co-operation of employers' and workers' organisations and other appropriate bodies in promoting the acceptance and observance of this policy;

(b) to enact such legislation and to promote such educational programmes as may be calculated to secure the acceptance and observance of the policy;

(c) to repeal any statutory provisions and modify any administrative instructions or practices which are inconsistent with the policy;

(d) to pursue the policy in respect of employment under the direct control of a national authority;

(e) to ensure observance of the policy in the activities of vocational guidance, vocational training and placement services under the direction of a national authority;

(f) to indicate in its annual reports on the application of the Convention the action taken in pursuance of the policy and the results secured by such action.

Article 4

Any measures affecting an individual who is justifiably suspected of, or engaged in, activities prejudicial to the security of the State shall not be deemed to be discrimination, provided that the individual concerned shall have the right to appeal to a competent body established in accordance with national practice.

Article 5

1. Special measures of protection or assistance provided for in other Conventions or Recommendations adopted by the International Labour Conference shall not be deemed to be discrimination.

2. Any Member may, after consultation with representative employers' and workers' organisations, where such exist, determine that other special measures designed to meet the particular requirements of persons who, for reasons such as sex, age, disablement, family responsibilities or social or cultural status, are generally recognised to require special protection or assistance, shall not be deemed to be discrimination.

Article 6

Each Member which ratifies this Convention undertakes to apply it to non-metropolitan territories in accordance with the provisions of the Constitution of the International Labour Organisation.

Article 7

The formal ratifications of this Convention shall be communicated to the Director-General of the International Labour Office for registration.

Article 8

1. This Convention shall be binding only upon those Members of the International Labour Organisation whose ratifications have been registered with the Director-General.

2. It shall come into force twelve months after the date on which the ratifications of two Members have been registered with the Director-General.

3. Thereafter, this Convention shall come into force for any Member twelve months after the date on which its ratification has been registered.

Article 9

1. A Member which has ratified this Convention may denounce it after the expiration of ten years from the date on which the Convention first comes into force, by an act communicated to the Director-General of the International Labour Office for registration. Such denunciation shall not take effect until one year after the date on which it is registered.

2. Each Member which has ratified this Convention and which does not, within the year following the expiration of the period of ten years mentioned in the preceding paragraph, exercise the right of denunciation provided for in this Article, will be bound for another period of ten years and, thereafter, may denounce this Convention at the expiration of each period of ten years under the terms provided for in this Article.

Article 10

1. The Director-General of the International Labour Office shall notify all Members of the International Labour Organisation of the registration of all ratifications and denunciations communicated to him by the Members of the Organisation.

2. When notifying the Members of the Organisation of the registration of the second ratification communicated to him, the Director-General shall draw the attention of the Members of the Organisation to the date upon which the Convention will come into force.

Article 11

The Director-General of the International Labour Office shall communicate to the Secretary-General of the United Nations for registration in accordance with Article 102 of the Charter of the United Nations full particulars of all ratifications and acts of denunciation registered by him in accordance with the provisions of the preceding Articles.

Article 12

At such times as it may consider necessary the Governing Body of the International Labour Office shall present to the General Conference a report on the working of this Convention and shall examine the desirability of placing on the agenda of the Conference the question of its revision in whole or in part.

Article 13

1. Should the Conference adopt a new Convention revising this Convention in whole or in part, then, unless the new Convention otherwise provides:

a) the ratification by a Member of the new revising Convention shall ipso jure involve the immediate denunciation of this Convention, notwithstanding the provisions of Article 9 above, if and when the new revising Convention shall have come into force;

b) as from the date when the new revising Convention comes into force, this Convention shall cease to be open to ratification by the Members.

2. This Convention shall in any case remain in force in its actual form and content for those Members which have ratified it but have not ratified the revising Convention.

The Workers with Family Responsibilities Convention, No. 156, 1981

...

Article 1

1. This Convention applies to men and women workers with responsibilities in relation to their dependent children, where such responsibilities restrict their possibilities of preparing for, entering, participating in or advancing in economic activity.

2. The provisions of this Convention shall also be applied to men and women workers with responsibilities in relation to other members of their immediate family who clearly need their care or support, where such responsibilities restrict their possibilities of preparing for, entering, participating in or advancing in economic activity.

3. For the purposes of this Convention, the terms dependent child and other member of the immediate family who clearly needs care or support mean persons defined as such in each country by one of the means referred to in Article 9 of this Convention.

4. The workers covered by virtue of paragraphs 1 and 2 of this Article are hereinafter referred to as *workers with family responsibilities*.

Article 2

This Convention applies to all branches of economic activity and all categories of workers.

Article 3

1. With a view to creating effective equality of opportunity and treatment for men and women workers, each Member shall make it an aim of national policy to enable persons with family responsibilities who are engaged or wish to engage in employment to exercise their right to do so without being subject to discrimination and, to the extent possible, without conflict between their employment and family responsibilities.

2. For the purposes of paragraph 1 of this Article, the term *discrimination* means discrimination in employment and occupation as defined by Articles 1 and 5 of the Discrimination (Employment and Occupation) Convention, 1958.

Article 4

With a view to creating effective equality of opportunity and treatment for men and women workers, all measures compatible with national conditions and possibilities shall be taken –

(a) to enable workers with family responsibilities to exercise their right to free choice of employment; and

(b) to take account of their needs in terms and conditions of employment and in social security.

Article 5

All measures compatible with national conditions and possibilities shall further be taken –

(a) to take account of the needs of workers with family responsibilities in community planning; and

(b) to develop or promote community services, public or private, such as child-care and family services and facilities.

Article 6

The competent authorities and bodies in each country shall take appropriate measures to promote information and education which engender broader public understanding of the principle of equality of opportunity and treatment for men and women workers and of the problems of workers with family responsibilities, as well as a climate of opinion conducive to overcoming these problems.

Article 7

All measures compatible with national conditions and possibilities, including measures in the field of vocational guidance and training, shall be taken to enable workers with family responsibilities to become and remain integrated in the labour force, as well as to re-enter the labour force after an absence due to those responsibilities.

Article 8

Family responsibilities shall not, as such, constitute a valid reason for termination of employment.

Article 9

The provisions of this Convention may be applied by laws or regulations, collective agreements, works rules, arbitration awards, court decisions or a combination of these methods, or in any other manner consistent with national practice which may be appropriate, account being taken of national conditions.

Article 10

1. The provisions of this Convention may be applied by stages if necessary, account being taken of national conditions: Provided that such measures of implementation as are taken shall apply in any case to all the workers covered by Article 1, paragraph 1.

2. Each Member which ratifies this Convention shall indicate in the first report on the application of the Convention submitted under Article 22 of the Constitution of the International Labour Organisation in what respect, if any, it intends to make use of the faculty given by paragraph 1 of this Article, and shall state in subsequent reports the extent to which effect has been given or is proposed to be given to the Convention in that respect.

Article 11

Employers' and workers' organisations shall have the right to participate, in a manner appropriate to national conditions and practice, in devising and applying measures designed to give effect to the provisions of this Convention.

Article 12

The formal ratifications of this Convention shall be communicated to the Director-General of the International Labour Office for registration.

Article 13

1. This Convention shall be binding only upon those Members of the International Labour Organisation whose ratifications have been registered with the Director-General.

2. It shall come into force twelve months after the date on which the ratifications of two Members have been registered with the Director-General.

3. Thereafter, this Convention shall come into force for any Member twelve months after the date on which its ratification has been registered.

Article 14

1. A Member which has ratified this Convention may denounce it after the expiration of ten years from the date on which the Convention first comes into force, by an act communicated to the Director-General of the International Labour Office for registration. Such denunciation shall not take effect until one year after the date on which it is registered.

2. Each Member which has ratified this Convention and which does not, within the year following the expiration of the period of ten years mentioned in the preceding paragraph, exercise the right of denunciation provided for in this Article, will be bound for another period of ten years and, thereafter, may denounce this Convention at the expiration of each period of ten years under the terms provided for in this Article.

Article 15

1. The Director-General of the International Labour Office shall notify all Members of the International Labour Organisation of the registration of all ratifications and denunciations communicated to him by the Members of the Organisation.

2. When notifying the Members of the Organisation of the registration of the second ratification communicated to him, the Director-General shall draw the attention of the Members of the Organisation to the date upon which the Convention will come into force.

Article 16

The Director-General of the International Labour Office shall communicate to the Secretary-General of the United Nations for registration in accordance with Article 102 of the Charter of the United Nations full particulars of all ratifications and acts of denunciation registered by him in accordance with the provisions of the preceding Articles.

Article 17

At such times as it may consider necessary the Governing Body of the International Labour Office shall present to the General Conference a report on the working of this Convention and shall examine the desirability of placing on the agenda of the Conference the question of its revision in whole or in part.

Article 18

1. Should the Conference adopt a new Convention revising this Convention in whole or in part, then, unless the new Convention otherwise provides:

a) the ratification by a Member of the new revising Convention shall ipso jure involve the immediate denunciation of this Convention, notwithstanding the provisions of Article 14 above, if and when the new revising Convention shall have come into force;

b) as from the date when the new revising Convention comes into force this Convention shall cease to be open to ratification by the Members.

2. This Convention shall in any case remain in force in its actual form and content for those Members which have ratified it but have not ratified the revising Convention.

The Part-Time Work Convention, No. 175, 1994

...

Article 1

For the purposes of this Convention:

(a) the term *part-time worker* means an employed person whose normal hours of work are less than those of comparable full-time workers;

(b) the normal hours of work referred to in subparagraph (a) may be calculated weekly or on average over a given period of employment;

(c) the term *comparable full-time worker* refers to a full-time worker who:

(i) has the same type of employment relationship;

(ii) is engaged in the same or a similar type of work or occupation; and

(iii) is employed in the same establishment or, when there is no comparable full-time worker in that establishment, in the same enterprise or, when there is no comparable full-time worker in that enterprise, in the same branch of activity,

as the part-time worker concerned;

(d) full-time workers affected by partial unemployment, that is by a collective and temporary reduction in their normal hours of work for economic, technical or structural reasons, are not considered to be part-time workers.

Article 2

This Convention does not affect more favourable provisions applicable to part-time workers under other international labour Conventions.

Article 3

1. This Convention applies to all part-time workers, it being understood that a Member may, after consulting the representative organizations of employers and workers concerned, exclude wholly or partly from its scope particular categories of workers or of establishments when its application to them would raise particular problems of a substantial nature.

2. Each Member having ratified this Convention which avails itself of the possibility afforded in the preceding paragraph shall, in its reports on the application of the Convention under article 22 of the Constitution of the International Labour Organization, indicate any particular category of workers or of establishments thus excluded and the reasons why this exclusion was or is still judged necessary.

Article 4

Measures shall be taken to ensure that part-time workers receive the same protection as that accorded to comparable full-time workers in respect of:

(a) the right to organize, the right to bargain collectively and the right to act as workers' representatives;

(b) occupational safety and health;

(c) discrimination in employment and occupation.

Article 5

Measures appropriate to national law and practice shall be taken to ensure that part-time workers do not, solely because they work part time, receive a basic wage which, calculated proportionately on an hourly, performance-related, or piece-rate basis, is lower than the basic wage of comparable full-time workers, calculated according to the same method.

Article 6

Statutory social security schemes which are based on occupational activity shall be adapted so that part-time workers enjoy conditions equivalent to those of comparable full-time workers; these conditions may be determined in proportion to hours of work, contributions or earnings, or through other methods consistent with national law and practice.

Article 7

Measures shall be taken to ensure that part-time workers receive conditions equivalent to those of comparable full-time workers in the fields of:

(a) maternity protection;

(b) termination of employment;

(c) paid annual leave and paid public holidays; and

(d) sick leave,

it being understood that pecuniary entitlements may be determined in proportion to hours of work or earnings.

Article 8

1. Part-time workers whose hours of work or earnings are below specified thresholds may be excluded by a Member:

(a) from the scope of any of the statutory social security schemes referred to in Article 6, except in regard to employment injury benefits;

(b) from the scope of any of the measures taken in the fields covered by Article 7, except in regard to maternity protection measures other than those provided under statutory social security schemes.

2. The thresholds referred to in paragraph 1 shall be sufficiently low as not to exclude an unduly large percentage of part-time workers.

3. A Member which avails itself of the possibility provided for in paragraph 1 above shall:

(a) periodically review the thresholds in force;

(b) in its reports on the application of the Convention under article 22 of the Constitution of the International Labour Organization, indicate the thresholds in force, the reasons therefor and whether consideration is being given to the progressive extension of protection to the workers excluded.

4. The most representative organizations of employers and workers shall be consulted on the establishment, review and revision of the thresholds referred to in this Article.

Article 9

1. Measures shall be taken to facilitate access to productive and freely chosen part-time work which meets the needs of both employers and workers, provided that the protection referred to in Articles 4 to 7 is ensured.

2. These measures shall include:

(a) the review of laws and regulations that may prevent or discourage recourse to or acceptance of part-time work;

(b) the use of employment services, where they exist, to identify and publicize possibilities for part-time work in their information and placement activities;

(c) special attention, in employment policies, to the needs and preferences of specific groups such as the unemployed, workers with family responsibilities, older workers, workers with disabilities and workers undergoing education or training.

3. These measures may also include research and dissemination of information on the degree to which part-time work responds to the economic and social aims of employers and workers.

Article 10

Where appropriate, measures shall be taken to ensure that transfer from full-time to part-time work or vice versa is voluntary, in accordance with national law and practice.

Article 11

The provisions of this Convention shall be implemented by laws or regulations, except in so far as effect is given to them by means of collective agreements or in any other manner consistent with national practice. The most representative organizations of employers and workers shall be consulted before any such laws or regulations are adopted.

Article 12

The formal ratifications of this Convention shall be communicated to the Director-General of the International Labour Office for registration.

Article 13

1. This Convention shall be binding only upon those Members of the International Labour Organization whose ratifications have been registered with the Director-General.

2. It shall come into force 12 months after the date on which the ratifications of two Members have been registered with the Director-General.

3. Thereafter, this Convention shall come into force for any Member 12 months after the date on which its ratification has been registered.

Article 14

1. A Member which has ratified this Convention may denounce it after the expiration of ten years from the date on which the Convention first comes into force, by an act communicated to the Director-General of the International Labour Office for registration. Such denunciation shall not take effect until one year after the date on which it is registered.

2. Each Member which has ratified this Convention and which does not, within the year following the expiration of the period of ten years mentioned in the preceding paragraph, exercise the right of denunciation provided for in this Article, will be bound for another period of ten years and, thereafter, may denounce this Convention at the expiration of each period of ten years under the terms provided for in this Article.

Article 15

1. The Director-General of the International Labour Office shall notify all Members of the International Labour Organization of the registration of all ratifications and denunciations communicated to him by the Members of the Organization.
2. When notifying the Members of the Organization of the registration of the second ratification communicated to him, the Director-General shall draw the attention of the Members of the Organization to the date upon which the Convention will come into force.

Article 16

The Director-General of the International Labour Office shall communicate to the Secretary-General of the United Nations for registration in accordance with Article 102 of the Charter of the United Nations full particulars of all ratifications and acts of denunciations registered by him in accordance with the provisions of the preceding Articles.

Article 17

At such times as it may consider necessary, the Governing Body of the International Labour Office shall present to the General Conference a report on the working of this Convention and shall examine the desirability of placing on the agenda of the Conference the question of its revision in whole or in part.

Article 18

1. Should the Conference adopt a new Convention revising this Convention in whole or in part, then, unless the new Convention otherwise provides –

(a) the ratification by a Member of the new revising Convention shall ipso jure involve the immediate denunciation of this Convention, notwithstanding the provisions of Article 14 above, if and when the new revising Convention shall have come into force;

(b) as from the date when the new revising Convention comes into force this Convention shall cease to be open to ratification by the Members.

2. This Convention shall in any case remain in force in its actual form and content for those Members which have ratified it but have not ratified the revising Convention.

SELECT EU LAWS – EXCERPTS

EC Treaty, Article 141 (ex Article 119)

OJ (2002) C 325/33

1. Each Member State shall ensure that the principle of equal pay for male and female workers for equal work or work of equal value is applied.

2. For the purpose of this Article, "pay" means the ordinary basic or minimum wage or salary and any other consideration, whether in cash or in kind, which the worker receives directly or indirectly, in respect of his employment, from his employer.

Equal pay without discrimination based on sex means:

(a) that pay for the same work at piece rates shall be calculated on the basis of the same unit of measurement;

(b) that pay for work at time rates shall be the same for the same job.

3. The Council, acting in accordance with the procedure referred to in Article 251, and after consulting the Economic and Social Committee, shall adopt measures to ensure the application of the principle of equal opportunities and equal treatment of men and women in matters of employment and occupation, including the principle of equal pay for equal work or work of equal value.

4. With a view to ensuring full equality in practice between men and women in working life, the principle of equal treatment shall not prevent any Member State from maintaining or adopting measures providing for specific advantages in order to make it easier for the under-represented sex to pursue a vocational activity or to prevent or compensate for disadvantages in professional careers.

Council Directive 75/117/EEC of 10 February 1975 on the approximation of the laws of the Member States relating to the application of the principle of equal pay for men and women

OJ (1975) L 45/19

Article 1

The principle of equal pay for men and women outlined in Article 119 of the Treaty, hereinafter called "principle of equal pay", means, for the same work or for work to which equal value is attributed, the elimination of all discrimination on grounds of sex with regard to all aspects and conditions of remuneration.

In particular, where a job classification system is used for determining pay, it must be based on the same criteria for both men and women and so drawn up as to exclude any discrimination on grounds of sex.

Article 2

Member States shall introduce into their national legal systems such measures as are necessary to enable all employees who consider themselves wronged by failure to apply the principle of equal pay to pursue their claims by judicial process after possible recourse to other competent authorities.

Article 3

Member States shall abolish all discrimination between men and women arising from laws, regulations or administrative provisions which is contrary to the principle of equal pay.

Article 4

Member States shall take the necessary measures to ensure that provisions appearing in collective agreements, wage scales, wage agreements or individual contracts of employment which are contrary to the principle of equal pay shall be, or may be declared, null and void or may be amended.

Article 5

Member States shall take the necessary measures to protect employees against dismissal by the employer as a reaction to a complaint within the undertaking or to any legal proceedings aimed at enforcing compliance with the principle of equal pay.

Article 6

Member States shall, in accordance with their national circumstances and legal systems, take the measures necessary to ensure that the priciple of equal pay is applied. They shall see that effective means are available to take care that this principle is observed.

Article 7

Member States shall take care that the provisions adopted pursuant to this Directive, together with the relevant provisions already in force, are brought to the attention of employees by all appropriate means, for example at their place of employment.

Article 8

1. Member States shall put into force the laws, regulations and administrative provisions necessary in order to comply with this Directive within one year of its notification and shall immediately inform the Commission thereof.

2. Member States shall communicate to the Commission the texts of the laws, regulations and administrative provisions which they adopt in the field covered by this Directive.

Article 9

Within two years of the expiry of the one-year period referred to in Article 8, Member States shall forward all necessary information to the Commission to enable it to draw up a report on the application of this Directive for submission to the Council.

Article 10

This Directive is addressed to the Member States.

Council Directive of 9 February 1976 on the implementation of the principle of equal treatment for men and women as regards access to employment, vocational training and promotion, and working conditions

76/207/EEC, OJ (1976) L 39/40

...

Article 1

1. The purpose of this Directive is to put into effect in the Member States the principle of equal treatment for men and women as regards access to employment, including promotion, and to vocational training and as regards working

conditions and, on the conditions referred to in paragraph 2, social security. This principle is herinafter referred to as "the principle of equal treatment."

2. With a view to ensuring the progressive implementation of the principle of equal treatment in matters of social security, the Council, acting on a proposal from the Commission, will adopt provisions defining its substance, its scope and the arrangements for its application.

Article 2

1. For the purposes of the following provisions, the principle of equal treatment shall mean that there shall be no discrimination whatsoever on grounds of sex either directly or indirectly by reference in particular to marital or family status.

2. This Directive shall be without prejudice to the right of Member States to exclude from its field of application those occupational activities and, where appropriate, the training leading thereto, for which, by reason of their nature or the context in which they are carried out, the sex of the worker constitutes a determining factor.

3. This Directive shall be without prejudice to provisions concerning the protection of women, particularly as regards pregnancy and maternity.

4. This Directive shall be without prejudice to measures to promote equal opportunity for men and women, in particular by removing existing inequalities which affect women's opportunities in the areas referred to in Article 1 (1).

Article 3

1. Application of the principle of equal treatment means that there shall be no discrimination whatsoever on grounds of sex in the conditions, including selection criteria, for access to all jobs or posts, whatever the sector or branch of activity, and to all levels of the occupational hierarchy.

2. To this end, Member States shall take the measures necessary to ensure that:

(a) any laws, regulations and administrative provisions contrary to the principle of equal treatment shall be abolished;

(b) any provisions contrary to the principle of equal treatment which are included in collective agreements, individual contracts of employment, internal rules of undertakings or in rules governing the independent occupations and professions shall be, or may be declared, null and void or may be amended;

(c) those laws, regulations and administrative provisions contrary to the principle of equal treatment when the concern for protection which originally inspired them is no longer well founded shall be revised; and that where similar provisions are included in collective agreements labour and management shall be requested to undertake the desired revision.

Article 4

Application of the principle of equal treatment with regard to access to all types and to all levels, of vocational guidance, vocational training, advanced vocational training and retraining, means that Member States shall take all necessary measures to ensure that:

(a) any laws, regulations and administrative provisions contrary to the principle of equal treatment shall be abolished;

(b) any provisions contrary to the principle of equal treatment which are included in collective agreements, individual contracts of employment, internal rules of undertakings or in rules governing the independent occupations and professions shall be, or may be declared, null and void or may be amended;

(c) without prejudice to the freedom granted in certain Member States to certain private training establishments, vocational guidance, vocational training, advanced vocational training and retraining shall be accessible on the basis of the same criteria and at the same levels without any discrimination on grounds of sex.

Article 5

1. Application of the principle of equal treatment with regard to working conditions, including the conditions governing dismissal, means that men and women shall be guaranteed the same conditions without discrimination on grounds of sex.

2. To this end, Member States shall take the measures necessary to ensure that:

(a) any laws, regulations and administrative provisions contrary to the principle of equal treatment shall be abolished;

(b) any provisions contrary to the principle of equal treatment which are included in collective agreements, individual contracts of employment, internal rules of undertakings or in rules governing the independent occupations and professions shall be, or may be declared, null and void or may be amended;

(c) those laws, regulations and administrative provisions contrary to the principle of equal treatment when the concern for protection which originally inspired them is no longer well founded shall be revised; and that where similar provisions are included in collective agreements labour and management shall be requested to undertake the desired revision.

Article 6

Member States shall introduce into their national legal systems such measures as are necessary to enable all persons who consider themselves wronged by failure to apply to them the principle of equal treatment within the meaning of Articles 3, 4 and 5 to pursue their claims by judicial process after possible recourse to other competent authorities.

Article 7

Member States shall take the necessary measures to protect employees against dismissal by the employer as a reaction to a complaint within the undertaking or to any legal proceedings aimed at enforcing compliance with the principle of equal treatment.

Article 8

Member States shall take care that the provisions adopted pursuant to this Directive, together with the relevant provisions already in force, are brought to the attention of employees by all appropriate means, for example at their place of employment.

Article 9

1. Member States shall put into force the laws, regulations and administrative provisions necessary in order to comply with this Directive within 30 months of its notification and shall immediately inform the Commission thereof.

However, as regards the first part of Article 3 (2) (c) and the first part of Article 5 (2) (c), Member States shall carry out a first examination and if necessary a first revision of the laws, regulations and administrative provisions referred to therein within four years of notification of this Directive.

2. Member States shall periodically assess the occupational activities referred to in Article 2 (2) in order to decide, in the light of social developments, whether there is justification for maintaining the exclusions concerned. They shall notify the Commission of the results of this assessment.

3. Member States shall also communicate to the Commission the texts of laws, regulations and administrative provisions which they adopt in the field covered by this Directive.

Article 10

Within two years following expiry of the 30-month period laid down in the first subparagraph of Article 9 (1), Member States shall forward all necessary information to the Commission to enable it to draw up a report on the application of this Directive for submission to the Council.

Council Directive of 3 June 1996 on the Framework Agreement on Parental Leave concluded by UNICE, CEEP and the ETUC

96/34/EC, OJ (1996) L 145/4

...

Article 1
Implementation of the framework agreement

The purpose of this Directive is to put into effect the annexed framework agreement on parental leave concluded on 14 December 1995 between the general cross-industry organizations (Unice, CEEP and the ETUC).

Article 2
Final provisions

1. The Member States shall bring into force the laws, regulations and administrative provisions necessary to comply with this Directive by 3 June 1998 at the latest or shall ensure by that date at the latest that management and labour have introduced the necessary measures by agreement, the Member States being required to take any necessary measure enabling them at any time to be in a position to guarantee the results imposed by this Directive. They shall forthwith inform the Commission thereof.

2. The Member States may have a maximum additional period of one year, if this is necessary to take account of special difficulties or implementation by a collective agreement.

They must forthwith inform the Commission of such circumstances.

3. When Member States adopt the measures referred to in paragraph 1, they shall contain a reference to this Directive or be accompanied by such reference on the occasion of their official publication. The methods of making such reference shall be laid down by Member States.

...

ANNEX

FRAMEWORK AGREEMENT ON PARENTAL LEAVE

...

THE SIGNATORY PARTIES HAVE AGREED THE FOLLOWING:

II. CONTENT

Clause 1: Purpose and scope

1. This agreement lays down minimum requirements designed to facilitate the reconciliation of parental and professional responsibilities for working parents.

2. This agreement applies to all workers, men and women, who have an employment contract or employment relationship as defined by the law, collective agreements or practices in force in each Member State.

Clause 2: Parental leave

1. This agreement grants, subject to clause 2.2, men and women workers an individual right to parental leave on the grounds of the birth or adoption of a child to enable them to take care of that child, for at least three months, until a given age up to 8 years to be defined by Member States and/or management and labour.

2. To promote equal opportunities and equal treatment between men and women, the parties to this agreement consider that the right to parental leave provided for under clause 2.1 should, in principle, be granted on a non-transferable basis.

3. The conditions of access and detailed rules for applying parental leave shall be defined by law and/or collective agreement in the Member States, as long as the minimum requirements of this agreement are respected. Member States and/or management and labour may, in particular:

(a) decide whether parental leave is granted on a full-time or part-time basis, in a piecemeal way or in the form of a time-credit system;

(b) make entitlement to parental leave subject to a period of work qualification and/or a length of service qualification which shall not exceed one year;

(c) adjust conditions of access and detailed rules for applying parental leave to the special circumstances of adoption;

(d) establish notice periods to be given by the worker to the employer when exercising the right to parental leave, specifying the beginning and the end of the period of leave;

(e) define the circumstances in which an employer, following consultation in accordance with national law, collective agreements and practices, is allowed to postpone the granting of parental leave for justifiable reasons related to the operation of the undertaking (e.g. where work is of a seasonal nature, where a replacement cannot be found within the notice period, where a significant proportion of the workforce applies for parental leave at the same time, where a specific function is of strategic importance). Any problem arising from the application of this provision should be dealt with in accordance with national law, collective agreements and practices;

(f) in addition to (e), authorize special arrangements to meet the operational and organizational requirements of small undertakings.

4. In order to ensure that workers can exercise their right to parental leave, Member States and/or management and labour shall take the necessary measures to protect workers against dismissal on the grounds of an application for, or the taking of, parental leave in accordance with national law, collective agreements or practices.

5. At the end of parental leave, workers shall have the right to return to the same job or, if that is not possible, to an equivalent or similar job consistent with their employment contract or employment relationship.

6. Rights acquired or in the process of being acquired by the worker on the date on which parental leave starts shall be maintained as they stand until the end of parental leave. At the end of parental leave, these rights, including any changes arising from national law, collective agreements or practice, shall apply.

7. Member States and/or management and labour shall define the status of the employment contract or employment relationship for the period of parental leave.

8. All matters relating to social security in relation to this agreement are for consideration and determination by Member States according to national law, taking into account the importance of the continuity of the entitlements to social security cover under the different schemes, in particular health care.

Clause 3: Time off from work on grounds of force majeure

1. Member States and/or management and labour shall take the necessary measures to entitle workers to time off from work, in accordance with national legislation, collective agreements and/or practice, on grounds of force majeure for urgent family reasons in cases of sickness or accident making the immediate presence of the worker indispensable.

2. Member States and/or management and labour may specify the conditions of access and detailed rules for applying clause 3.1 and limit this entitlement to a certain amount of time per year and/or per case.

Clause 4: Final provisions

1. Member States may apply or introduce more favourable provisions that those set out in this agreement.

2. Implementation of the provisions of this agreement shall not constitute valid grounds for reducing the general level of protection afforded to workers in the field covered by this agreement. This shall not prejudice the right of Member States and/or management and labour to develop different legislative, regulatory or contractual provisions, in the light of changing circumstances (including the introduction of non-transferability), as long as the minimum requirements provided for in the present agreement are complied with.

3. The present agreement shall not prejudice the right of management and labour to conclude, at the appropriate level including European level, agreements adapting and/or complementing the provisions of this agreement in order to take into account particular circumstances.

4. Member States shall adopt the laws, regulations and administrative provisions necessary to comply with the Council decision within a period of two years from its adoption or shall ensure that management and labour (1) introduce the necessary measures by way of agreement by the end of this period. Member States may, if necessary to take account of particular difficulties or implementation by collective agreement, have up to a maximum of one additional year to comply with this decision.

5. The prevention and settlement of disputes and grievances arising from the application of this agreement shall be dealt with in accordance with national law, collective agreements and practices.

6. Without prejudice to the respective role of the Commission, national courts and the Court of Justice, any matter relating to the interpretation of this agreement at European level should, in the first instance, be referred by the Commission to the signatory parties who will give an opinion.

7. The signatory parties shall review the application of this agreement five years after the date of the Council decision if requested by one of the parties to this agreement.

Council Directive of 15 December 1997 concerning the Framework Agreement on part-time work concluded by UNICE, CEEP and the ETUC – Annex: Framework Agreement on part-time work

97/81/EC, OJ (1997) L 14/9

...

Article 1

The purpose of this Directive is to implement the Framework Agreement on part-time work concluded on 6 June 1997 between the general cross-industry organizations (UNICE, CEEP and the ETUC) annexed hereto.

Article 2

1. Member States shall bring into force the laws, regulations and administrative provisions necessary to comply with this Directive not later than 20 January 2000, or shall ensure that, by that date at the latest, the social partners have introduced the necessary measures by agreement, the Member States being required to take any necessary measures to enable them at any time to be in a position to guarantee the results imposed by this Directive. They shall forthwith inform the Commission thereof.

Member States may have a maximum of one more year, if necessary, to take account of special difficulties or implementation by a collective agreement.

They shall inform the Commission forthwith in such circumstances.

When Member States adopt the measures referred to in the first subparagraph, they shall contain a reference to this Directive or shall be accompanied by such reference on the occasion of their official publication. The methods of making such a reference shall be laid down by the Member States.

2. Member States shall communicate to the Commission the text of the main provisions of domestic law which they have adopted or which they adopt in the field governed by this Directive.

Article 3

This Directive shall enter into force on the day of its publication in the Official Journal of the European Communities.

...

ANNEX

UNION OF INDUSTRIAL AND EMPLOYERS' CONFEDERATIONS OF EUROPE EUROPEAN TRADE UNION CONFEDERATION EUROPEAN CENTRE OF ENTERPRISES WITH PUBLIC PARTICIPATION

FRAMEWORK AGREEMENT ON PART-TIME WORK

...

THE SIGNATORY PARTIES HAVE AGREED THE FOLLOWING:

Clause 1: Purpose

The purpose of this Framework Agreement is:

(a) to provide for the removal of discrimination against part-time workers and to improve the quality of part-time work;

(b) to facilitate the development of part-time work on a voluntary basis and to contribute to the flexible organization of working time in a manner which takes into account the needs of employers and workers.

Clause 2: Scope

1. This Agreement applies to part-time workers who have an employment contract or employment relationship as defined by the law, collective agreement or practice in force in each Member State.

2. Member States, after consultation with the social partners in accordance with national law, collective agreements or practice, and/or the social partners at the appropriate level in conformity with national industrial relations practice may, for objective reasons, exclude wholly or partly from the terms of this Agreement part-time workers who work on a casual basis. Such exclusions should be reviewed periodically to establish if the objective reasons for making them remain valid.

Clause 3: Definitions

For the purpose of this agreement:

1. The term 'part-time worker` refers to an employee whose normal hours of work, calculated on a weekly basis or on average over a period of employment of up to one year, are less than the normal hours of work of a comparable full-time worker.

2. The term 'comparable full-time worker` means a full-time worker in the same establishment having the same type of employment contract or relationship, who is engaged in the same or a similar work/occupation, due regard being given to other considerations which may include seniority and qualification/skills.

Where there is no comparable full-time worker in the same establishment, the comparison shall be made by reference to the applicable collective agreement or, where there is no applicable collective agreement, in accordance with national law, collective agreements or practice.

Clause 4: Principle of non-discrimination

1. In respect of employment conditions, part-time workers shall not be treated in a less favourable manner than comparable full-time workers solely because they work part time unless different treatment is justified on objective grounds.

2. Where appropriate, the principle of pro rata temporis shall apply.

3. The arrangements for the application of this clause shall be defined by the Member States and/or social partners, having regard to European legislation, national law, collective agreements and practice.

4. Where justified by objective reasons, Member States after consultation of the social partners in accordance with national law, collective agreements or practice and/or social partners may, where appropriate, make access to particular conditions of employment subject to a period of service, time worked or earnings qualification. Qualifications relating to access by part-time workers to particular conditions of employment should be reviewed periodically having regard to the principle of non-discrimination as expressed in Clause 4.1.

Clause 5: Opportunities for part-time work

1. In the context of Clause 1 of this Agreement and of the principle of non-discrimination between part-time and full-time workers:

(a) Member States, following consultations with the social partners in accordance with national law or practice, should identify and review obstacles of a legal or administrative nature which may limit the opportunities for part-time work and, where appropriate, eliminate them;

(b) the social partners, acting within their sphere of competence and through the procedures set out in collective agreements, should identify and review obstacles which may limit opportunities for part-time work and, where appropriate, eliminate them.

2. A worker's refusal to transfer from full-time to part-time work or vice-versa should not in itself constitute a valid reason for termination of employment, without prejudice to termination in accordance with national law, collective agreements and practice, for other reasons such as may arise from the operational requirements of the establishment concerned.

3. As far as possible, employers should give consideration to:

(a) requests by workers to transfer from full-time to part-time work that becomes available in the establishment;

(b) requests by workers to transfer from part-time to full-time work or to increase their working time should the opportunity arise;

(c) the provision of timely information on the availability of part-time and full-time positions in the establishment in order to facilitate transfers from full-time to part-time or vice versa;

(d) measures to facilitate access to part-time work at all levels of the enterprise, including skilled and managerial positions, and where appropriate, to facilitate access by part-time workers to vocational training to enhance career opportunities and occupational mobility;

(e) the provision of appropriate information to existing bodies representing workers about part-time working in the enterprise.

Clause 6: Provisions on implementation

1. Member States and/or social partners may maintain or introduce more favourable provisions than set out in this agreement.

2. Implementation of the provisions of this Agreement shall not constitute valid grounds for reducing the general level of protection afforded to workers in the field of this agreement. This does not prejudice the right of Member States and/or social partners to develop different legislative, regulatory or contractual provisions, in the light of changing circumstances, and does not prejudice the application of Clause 5.1 as long as the principle of non-discrimination as expressed in Clause 4.1 is complied with.

3. This Agreement does not prejudice the right of the social partners to conclude, at the appropriate level, including European level, agreements adapting and/or complementing the provisions of this Agreement in a manner which will take account of the specific needs of the social partners concerned.

4. This Agreement shall be without prejudice to any more specific Community provisions, and in particular Community provisions concerning equal treatment or opportunities for men and women.

5. The prevention and settlement of disputes and grievances arising from the application of this Agreement shall be dealt with in accordance with national law, collective agreements and practice.

6. The signatory parties shall review this Agreement, five years after the date of the Council decision, if requested by one of the parties to this Agreement.

Directive of the European Parliament and of the Council of 23 September 2002 amending Council Directive 76/207/EEC on the implementation of the principle of equal treatment for men and women as regards access to employment, vocational training and promotion, and working conditions

2002/73/EC, OJ (2002) L 269/15

…

Article 1

Directive 76/207/EEC is hereby amended as follows:

1. in Article 1, the following paragraph shall be inserted: "1a. Member States shall actively take into account the objective of equality between men and women when formulating and implementing laws, regulations, administrative provisions, policies and activities in the areas referred to in paragraph 1.";

2. Article 2 shall be replaced by the following:

"Article 2

1. For the purposes of the following provisions, the principle of equal treatment shall mean that there shall be no discrimination whatsoever on grounds of sex either directly or indirectly by reference in particular to marital or family status.

2. For the purposes of this Directive, the following definitions shall apply:

- direct discrimination: where one person is treated less favourably on grounds of sex than another is, has been or would be treated in a comparable situation,
- indirect discrimination: where an apparently neutral provision, criterion or practice would put persons of one sex at a particular disadvantage compared with persons of the other sex, unless that provision, criterion or practice is objectively justified by a legitimate aim, and the means of achieving that aim are appropriate and necessary,
- harassment: where an unwanted conduct related to the sex of a person occurs with the purpose or effect of violating the dignity of a person, and of creating an intimidating, hostile, degrading, humiliating or offensive environment,
- sexual harassment: where any form of unwanted verbal, non-verbal or physical conduct of a sexual nature occurs, with the purpose

or effect of violating the dignity of a person, in particular when creating an intimidating, hostile, degrading, humiliating or offensive environment.

3. Harassment and sexual harassment within the meaning of this Directive shall be deemed to be discrimination on the grounds of sex and therefore prohibited.

A person's rejection of, or submission to, such conduct may not be used as a basis for a decision affecting that person.

4. An instruction to discriminate against persons on grounds of sex shall be deemed to be discrimination within the meaning of this Directive.

5. Member States shall encourage, in accordance with national law, collective agreements or practice, employers and those responsible for access to vocational training to take measures to prevent all forms of discrimination on grounds of sex, in particular harassment and sexual harassment at the workplace.

6. Member States may provide, as regards access to employment including the training leading thereto, that a difference of treatment which is based on a characteristic related to sex shall not constitute discrimination where, by reason of the nature of the particular occupational activities concerned or of the context in which they are carried out, such a characteristic constitutes a genuine and determining occupational requirement, provided that the objective is legitimate and the requirement is proportionate.

7. This Directive shall be without prejudice to provisions concerning the protection of women, particularly as regards pregnancy and maternity.

A woman on maternity leave shall be entitled, after the end of her period of maternity leave, to return to her job or to an equivalent post on terms and conditions which are no less favourable to her and to benefit from any improvement in working conditions to which she would be entitled during her absence.

Less favourable treatment of a woman related to pregnancy or maternity leave within the meaning of Directive 92/85/EEC shall constitute discrimination within the meaning of this Directive.

This Directive shall also be without prejudice to the provisions of Council Directive 96/34/EC of 3 June 1996 on the framework agreement on parental leave concluded by UNICE, CEEP and the ETUC(14) and of Council Directive 92/85/EEC of 19 October 1992 on the introduction of measures to encourage improvements in the safety and health at work of pregnant workers and workers who have recently given birth or are breastfeeding (tenth individual Directive within the meaning of Article

16(1) of Directive 89/391/EEC)(15). It is also without prejudice to the right of Member States to recognise distinct rights to paternity and/or adoption leave. Those Member States which recognise such rights shall take the necessary measures to protect working men and women against dismissal due to exercising those rights and ensure that, at the end of such leave, they shall be entitled to return to their jobs or to equivalent posts on terms and conditions which are no less favourable to them, and to benefit from any improvement in working conditions to which they would have been entitled during their absence.

8. Member States may maintain or adopt measures within the meaning of Article 141(4) of the Treaty with a view to ensuring full equality in practice between men and women.";

3. Article 3 shall be replaced by the following:

"Article 3

1. Application of the principle of equal treatment means that there shall be no direct or indirect discrimination on the grounds of sex in the public or private sectors, including public bodies, in relation to:

(a) conditions for access to employment, to self-employment or to occupation, including selection criteria and recruitment conditions, whatever the branch of activity and at all levels of the professional hierarchy, including promotion;

(b) access to all types and to all levels of vocational guidance, vocational training, advanced vocational training and retraining, including practical work experience;

(c) employment and working conditions, including dismissals, as well as pay as provided for in Directive 75/117/EEC;

(d) membership of, and involvement in, an organisation of workers or employers, or any organisation whose members carry on a particular profession, including the benefits provided for by such organisations.

2. To that end, Member States shall take the necessary measures to ensure that:

(a) any laws, regulations and administrative provisions contrary to the principle of equal treatment are abolished;

(b) any provisions contrary to the principle of equal treatment which are included in contracts or collective agreements, internal rules of undertakings or rules governing the independent occupations and professions and workers' and employers' organisations shall be, or may be declared, null and void or are amended.";

4. Articles 4 and 5 shall be deleted;

5. Article 6 shall be replaced by the following:

"Article 6

1. Member States shall ensure that judicial and/or administrative procedures, including where they deem it appropriate conciliation procedures, for the enforcement of obligations under this Directive are available to all persons who consider themselves wronged by failure to apply the principle of equal treatment to them, even after the relationship in which the discrimination is alleged to have occurred has ended.

2. Member States shall introduce into their national legal systems such measures as are necessary to ensure real and effective compensation or reparation as the Member States so determine for the loss and damage sustained by a person injured as a result of discrimination contrary to Article 3, in a way which is dissuasive and proportionate to the damage suffered; such compensation or reparation may not be restricted by the fixing of a prior upper limit, except in cases where the employer can prove that the only damage suffered by an applicant as a result of discrimination within the meaning of this Directive is the refusal to take his/her job application into consideration.

3. Member States shall ensure that associations, organisations or other legal entities which have, in accordance with the criteria laid down by their national law, a legitimate interest in ensuring that the provisions of this Directive are complied with, may engage, either on behalf or in support of the complainants, with his or her approval, in any judicial and/or administrative procedure provided for the enforcement of obligations under this Directive.

4. Paragraphs 1 and 3 are without prejudice to national rules relating to time limits for bringing actions as regards the principle of equal treatment.";

6. Article 7 shall be replaced by the following:

"Article 7

Member States shall introduce into their national legal systems such measures as are necessary to protect employees, including those who are employees' representatives provided for by national laws and/or practices, against dismissal or other adverse treatment by the employer as a reaction to a complaint within the undertaking or to any legal proceedings aimed at enforcing compliance with the principle of equal treatment.";

7. The following Articles shall be inserted:

"Article 8a

1. Member States shall designate and make the necessary arrangements for a body or bodies for the promotion, analysis, monitoring and support of equal treatment of all persons without discrimination on the grounds of sex. These bodies may form part of agencies charged at national level with the defence of human rights or the safeguard of individuals' rights.

2. Member States shall ensure that the competences of these bodies include:

(a) without prejudice to the right of victims and of associations, organisations or other legal entities referred to in Article 6(3), providing independent assistance to victims of discrimination in pursuing their complaints about discrimination;

(b) conducting independent surveys concerning discrimination;

(c) publishing independent reports and making recommendations on any issue relating to such discrimination.

Article 8b

1. Member States shall, in accordance with national traditions and practice, take adequate measures to promote social dialogue between the social partners with a view to fostering equal treatment, including through the monitoring of workplace practices, collective agreements, codes of conduct, research or exchange of experiences and good practices.

2. Where consistent with national traditions and practice, Member States shall encourage the social partners, without prejudice to their autonomy, to promote equality between women and men and to conclude, at the appropriate level, agreements laying down anti-discrimination rules in the fields referred to in Article 1 which fall within the scope of collective bargaining. These agreements shall respect the minimum requirements laid down by this Directive and the relevant national implementing measures.

3. Member States shall, in accordance with national law, collective agreements or practice, encourage employers to promote equal treatment for men and women in the workplace in a planned and systematic way.

4. To this end, employers should be encouraged to provide at appropriate regular intervals employees and/or their representatives with appropriate information on equal treatment for men and women in the undertaking.

Such information may include statistics on proportions of men and women at different levels of the organisation and possible measures to improve the situation in cooperation with employees' representatives.

Article 8c

Member States shall encourage dialogue with appropriate non-governmental organisations which have, in accordance with their national law and practice, a legitimate interest in contributing to the fight against discrimination on grounds of sex with a view to promoting the principle of equal treatment.

Article 8d

Member States shall lay down the rules on sanctions applicable to infringements of the national provisions adopted pursuant to this Directive, and shall take all measures necessary to ensure that they are applied.

The sanctions, which may comprise the payment of compensation to the victim, must be effective, proportionate and dissuasive. The Member States shall notify those provisions to the Commission by 5 October 2005 at the latest and shall notify it without delay of any subsequent amendment affecting them.

Article 8e

1. Member States may introduce or maintain provisions which are more favourable to the protection of the principle of equal treatment than those laid down in this Directive.

2. The implementation of this Directive shall under no circumstances constitute grounds for a reduction in the level of protection against discrimination already afforded by Member States in the fields covered by this Directive."

Article 2

1. Member States shall bring into force the laws, regulations and administrative provisions necessary to comply with this Directive by 5 October 2005 at the latest or shall ensure, by that date at the latest, that management and labour introduce the requisite provisions by way of agreement. Member States shall take all necessary steps to enable them at all times to guarantee the results imposed by this Directive. They shall immediately inform the Commission thereof.

When Member States adopt those measures, they shall contain a reference to this Directive or be accompanied by such reference on the occasion of their official publication. Member States shall determine how such reference is to be made.

2. The Member States shall communicate to the Commission, within three years of the entry into force of this Directive, all the information necessary for the Commission to draw up a report to the European Parliament and the Council on the application of this Directive.

3. Without prejudice to paragraph 2, Member States shall communicate to the Commission, every four years, the texts of laws, regulations and administrative provisions of any measures adopted pursuant to Article 141(4) of the Treaty, as well as reports on these measures and their implementation. On the basis of that information, the Commission will adopt and publish every four years a report establishing a comparative assessment of any measures in the light of Declaration No 28 annexed to the Final Act of the Treaty of Amsterdam.

Article 3

This Directive shall enter into force on the day of its publication in the Official Journal of the European Communities.

Directive of the European Parliament and of the Council of 5 July 2006 on the implementation of the principle of equal opportunities and equal treatment of men and women in matters of employment and occupation (recast)

2006/54/EC, OJ (2006) L 204/30

...

Whereas:

(1) Council Directive 76/207/EEC of 9 February 1976 on the implementation of the principle of equal treatment for men and women as regards access to employment, vocational training and promotion, and working conditions (3) and Council Directive 86/378/EEC of 24 July 1986 on the implementation of the principle of equal treatment for men and women in occupational social security schemes (4) have been significantly amended (5). Council Directive 75/117/EEC of 10 February 1975 on the approximation of the laws of the Member States relating to the application of the principle of equal pay for men and women (6) and Council Directive 97/80/EC of 15 December 1997 on the burden of proof in cases of discrimination based on sex (7) also contain provisions which have as their purpose the implementation of the principle of equal treatment between men and women. Now that new amendments are being made to the

said Directives, it is desirable, for reasons of clarity, that the provisions in question should be recast by bringing together in a single text the main provisions existing in this field as well as certain developments arising out of the case-law of the Court of Justice of the European Communities (hereinafter referred to as the Court of Justice).

(2) Equality between men and women is a fundamental principle of Community law under Article 2 and Article 3 (2) of the Treaty and the case-law of the Court of Justice. Those Treaty provisions proclaim equality between men and women as a 'task' and an 'aim' of the Community and impose a positive obligation to promote it in all its activities.

...

(4) Article 141(3) of the Treaty now provides a specific legal basis for the adoption of Community measures to ensure the application of the principle of equal opportunities and equal treatment in matters of employment and occupation, including the principle of equal pay for equal work or work of equal value.

(5) Articles 21 and 23 of the Charter of Fundamental Rights of the European Union also prohibit any discrimination on grounds of sex and enshrine the right to equal treatment between men and women in all areas, including employment, work and pay.

(6) Harassment and sexual harassment are contrary to the principle of equal treatment between men and women and constitute discrimination on grounds of sex for the purposes of this Directive. These forms of discrimination occur not only in the workplace, but also in the context of access to employment, vocational training and promotion. They should therefore be prohibited and should be subject to effective, proportionate and dissuasive penalties.

(7) In this context, employers and those responsible for vocational training should be encouraged to take measures to combat all forms of discrimination on grounds of sex and, in particular, to take preventive measures against harassment and sexual harassment in the workplace and in access to employment, vocational training and promotion, in accordance with national law and practice.

(8) The principle of equal pay for equal work or work of equal value as laid down by Article 141 of the Treaty and consistently upheld in the case-law of the Court of Justice constitutes an important aspect of the principle of equal treatment between men and women and an essential and indispensable part of the *acquis communautaire*, including the case-law of the Court concerning sex discrimination. It is therefore appropriate to make further provision for its implementation.

(9) In accordance with settled case-law of the Court of Justice, in order to assess whether workers are performing the same work or work of equal value, it should be determined whether, having regard to a range of factors including

the nature of the work and training and working conditions, those workers may be considered to be in a comparable situation.

(10) The Court of Justice has established that, in certain circumstances, the principle of equal pay is not limited to situations in which men and women work for the same employer.

(11) The Member States, in collaboration with the social partners, should continue to address the problem of the continuing gender-based wage differentials and marked gender segregation on the labour market by means such as flexible working time arrangements which enable both men and women to combine family and work commitments more successfully. This could also include appropriate parental leave arrangements which could be taken up by either parent as well as the provision of accessible and affordable child-care facilities and care for dependent persons.

...

(20) This Directive does not prejudice freedom of association, including the right to establish unions with others and to join unions to defend one's interests. Measures within the meaning of Article 141(4) of the Treaty may include membership or the continuation of the activity of organisations or unions whose main objective is the promotion, in practice, of the principle of equal treatment between men and women.

(21) The prohibition of discrimination should be without prejudice to the maintenance or adoption of measures intended to prevent or compensate for disadvantages suffered by a group of persons of one sex. Such measures permit organisations of persons of one sex where their main object is the promotion of the special needs of those persons and the promotion of equality between men and women.

(22) In accordance with Article 141(4) of the Treaty, with a view to ensuring full equality in practice between men and women in working life, the principle of equal treatment does not prevent Member States from maintaining or adopting measures providing for specific advantages in order to make it easier for the under-represented sex to pursue a vocational activity or to prevent or compensate for disadvantages in professional careers. Given the current situation and bearing in mind Declaration No 28 to the Amsterdam Treaty, Member States should, in the first instance, aim at improving the situation of women in working life.

(23) It is clear from the case-law of the Court of Justice that unfavourable treatment of a woman related to pregnancy or maternity constitutes direct discrimination on grounds of sex. Such treatment should therefore be expressly covered by this Directive.

(24) The Court of Justice has consistently recognised the legitimacy, as regards the principle of equal treatment, of protecting a woman's biological condition during

pregnancy and maternity and of introducing maternity protection measures as a means to achieve substantive equality. This Directive should therefore be without prejudice to Council Directive 92/85/EEC of 19 October 1992 on the introduction of measures to encourage improvements in the safety and health at work of pregnant workers and workers who have recently given birth or are breastfeeding. This Directive should further be without prejudice to Council Directive 96/34/EC of 3 June 1996 on the framework agreement on parental leave concluded by UNICE, CEEP and the ETUC.

(25) For reasons of clarity, it is also appropriate to make express provision for the protection of the employment rights of women on maternity leave and in particular their right to return to the same or an equivalent post, to suffer no detriment in their terms and conditions as a result of taking such leave and to benefit from any improvement in working conditions to which they would have been entitled during their absence.

(26) In the Resolution of the Council and of the Ministers for Employment and Social Policy, meeting within the Council, of 29 June 2000 on the balanced participation of women and men in family and working life, Member States were encouraged to consider examining the scope for their respective legal systems to grant working men an individual and non-transferable right to paternity leave, while maintaining their rights relating to employment.

(27) Similar considerations apply to the granting by Member States to men and women of an individual and nontransferable right to leave subsequent to the adoption of a child. It is for the Member States to determine whether or not to grant such a right to paternity and/or adoption leave and also to determine any conditions, other than dismissal and return to work, which are outside the scope of this Directive.

(28) The effective implementation of the principle of equal treatment requires appropriate procedures to be put in place by the Member States.

(29) The provision of adequate judicial or administrative procedures for the enforcement of the obligations imposed by this Directive is essential to the effective implementation of the principle of equal treatment.

(30) The adoption of rules on the burden of proof plays a significant role in ensuring that the principle of equal treatment can be effectively enforced. As the Court of Justice has held, provision should therefore be made to ensure that the burden of proof shifts to the respondent when there is a *prima facie* case of discrimination, except in relation to proceedings in which it is for the court or other competent national body to investigate the facts. It is however necessary to clarify that the appreciation of the facts from which it may be presumed that there has been direct or indirect discrimination remains a matter for the relevant national body in accordance with national law or practice. Further, it is for the

Member States to introduce, at any appropriate stage of the proceedings, rules of evidence which are more favourable to plaintiffs.

(31) With a view to further improving the level of protection offered by this Directive, associations, organisations and other legal entities should also be empowered to engage in proceedings, as the Member States so determine, either on behalf or in support of a complainant, without prejudice to national rules of procedure concerning representation and defence.

(32) Having regard to the fundamental nature of the right to effective legal protection, it is appropriate to ensure that workers continue to enjoy such protection even after the relationship giving rise to an alleged breach of the principle of equal treatment has ended. An employee defending or giving evidence on behalf of a person protected under this Directive should be entitled to the same protection.

(33) It has been clearly established by the Court of Justice that in order to be effective, the principle of equal treatment implies that the compensation awarded for any breach must be adequate in relation to the damage sustained. It is therefore appropriate to exclude the fixing of any prior upper limit for such compensation, except where the employer can prove that the only damage suffered by an applicant as a result of discrimination within the meaning of this Directive was the refusal to take his/her job application into consideration.

(34) In order to enhance the effective implementation of the principle of equal treatment, Member States should promote dialogue between the social partners and, within the framework of national practice, with non-governmental organisations.

(35) Member States should provide for effective, proportionate and dissuasive penalties for breaches of the obligations under this Directive.

(36) Since the objectives of this Directive cannot be sufficiently achieved by the Member States and can therefore be better achieved at Community level, the Community may adopt measures in accordance with the principle of subsidiarity as set out in Article 5 of the Treaty. In accordance with the principle of proportionality, as set out in that Article, this Directive does not go beyond what is necessary in order to achieve those objectives.

(37) For the sake of a better understanding of the different treatment of men and women in matters of employment and occupation, comparable statistics disaggregated by sex should continue to be developed, analysed and made available at the appropriate levels.

(38) Equal treatment of men and women in matters of employment and occupation cannot be restricted to legislative measures. Instead, the European Union and the Member States should continue to promote the raising of public awareness of wage discrimination and the changing of public attitudes, involving all parties

concerned at public and private level to the greatest possible extent. The dialogue between the social partners could play an important role in this process.

(39) The obligation to transpose this Directive into national law should be confined to those provisions which represent a substantive change as compared with the earlier Directives. The obligation to transpose the provisions which are substantially unchanged arises under the earlier Directives.

(40) This Directive should be without prejudice to the obligations of the Member States relating to the time limits for transposition into national law and application of the Directives set out in Annex I, Part B.

(41) In accordance with paragraph 34 of the Interinstitutional agreement on better law-making (1), Member States are encouraged to draw up, for themselves and in the interest of the Community, their own tables, which will, as far as possible, illustrate the correlation between this Directive and the transposition measures and to make them public, HAVE ADOPTED THIS DIRECTIVE:

TITLE I
GENERAL PROVISIONS

Article 1
Purpose

The purpose of this Directive is to ensure the implementation of the principle of equal opportunities and equal treatment of men and women in matters of employment and occupation.

To that end, it contains provisions to implement the principle of equal treatment in relation to:

(a) access to employment, including promotion, and to vocational training;

(b) working conditions, including pay;

(c) occupational social security schemes.

It also contains provisions to ensure that such implementation is made more effective by the establishment of appropriate procedures.

Article 2
Definitions

1. For the purposes of this Directive, the following definitions shall apply:

(a) 'direct discrimination': where one person is treated less favourably on grounds of sex than another is, has been or would be treated in a comparable situation;

(b) 'indirect discrimination': where an apparently neutral provision, criterion or practice would put persons of one sex at a particular disadvantage compared with persons of the other sex, unless that provision, criterion or practice is objectively justified by a legitimate aim, and the means of achieving that aim are appropriate and necessary;

(c) 'harassment': where unwanted conduct related to the sex of a person occurs with the purpose or effect of violating the dignity of a person, and of creating an intimidating, hostile, degrading, humiliating or offensive environment;

(d) 'sexual harassment': where any form of unwanted verbal, non-verbal or physical conduct of a sexual nature occurs, with the purpose or effect of violating the dignity of a person, in particular when creating an intimidating, hostile, degrading, humiliating or offensive environment;

(e) 'pay': the ordinary basic or minimum wage or salary and any other consideration, whether in cash or in kind, which the worker receives directly or indirectly, in respect of his/her employment from his/her employer;

...

2. For the purposes of this Directive, discrimination includes:

(a) harassment and sexual harassment, as well as any less favourable treatment based on a person's rejection of or submission to such conduct;

(b) instruction to discriminate against persons on grounds of sex;

(c) any less favourable treatment of a woman related to pregnancy or maternity leave within the meaning of Directive 92/85/EEC.

Article 3
Positive action

Member States may maintain or adopt measures within the meaning of Article 141(4) of the Treaty with a view to ensuring full equality in practice between men and women in working life.

TITLE II
SPECIFIC PROVISIONS

CHAPTER 3
Equal treatment as regards access to employment, vocational training and promotion and working conditions

Article 14
Prohibition of discrimination

1. There shall be no direct or indirect discrimination on grounds of sex in the public or private sectors, including public bodies, in relation to:

(a) conditions for access to employment, to self-employment or to occupation, including selection criteria and recruitment conditions, whatever the branch of activity and at all levels of the professional hierarchy, including promotion;

(b) access to all types and to all levels of vocational guidance, vocational training, advanced vocational training and retraining, including practical work experience;

(c) employment and working conditions, including dismissals, as well as pay as provided for in Article 141 of the Treaty;

(d) membership of, and involvement in, an organisation of workers or employers, or any organisation whose members carry on a particular profession, including the benefits provided for by such organisations.

2. Member States may provide, as regards access to employment including the training leading thereto, that a difference of treatment which is based on a characteristic related to sex shall not constitute discrimination where, by reason of the nature of the particular occupational activities concerned or of the context in which they are carried out, such a characteristic constitutes a genuine and determining occupational requirement, provided that its objective is legitimate and the requirement is proportionate.

Article 15
Return from maternity leave

A woman on maternity leave shall be entitled, after the end of her period of maternity leave, to return to her job or to an equivalent post on terms and conditions which are no less favourable to her and to benefit from any improvement in working conditions to which she would have been entitled during her absence.

Article 16
Paternity and adoption leave

This Directive is without prejudice to the right of Member States to recognise distinct rights to paternity and/or adoption leave. Those Member States which recognise such rights shall take the necessary measures to protect working men and women against dismissal due to exercising those rights and ensure that, at the end of such leave, they are entitled to return to their jobs or to equivalent posts on terms and conditions which are no less favourable to them, and to benefit from any improvement in working conditions to which they would have been entitled during their absence.

TITLE III
HORIZONTAL PROVISIONS

CHAPTER 1
Remedies and enforcement

Section 1
Remedies

Article 17
Defence of rights

1. Member States shall ensure that, after possible recourse to other competent authorities including where they deem it appropriate conciliation procedures, judicial procedures for the enforcement of obligations under this Directive are available to all persons who consider themselves wronged by failure to apply the principle of equal treatment to them, even after the relationship in which the discrimination is alleged to have occurred has ended.

2. Member States shall ensure that associations, organisations or other legal entities which have, in accordance with the criteria laid down by their national law, a legitimate interest in ensuring that the provisions of this Directive are complied with, may engage, either on behalf or in support of the complainant, with his/her approval, in any judicial and/or administrative procedure provided for the enforcement of obligations under this Directive.

3. Paragraphs 1 and 2 are without prejudice to national rules relating to time limits for bringing actions as regards the principle of equal treatment.

Article 18
Compensation or reparation

Member States shall introduce into their national legal systems such measures as are necessary to ensure real and effective compensation or reparation as the

Member States so determine for the loss and damage sustained by a person injured as a result of discrimination on grounds of sex, in a way which is dissuasive and proportionate to the damage suffered. Such compensation or reparation may not be restricted by the fixing of a prior upper limit, except in cases where the employer can prove that the only damage suffered by an applicant as a result of discrimination within the meaning of this Directive is the refusal to take his/her job application into consideration.

Section 2
Burden of proof

Article 19
Burden of proof

1. Member States shall take such measures as are necessary, in accordance with their national judicial systems, to ensure that, when persons who consider themselves wronged because the principle of equal treatment has not been applied to them establish, before a court or other competent authority, facts from which it may be presumed that there has been direct or indirect discrimination, it shall be for the respondent to prove that there has been no breach of the principle of equal treatment.

2. Paragraph 1 shall not prevent Member States from introducing rules of evidence which are more favourable to plaintiffs.

3. Member States need not apply paragraph 1 to proceedings in which it is for the court or competent body to investigate the facts of the case.

4. Paragraphs 1, 2 and 3 shall also apply to:

(a) the situations covered by Article 141 of the Treaty and, insofar as discrimination based on sex is concerned, by Directives 92/85/EEC and 96/34/EC;

(b) any civil or administrative procedure concerning the public or private sector which provides for means of redress under national law pursuant to the measures referred to in (a) with the exception of out-of-court procedures of a voluntary nature or provided for in national law.

5. This Article shall not apply to criminal procedures, unless otherwise provided by the Member States.

CHAPTER 2
Promotion of equal treatment – dialogue

Article 20
Equality bodies

1. Member States shall designate and make the necessary arrangements for a body or bodies for the promotion, analysis, monitoring and support of equal treatment of all persons without discrimination on grounds of sex. These bodies may form part of agencies with responsibility at national level for the defence of human rights or the safeguard of individuals' rights.

2. Member States shall ensure that the competences of these bodies include:

(a) without prejudice to the right of victims and of associations, organisations or other legal entities referred to in Article 17(2), providing independent assistance to victims of discrimination in pursuing their complaints about discrimination;

(b) conducting independent surveys concerning discrimination;

(c) publishing independent reports and making recommendations on any issue relating to such discrimination;

(d) at the appropriate level exchanging available information with corresponding European bodies such as any future European Institute for Gender Equality.

Article 21
Social dialogue

1. Member States shall, in accordance with national traditions and practice, take adequate measures to promote social dialogue between the social partners with a view to fostering equal treatment, including, for example, through the monitoring of practices in the workplace, in access to employment, vocational training and promotion, as well as through the monitoring of collective agreements, codes of conduct, research or exchange of experience and good practice.

2. Where consistent with national traditions and practice, Member States shall encourage the social partners, without prejudice to their autonomy, to promote equality between men and women, and flexible working arrangements, with the aim of facilitating the reconciliation of work and private life, and to conclude, at the appropriate level, agreements laying down antidiscrimination rules in the fields referred to in Article 1 which fall within the scope of collective bargaining. These agreements shall respect the provisions of this Directive and the relevant national implementing measures.

3. Member States shall, in accordance with national law, collective agreements or practice, encourage employers to promote equal treatment for men and women in a planned and systematic way in the workplace, in access to employment, vocational training and promotion.

4. To this end, employers shall be encouraged to provide at appropriate regular intervals employees and/or their representatives with appropriate information on equal treatment for men and women in the undertaking. Such information may include an overview of the proportions of men and women at different levels of the organisation; their pay and pay differentials; and possible measures to improve the situation in cooperation with employees' representatives.

Article 22
Dialogue with non-governmental organisations

Member States shall encourage dialogue with appropriate nongovernmental organisations which have, in accordance with their national law and practice, a legitimate interest in contributing to the fight against discrimination on grounds of sex with a view to promoting the principle of equal treatment.

CHAPTER 3
General horizontal provisions

Article 23
Compliance

Member States shall take all necessary measures to ensure that:

(a) any laws, regulations and administrative provisions contrary to the principle of equal treatment are abolished;

(b) provisions contrary to the principle of equal treatment in individual or collective contracts or agreements, internal rules of undertakings or rules governing the independent occupations and professions and workers' and employers' organisations or any other arrangements shall be, or may be, declared null and void or are amended;

(c) occupational social security schemes containing such provisions may not be approved or extended by administrative measures.

Article 24
Victimisation

Member States shall introduce into their national legal systems such measures as are necessary to protect employees, including those who are employees' representatives provided for by national laws and/or practices, against dismissal or other adverse treatment by the employer as a reaction to a complaint within the undertaking or to any legal proceedings aimed at enforcing compliance with the principle of equal treatment.

Article 25
Penalties

Member States shall lay down the rules on penalties applicable to infringements of the national provisions adopted pursuant to this Directive, and shall take all measures necessary to ensure that they are applied. The penalties, which may comprise the payment of compensation to the victim, must be effective, proportionate and dissuasive. The Member States shall notify those provisions to the Commission by 5 October 2005 at the latest and shall notify it without delay of any subsequent amendment affecting them.

Article 26
Prevention of discrimination

Member States shall encourage, in accordance with national law, collective agreements or practice, employers and those responsible for access to vocational training to take effective measures to prevent all forms of discrimination on grounds of sex, in particular harassment and sexual harassment in the workplace, in access to employment, vocational training and promotion.

Article 27
Minimum requirements

1. Member States may introduce or maintain provisions which are more favourable to the protection of the principle of equal treatment than those laid down in this Directive.

2. Implementation of this Directive shall under no circumstances be sufficient grounds for a reduction in the level of protection of workers in the areas to which it applies, without prejudice to the Member States' right to respond to changes in the situation by introducing laws, regulations and administrative provisions which differ from those in force on the notification of this Directive, provided that the provisions of this Directive are complied with.

Article 28
Relationship to Community and national provisions

1. This Directive shall be without prejudice to provisions concerning the protection of women, particularly as regards pregnancy and maternity.

2. This Directive shall be without prejudice to the provisions of Directive 96/34/EC and Directive 92/85/EEC.

Article 29
Gender mainstreaming

Member States shall actively take into account the objective of equality between men and women when formulating and implementing laws, regulations, administrative provisions, policies and activities in the areas referred to in this Directive.

Article 30
Dissemination of information

Member States shall ensure that measures taken pursuant to this Directive, together with the provisions already in force, are brought to the attention of all the persons concerned by all suitable means and, where appropriate, at the workplace.

TITLE IV
FINAL PROVISIONS

Article 31
Reports

1. By 15 February 2011, the Member States shall communicate to the Commission all the information necessary for the Commission to draw up a report to the European Parliament and the Council on the application of this Directive.

2. Without prejudice to paragraph 1, Member States shall communicate to the Commission, every four years, the texts of any measures adopted pursuant to Article 141(4) of the Treaty, as well as reports on these measures and their implementation. On the basis of that information, the Commission will adopt and publish every four years a report establishing a comparative assessment of any measures in the light of Declaration No 28 annexed to the Final Act of the Treaty of Amsterdam.

3. Member States shall assess the occupational activities referred to in Article 14(2), in order to decide, in the light of social developments, whether there is justification for maintaining the exclusions concerned. They shall notify the Commission of the results of this assessment periodically, but at least every 8 years.

Article 32
Review

By 15 February 2011 at the latest, the Commission shall review the operation of this Directive and if appropriate, propose any amendments it deems necessary.

Article 33
Implementation

Member States shall bring into force the laws, regulations and administrative provisions necessary to comply with this Directive by 15 August 2008 at the latest or shall ensure, by that date, that management and labour introduce the requisite provisions by way of agreement. Member States may, if necessary to take account of particular difficulties, have up to one additional year to comply with this Directive. Member States shall take all necessary steps to be able to guarantee the results imposed by this Directive. They shall forthwith communicate to the Commission the texts of those measures.

When Member States adopt these measures, they shall contain a reference to this Directive or be accompanied by such reference on the occasion of their official publication. They shall also include a statement that references in existing laws, regulations and administrative provisions to the Directives repealed by this Directive shall be construed as references to this Directive. Member States shall determine how such reference is to be made and how that statement is to be formulated.

The obligation to transpose this Directive into national law shall be confined to those provisions which represent a substantive change as compared with the earlier Directives. The obligation to transpose the provisions which are substantially unchanged arises under the earlier Directives.

Member States shall communicate to the Commission the text of the main provisions of national law which they adopt in the field covered by this Directive.

Article 34
Repeal

1. With effect from 15 August 2009 Directives 75/117/EEC, 76/207/EEC, 86/378/EEC and 97/80/EC shall be repealed without prejudice to the obligations of the Member States relating to the time-limits for transposition into national law and application of the Directives set out in Annex I, Part B.

2. References made to the repealed Directives shall be construed as being made to this Directive and should be read in accordance with the correlation table in Annex II.

Article 35
Entry into force

This Directive shall enter into force on the 20th day following its publication in the *Official Journal of the European Union.*

Charter of Fundamental Rights of the European Union

OJ (2000) C 364/01

CHAPTER I: DIGNITY

Article 1
Human dignity

Human dignity is inviolable. It must be respected and protected.

...

CHAPTER III: EQUALITY

...

Article 21
Non-discrimination

1. Any discrimination based on any ground such as sex, race, colour, ethnic or social origin, genetic features, language, religion or belief, political or any other opinion, membership of a national minority, property, birth, disability, age or sexual orientation shall be prohibited.

...

Article 23

Equality between men and women

Equality between men and women must be ensured in all areas, including employment, work and pay.

The principle of equality shall not prevent the maintenance or adoption of measures providing for specific advantages in favour of the under-represented sex.

...

CHAPTER IV: SOLIDARITY

Article 27
Workers' right to information and consultation within the undertaking

Workers or their representatives must, at the appropriate levels, be guaranteed information and consultation in good time in the cases and under the conditions provided for by Community law and national laws and practices.

Article 28
Right of collective bargaining and action

Workers and employers, or their respective organisations, have, in accordance with Community law and national laws and practices, the right to negotiate and conclude collective agreements at the appropriate levels and, in cases of conflicts of interest, to take collective action to defend their interests, including strike action. ...

Article 30
Protection in the event of unjustified dismissal

Every worker has the right to protection against unjustified dismissal, in accordance with Community law and national laws and practices.

Article 31
Fair and just working conditions

1. Every worker has the right to working conditions which respect his or her health, safety and dignity.

2. Every worker has the right to limitation of maximum working hours, to daily and weekly rest periods and to an annual period of paid leave.

...

Article 33
Family and professional life

1. The family shall enjoy legal, economic and social protection.

2. To reconcile family and professional life, everyone shall have the right to protection from dismissal for a reason connected with maternity and the right to paid maternity leave and to parental leave following the birth or adoption of a child. ...

CHAPTER VI: JUSTICE

Article 47
Right to an effective remedy and to a fair trial

Everyone whose rights and freedoms guaranteed by the law of the Union are violated has the right to an effective remedy before a tribunal in compliance with the conditions laid down in this Article.

Everyone is entitled to a fair and public hearing within a reasonable time by an independent and impartial tribunal previously established by law. Everyone shall have the possibility of being advised, defended and represented.

Legal aid shall be made available to those who lack sufficient resources in so far as such aid is necessary to ensure effective access to justice.

Alphabetical List of Cited Cases of the European Court of Justice

Abdoulaye v. *Regie Nationale des Usines Renault,*1999 Case C-218/98 (1999) ECR I-5723.

Abrahamsson and Anderson v. *Fogalqvist,* 2000, Case C-407/98 (2000) ECR I-5539.

Airola v. *Commission,*1975, Case 21/74 (1975) ECR 221.

Alabaster v. *Woolich plc. and Secretary of State for Social Security,* 2004 Case C-147/02 (2004) ECR I-3101.

Allonby v. *Accrington and Rossendale College,*2004 Case C-256/01 OJ (2004) C 47 (21.02.2004) p. 4.

Angestelten Betriebsrat der Wiener Gebietskrankenkasse v. *Wiener Gebietskrankenkasse* 1999, Case 309/97 (1999) ECR I-2865.

Austrian Trade Unions v. *Austrian Wirtschsftskammer* 2004 Case C-220/02 (2004) ECR I-5907.

Badeck and Others v. *Land Hessen case,* 2000, Case C-158/97 (2000) ECR I-1875.

Barbel Kachelmann v. *Bankhaus Hermann Lampe KG.* 2000, Case C-322/98 (2000) ECR I-7505.

Barber v. *Guardian Royal Exchange Assurance group,*1991 Case C-262/88 (1991) ECR I-1889.

Beets-Proper v. *F. van Landschot Bankiers NV,* 1986, Case C-262/84 (1986) ECR 773.

Bilka Kaufhaus GmbH v. *Weber Von Hartz,* 1986, Case C-170/84 (1986) ECR I-1607.

Boyle and Others v. *Equal Opportunities Commission* Case C-411/96 (1998) ECR I-6401.

Brown v. *Rentokil Ltd,* 1998, Case C-394/96 (1998) ECR I-4185.

Brunnhofer v. *Bank der Osterreichischen Postsparkasse AG*, 2001, Case C-381/99 (2001) ECR I-4961.

Burton v. *British Railways Board,* 1982, Case C-19/81 (1982) ECR 555.

Busch v. *Klinikum Neustadt GmbH & Co. Betriebs-KG* 2003, Case C-320/01 (2003) ECR I-2041.

Cadman v. *Health and Safety Executive* 2006 Case 17/05 OJ (2006) C 294 (2.12.2006) p. 10.

City of Berlin v. *Botel,* 1992, Case C-360/90 (1992) ECR I-3589.

Commission v. *Austria,* 2004, Case C-203.03 (2004) ECR I-935.

Commission v. *Belgium* 1993 Case C-173/91 (1993) ECR I-673.

Commission v. *Denmark* 1985 Case 143(83 (1985) ECR 427.

Commission v. *France* 1988, Case C-312/86 (1988) ECR 6315.

Commission v. *France* 1996, Case C-334/94 (1996) ECR I-1307.

Commission v. *France,* 1997, Case C-197/96 (1997) ECR I-1489.

Commission v. *France,* 1998, Case C-318/86 (1998) ECR 3559.

Commission v. *Germany* 1985 Case C-248/83 (1985) ECR 1459.

Commission v. *Greece* 1999 Case C-187/98 (1999) ECR I-7713.

Commission v. *Italy,* 1997, Case C-207/96 (1997) ECR I-6869.

Commission v. *Luxembourg* 1982 Case C-58/81 (1982) ECR 2175.

Commission v. *Luxembourg* 2005 Case C-519/03 OJ (2005) C (11.06.2005) p. 11.

Commission v. *UK (Re Equal Pay for Equal Work)*, 1982, Case C-61/81 (1982) ECR 2601.

Commission v. *UK (Re Equal Treatment for Men and Women)*, 1983, Case C-165/82 (1983) ECR I-3431.

Costa v. *ENEL,* 1964, Case 6/64 (1964) ECR 585.

Danfoss Case, 1989, Case C-109/88 (1989) ECR I-3199.

Defrenne v. *Belgium (No.1)*, 1971, Case 80/70 (1971) ECR 445.

Defrenne v. *SABENA (No. 2)*, 1976, Case 43/75 (1976) ECR 455.

Defrenne v. *SABENA (No.3)*, 1978, Case 149/77 (1978) ECR 1365.

Dekker v. *Stichting Vormingscentrum voor Jong Volwassenen (VJV-Centrum) Plus,* 1990, Case C-177/88 (1990) ECR I-3941.

Deutsche Post AG v. Sievers 2000, Case C-270/97 and C-271/97 (2000) ECR I-929.

Deutsche Telekom AG v. *Schroder,* 2000, C-50/96 (2000) ECR I-799.

*De Weerd (née Roks) and Others,*1994, Case C-343/92 (1994) ECR I-571.

Dietz Case, 1996, Case C-435/93 (1996) ECR.I-5223.

Dori v. *Recreb Srl,* 1993, Case C-91/92 (1993) ECR I-3325.

Dorit Harz v. *Deutsche Tradax GmbH,,* 1984, Case C-79/83 (1984) ECR I-1921.

Draehmpaehl v. Urania, 1997, Case C-180/95 (1997) ECR I -2195.

Elsner-Lakeberg v. *Land Nordrhein-Westfalen,* 2004, Case C-285/02 (2004) ECR I-05861.

Enderby v. *Frenchay Health Authority and Secretary of State for Health* 1993 Case C-127/92 (1993) ECR I-5535.

Finanzamt Köln-Altstadt v. *Roland Schumacker* (1995) Case C-279/93 (1995) ECR I-225.

Francovich v. *Italy* 1991 Case C-6 & 9/90 (1991) ECR I-5357.

Freers, and Speckmann, v. *Deutsche Bundespost,* 1996 Case C-278/93 (1996) ECR I -1165.

Garland v. *British Rail Engineering Ltd.* 1982, Case 12/81 (1982) ECR 359.

Gerster v. *Bavaria* 1997 Case C-1/95 (1997) ECR. I-5253.

Gillespie and others v. *Northern Health and Social Services Boards, Department of Health and Social Services, Eastern Health and Social Services Board and Southern Health and Social Services Board* 1996 Case C-342/93 (1996) ECR I-475.

Gomez v. *Contintental Industrias* 2004 Case C-342/01 (2004) ECR I-2605.

Gruber v. *Silhouett* 1999 Case 249/97 (1999) ECR I-5295.

Habermann-Beltermann v. *Arbeiterwohlfahrt, Bezirksverband Ndb./Opf.e.V.* 1994 Case C-421/92 (1994) ECR I-1657.

Handels-og Kontorfunktionaerernes Forbund i Danmark v. *Dansk Arbejsgiverforening* 1990 Case C-179/88 (1990) ECR I-3979.

Handels- og Kontorfunctionaernes Forbund I Danmark, acting on behalf of Larsson v. *Dansk Handel & Service, acting on behalf of Fotex Supermarked A/S* 1997 Case C-400/95 (1997) ECR I-2757.

Harz v. *Tradax* 1984, Case 79/83 (1984) ECR 1921.

Hofmann v. Barmer Ersatzkasse 1984 Case C-184/83 (1984) ECR I-3047.

Internationale Handelsgesellschaft mbH v. *Einfuhr- und Vorratsstele für Getreide und Futtermittel* 1970 Case 11/70 (1970) ECR 1125.

Jamstalldhetsombudsmannen v. *Orebo ians Landsting* 2000 Case C-236/98 (2000) ECR 2189.

Jenkins v. *Kingsgate (Clothing Productions) Ltd.* 1981 Case C-96/80 ECR I-911.

Johnston v. *Chief Constable of the Royal Ulster Constabulary* 1986, Case C-222/84 (1986) ECR I-1651.

Jørgensen Case 2000 Case C-226/98 (2000) ECR I-2447.

Kalanke v. *Freie Hansestadt Bremen* (1995) (Case C-450/93 (1995) ECR I-3051.

Kirsammer-Hack v. *Sidal* 1993 Case C-189/91 (1993) ECR I-6205.

Kording v. *Senator fur Finanzen* 1997 Case C-100/95 (1997) ECR. I-5289.

Kowalska v. *Freie Hansastadt Hambourg* 1990 case 33/89 (1990) ECR I-2591.

Kreil v. *Germany* 2000 Case C-285/98 (2000) ECR I-69.

Kruger v. *Kreiskrankenhaus Ebersberg* 1999 Case C-281/97 (1999) ECR 5127.

Kuratorium für Dialyse und Nierentransplantation e.V. Lewark 1996 Case C-457/93 (1996) ECR I-243.

Land Brandeburg v. *Sass* Case C-284/02 (2004) ECR I-11143.

Levez v. *Jennings (Harlow Pools) Ltd.* 1998 Case C-326/96 (1998) ECR 7835.

Lewen v. *Denda* 1999 Case C-333/97 (1999) ECR I-7243.

Liefting v. *The University of Amsterdam Case*, 1984, Case 23/83 (1984) ECR 3225.

Lommers v. *Dutch Ministry of Agriculture* 2002 Case C-476/99 (2002) ECR I -2891.

Macarthy Ltd v. *Smith* (1980) Case 129/79 (1980) ECR 1275.

Mahlburg v. *Land Mecklenburg* 2000 Case C-207/98 (2000) ECR-I 549.

Marschall, Helmut v. *Land Nord-Rhein-Westfalen*, 1997 Case C-409/95 (1997) ECR I-6363.

Marshall v. *Southampton and South West Hampshire Area Health Authority* (Teaching) 1986 Case C-152/84 (1986) Case 152/84 (1986) ECR I-723.

Marshall v. *Southampton and South West Hampshire Area Health Authority (No. 2).*

1993 Case C-271/91 (1993) ECR I-4367.

Megner and Scheffel v. *Innungskrankenkasse Rheinhessen-Pfalz* 1995 Case C-444/93 (1995) ECR I-4741.

Melgar v. *Ayuntamiento de Los Barrios* 2001 Case C-438/99 (2001) ECR I-6915.

Ministère public v. *Levy* 1993 Case C-158/91 (1993) ECR I-4287.

Ministère public v. *Stoeckel,*1991 Case C-345/89 (1989) ECR I-4047.

Murphy v. *Bord Telecom Eireann Case* 1988 Case 157/86(1988) ECR I – 673.

Nikoloudi v. *OTE 2005* Case C-196/02 (2005) ECR I-1789.

Nimz v. *Freie und Hansestadt Hamburg* 1991 Case C-184/89 (1991) ECR I-297.

Office National de l'Emploi v. *Minne* 1994 Case C-13/93 (1994) ECRI-371.

Preston, Shirley and Others 2000 (Case C-78/98 (2000) ECR I-3201.

Razzouk and Beydoun v. *Commission.*1984 Cases 75 &117/82 (1984) ECR 1509.

Rinke, Katharina, v. *Artztekammer Hamburg* 2003 Case C-25/02 (2003) ECR I-8349.

Rinner-Kühn v. *FWW Spezial-Gebaudereinigung GmbH* 1989 Case C-171/88 (1989) ECR I-2743.

Royal Copenhagen Case 1995 Case C-400/93 (1995) ECR I-1275.

Rummler v. *Dato-Druck GmbH* 1986 Case 237/85 (1986) ECR I-2101.

R v. Secretary of State for Employment, ex parte Seymour-Smith and Perez.

1999 Case C-167/99 (1999) ECR I-623.

Sabbatini-Bertoni v. *European Parliament* and *Chollet-Baudain* v.*Commission* 1972 Case 32/71 (1972) ECR I-345.

Schnorbus v. *Land Hessen,* 2000 Case C-79/99 (2000) ECR I-10997.

Schonheit v. *Stadt Frankfurt am* 2003 Cases C-4 and 5-02 OJ (2003) C 304 (13.12.2003) p. 6.

Sirdar v. *Army Board and Secretary of Defence* 1999 Case C-273/97 (1999) ECR I-7403.

Stadt Lengerich v. *Helmig* 1994 Cases C-399 et al (1994) ECR I-5727.

Stauder v. *City of Ulm* 1969 Case 29/69 (1969) ECR I-419.

Steinicke v. *Bundesanstalt für Arbeit,* 2003 Case C-77/02 (2003) ECR I-9027.

Tele Danmark A/S v. *Handels-og Kontorfunktionaerernes Forbund i Danmark (HK),* 2001 Case C-109/00 (2001) ECR I-6993.

Van Duyn v. *Home office* 1974 Case 41/74 (1974) ECR 1337.

Van Gend & Loos Case 1963 Case 26/62 (1963) ECR 1.

Von Colson and Kamman v. *Land North Rhein Westphalia* 1984 Case C-14/83 (1984) ECR I-1891.

Webb v. *EMO Air Cargo (UK) Ltd* 1994 Case C-32/93 (1994) ECR I-3567.

Wippel, Nicole, v. *Peek & Cloppenburg GmbH & Co. KG.*,2004 Case C-313/02 (2004) ECR I-9483.

Worringham v. *Lloyds Bank Ltd* 1981 Case 69/80 (1981) ECR I-767.

Opinion 2/91 Re ILO Convention No. 170 (1993) ECR I-1061.

SELECT BIBLIOGRAPHY

ILO Publications

Constitution of the International Labour Organization and Standing Orders of the International Labour Conference, Constitution de l'Organisation internationale du Travail et Règlement de la Conférence internationale du Travail (ILO, Geneva, December 1994).

Amendments to the Standing Orders of the InternationalLabour Conference adopted by the Conference at its 82nd Session (June 1995), Amendements au Règlement de la Conférence internationale du Travail adoptés par la Conférence à sa 82e session (juin 1995) (ILO, Geneva, June 1995).

Equality in Employment and Occupation, Special Survey in respect of Convention No.111, Report of the Committee of Experts, International Labour Conference, 83rd session 1996.

Report of the Director-General, Reducing the Decent Work Deficit, A global challenge, International Labour Conference, 89th Session 2001.

Javillier, Jean-Claude et Gernigon, Bernard, Politakis, Georges P. (Coordinateur), *Les normes internationales du travail: un patrimoine pour l'avenir, Mélanges en l'honneur de Nicolas Valticos* (ILO, Geneva, 2004).

Wisskircher, Alfred, *The standard-setting and monitoring activity of the ILO: Legal questions and practical experience* (ILO, Geneva, 2005).

Equality at work: Tackling the challenges, Global Report under the follow-up to the ILO Declaration on Fundamental Principles and Rights at work (ILO, Geneva, 2007).

EU Documentation

Network of Experts on the Implementation of the Equality Directives, Final Consolidated Report 1987 (V/1987/88/EN)

The Rubenstein Report, "The Dignity of Women at Work:Report on the Problem of Sexual Harassment in th Member States of the European Communities" Part II : Appendix: October 1987 (Commission of the European Communities, Doc. V/412/1/87-EN)

European Commission Communication COM (96) 88 final

European Parliament, Directorate General for Research, Working Paper on Women's Rights and the Treaty of Amsterdam, 1998 - COM (96) 88 final

Working Paper on Atypical Work in the EU, Social Affairs Series 3-2000, European Parliament, 2000

Copenhagen Conference on Gender Equality for EU Candidate Countries, November 29, 2002.

Report on Equal Opportunities for Women and Men (COM) (2003) 93 final

Regulation 29/2004/EC of 8 January 2004 adopting the specifications of the 2005 ad hoc module on reconciliation between work and Family Life provided for by Council Regulation 577/98/EC (OJ (2004) L 5/57)

Eurostat, The Labour Force Survey, 2005 http://epp.eurostat.ec.eu.

Report on Equal Opportunities for Women and Men (COM) (2003) 93 final)

European Commission Road Map for Equality between Women and Men for the period 2006-2010, Doc. COM (2006) 92 final.

EU Doc. COM (2006) 71 final Section 3 "Challenges and Policy Orientation"

Report from the Commission to the Council, the European Parliament, the Economic and Social Committee and the Committee of the Regions on Equality between Women and Men 2007, Doc. COM (2007) 49 final, 7 February 2007 and Annex.

Other Publications

Alston, P., "Core Labour Standards and the Transformation of International Labour Rights Regime", (2004) 15 *European Journal of International Law* 457-521.

Arnull, A., "Out with the Old" (Editorial), (2006) 31 *EL Rev.* 1-2.

Arseguel, A., and Reynes, B., in *Equality Law Between Men and Women in the European Community* (Louvain-La-Neuve, 1986).

Barnard, C., Deakin S and Morris G, *The Future of Labour Law: Liber amicorum Bob Hepple* (Oxford, Hart, 2004).

Biagi M., "Social Europe and Labour Law: The Role of the European Social Charter", *The Council of Europe and the Social Challenges of the XXIst Century* (2001), 71-85.

Birk, R., "The European Social Charter and the European Union", *The Council of Europe and Social Challenges of the XXIst Century* (2001), 41-48.

Blanpain, R., "Equal Treatment and the prohibition of Discrimination in Employment and Occupation: Implementation in the European Union and in Belgium", *The Council of Europe and the Social Challenges of the XXIst Century* (2001), 121-155.

Blanpain, R. (ed.), *EC Law on Justification for Sex Discrimination in Working Life, Collective bargaining, Discrimination, Social Security and European Integration* (Kluwer, Deventer, 2003).

Blanpain R. *European Labour Law* (10th rev. edn, Kluwer Law International, 2006).

Clark, Jon and Wedderburg, Lord, *Labour Law and Industrial Relations* (Oxford, 1983).

Colling, Trevor and Dickens, Linda, *Equality Bargaining – Why Not?* (HMSO, London, 1989).

Coussey, Mary and Jackson, Hilary, *Making Equal Opportunities Work* (London, 1991).

Craiq and Burca, *EU Law: Text, Cases and Materials* (3rd edn, Oxford University Press, Oxford, 2003).

Dashwood, A., and O'Leary, S., *The Principle of Equal Treatment in EC Law* (Sweet & Maxwell, London, 1997).

Dickens, Linda, "Anti-discrimination Legislation: Exploring and Explaining the Impact of Women's Employment", in McCarthy, W. (ed.), *Legal Intervention in Industrial Relations: Gains and Losses,* (Oxford, 1993).

Docksey, C., "The Principle of Equality Between Women and Men as a Fundamental Right under Community Law", (1991) 20 *ILJ* 258.

Ellis, Evelyn, *European Community Sex Equality Law* (2nd edn, Oxford University Press, Oxford, 1998).

Ellis, Evelyn, *EU Anti-Discrimination Law* (Oxford University Press, Oxford EC Law Library, Oxford, 2005).

Fredman, Sandra, "European Community Discrimination Law: A Critique", (1992) 21 *ILJ* 119.

Fredman, Sandra, "A Difference with Disctinction: Pregnancy and Parenthood Reassesed", (1994) 110 *Law Quarterly Review* 106.

Frid, R., "European Community, Membership in International Organisations or Institutions", in Professor R. Wolfrum, Director of the Max Planck Institute for Comparative Public Law and International Law (ed.), *Max Planck Encyclopedia of Public International Law* (Oxford University Press, expected 2008).

Hepple, B., "Equality and Discrimination", *Principles and Perspectives on European Labour Law: Liber amicorum Lord Wedderburn* (Clarendon Oxford Press, 1996) 237-259.

Hervey, T., and O'Keeffe, D., *Sex Equality Law in the European Union* (J. Wiley & Son, 1995).

Hervey, T., *European Social Law and Policy* (Longsman, London, 1998).

Kenner, J., *EU Employment Law: From Rome to Amsterdam* (Hart Publishing, Oxford, 2002).

Kombos, Constantinos and Hadjisolomou, Maria, "The Mechanisms Used by the ILO and the EU in Combating Employment Discrimination in Pay: Converging Divergence?", (September 2007) 11.2 *Electronic Journal of Comparative Law* <www.ejcl.org/112/art112-1.pdf>.

Lacey, N., "Legislation against Sex Discrimination: Questions from a Feminist Perspective", (1987) 14 *Journal of Law and Society* 114.

Landau, Eve C., *The Rights of Working Women in the European Community* (The European Perspectives Series, Brussels/Luxembourg, 1985).

Landau, Eve C. (Project Director) *The Status of Women at the Dawn of the Twenty-first Century, Proceedings of the Conference held under the Auspices of the International Association of Legal Science and the Minerva Center for Human Rights* (Unesco, Paris, 2001).

Landau, Eve C., "International Labour Standards: The Case of Equal Pay – European Community Perspective", in Gladstone *et al.*, (eds), *Labour Relations in a Changing Environment* (Walter de Gruyter, Berlin, New York, 1992).

Lenaerts K. and Foubert, P., "Social Rights in the Case Law of the European Court of Justice: The Impact of the Charter of Fundamental Rights of the European Union on Standing Case-Law", (2001) 28 *Legal Issues of European Integration* 267-296.

Lester, Sir Anthony, "Equal Pay and Equal Treatment without Sex Discrimination: Community and United Kingdom Law", in *Records of the Proceedings of the European Conference, Brussels, May 1985* (Louvain, 1986).

McCrudden, C. (ed.), *Women, Employment and European Equality Law* (London, 1987).

Murray J., *Transnational Labour Regulation: The ILO and EC Compared* (Kluwer, The Hague, 1999).

Nielsen, R., and Szyszczak, E., *The Social Dimension of the European Community* (3rd edn, Handelshojskolen Forlag, 1997).

O'Donovan and Szyszczak, *Equality and Sex Discrimination Law* (Oxford, 1988).

Plender, R., "Equal Pay for Men and Women; Two Recent Decisions of the European Court", (1982) *American Journal of Comparative Law* 627-653 at p. 650.

Politakis, G., "Deconstructing Flexibility in International Labour Conventions", in *Mélanges en honneur de Nicolas Valticos, Les normes internationales du travail: Un patrimoine pour l'avenir* (B.I.T. Genève, 2004).

Posner, Richard A., "An Economic Analysis of Sex Discrimination Laws", (1989) 56 *U Chi. LR* 1311.

Rubery, Jill, and Fagan, Collette, *Occupational Segregation of Women and Men in the European Community*, Social Europe, Supplement 3/93.

Samuel, Lenia, *Fundamental Social Rights, Case Law of the European Social Charter* (2nd edn, Council of Europe Publishing, Strasbourg, 2002).

Smit and Herzog, *The Law of the EEC (Commentary)* Vol. 3. (Matthew Bender, New York 1976).

Steiner, Josephine, and Woods, Lorna, *Textbook on EU Law* (9th edn, Oxford University Press, Oxford, 2006), chapter 25.

Szysczczak, Erika, "Differences in Pay for Part-Time Work", (1981) 44 *Modern Law Review* 672-682.

Symonides, Janusz and Volodin, Vladimir, *Human Rights of Women, A Collection of International and Regional Normative Instruments* (UNESCO, Paris, 1999).

Warner, J. "EC Social Policy in Practice: Community Action on Behalf of Women and its Impact in the Member States", (1984) 23 *Journal of Common Market Studies*.

Wedderburn, Lord, *The Worker and the Law* (3rd edn, Harmondsworth, 1986).

Wedderburn, Lord, "The New Politics of Labour Law: Immunities or Positive Rights?", in *Employment Rights in Britain and Europe* (London, 1991).

INDEX

www.ingramcontent.com/pod-product-compliance
Lightning Source LLC
LaVergne TN
LVHW081514300926
849161LV00006B/1174